FAIR TRADE

Michael Barratt Brown is Chair of Third World Information Network (TWIN) and Twin Trading Ltd, London, both of which organisations have since 1985 helped pioneer alternative trading links between North and South. After his university education at Corpus Christi College, Oxford, and war-time service, Michael Barratt Brown has spent a lifetime in adult education. From 1950 to 1959 he was a tutor for Cambridge University's Department of Extra-Mural Studies and the Workers' Educational Association. He then joined the Extramural Department of Sheffield University where he taught for 14 years until becoming Founding Principal of the Northern College in 1977. He has also held visiting appointments at various universities in Canada, India, Japan and the United States. In 1970 he became Chairman and later President of the Society of Industrial Tutors and in 1980 a director of the Bertrand Russell Peace Foundation. He is an Honorary Fellow of the Institute of Development Studies, University of Sussex, and has an honorary doctorate from the Open University.

He has served on the editorial boards of numerous journals, including *New Left Review*, *Capital and Class*, the *Institute for Workers' Control Bulletin*, *Spokesman*, *New Socialist*, and *European Labour Forum*. He is also the author of nine books on economic and political subjects, some of which have been translated into several European languages.

D0781648

Also by Michael Barratt Brown:

AFTER IMPERIALISM
(London: Heinemann, 1963)

WHAT ECONOMICS IS ABOUT
(London: Weidenfeld and Nicolson, 1970)

ESSAYS ON IMPERIALISM
(Nottingham: Spokesman, 1972)

FROM LABOURISM TO SOCIALISM
(Nottingham: Spokesman, 1972)

ECONOMICS OF IMPERIALISM
(Harmondsworth: Penguin, 1974)

RESOURCES AND THE ENVIRONMENT
(Nottingham: Spokesman, 1976)

INFORMATION AT WORK
(London: Hutchinson, 1978)

MODELS IN POLITICAL ECONOMY
(Harmondsworth: Penguin, 1984; Boulder, Co.: Rionner, 1985)

EUROPEAN UNION: FORTRESS OR DEMOCRACY?
(Nottingham: Spokesman, 1991)

SHORTCHANGED: AFRICA IN WORLD TRADE
(*with Pauline Tiffen*; London: Pluto, 1992)

MICHAEL BARRATT BROWN

Fair Trade

Reform and Realities in the
International Trading System

ZED BOOKS

London & New Jersey

Fair Trade was first published by Zed Books Ltd,
57 Caledonian Rd, London N1 9BU and 165
First Avenue, Atlantic Avenue, New Jersey 07716, in 1993.

Copyright © Michael Barratt Brown 1993

Cover by Andrew Corbett.
Printed and bound in the United Kingdom
by Biddles Ltd, Guilford and King's Lynn.

The right of Michael Barratt Brown, author of this work,
has been asserted by him in accordance with the Copyright,
Designs and Patents Act 1988.

A catalogue record for this book is available from the British Library
US CIP data is available from the Library of Congress

ISBN 1 85649 073 4 Hb
ISBN 1 85649 074 2 Pb

CONTENTS

Boxes

Tables

Charts

Acknowledgements

Grateful acknowledgement is hereby accorded to the following for permission to publish the charts and statistical tables appearing in this book: Basil Davidson for the map on The Triangular Trade (p.14) from *Discovering Africa's Past*, Longman, 1978; the Overseas Development Institute for the graph on Commodity Prices (p.39) from *Briefing Paper*, March 1988; the *Economist* for the chart on Korean Trade incentives (p.48) from the issue of September 1989; F. Clairmont and J. Cavanagh for the tables on Corporate Commodity Control (pp.51 and 71) from *Merchants of Drink*, Third World Network, 1984; the International Chamber of Commerce for the tables on Futures Trading (pp.58 and 59) from *Futures Trading in Commodity Markets*, Paris 1983; Spokesman Books for the table on Aid Beneficiaries (p.97) from M. Barratt Brown, *From Labourism to Socialism*, Spokesman, 1972; Harold Lever and Christopher Huhne for the table on Third World debtors (p.114) from *Debt and Danger*, Penguin, 1985; the National Westminster Bank Review for the graph on Common Agricultural Policy (p.132) from the issue of Autumn 1986; Third World Information Network for the tables on Countertrading (pp.139-140), from *Countertrade*, TWIN, 1987; Traidcraft for their catalogue reproduced (pp. 160-1); to the Food and Agriculture Organisation, for the diagram of Networks (p.167) from *Indonesian Action*, FAO, 1989; the Fair Trade Foundation for the reproduction of their logo (p.183); Spokesman Books for the quotation (pp.187-189) from M. Barratt Brown, *European Union Fortress or Democracy*, Spokesman, 1991.

PREFACE

This book could not have been written without the experience of my colleagues in TWIN and Twin Trading in trying to make Fair Trade a reality. I have learned so much from them that it has been hard for me to resist referring to them constantly in the text. It is what they have done in practice that has encouraged me to believe that my vision of a world of fair trade could one day be realised. I am particularly grateful to Pauline Tiffen who read through the whole of the book in draft and provided invaluable criticisms and corrections, and also to Dick Day and Peter Robbins who read and commented on several chapters at an early stage of the writing. At the same time, I have to say that this is not a TWIN book. I wrote it and I take full responsibility for whatever strengths and weaknesses it has. None of the opinions and judgements in it should be attributed to TWIN or to any of the organisations with which TWIN and Twin Trading are working.

Not least among my debts is the debt I owe to members of the cooperatives and producers' associations in the Third World, with which alternative trade organisations like TWIN have been working. It is the total commitment of these small-scale producers to new forms of independent development, which involve both popular participation and environmental protection, that has encouraged us in the rich, industrialised countries to believe in a future of more equal exchange and more sustainable development. It is to them and their families that this book is dedicated with deep respect and admiration.

Michael Barratt Brown
Third World Information Network
London

Part One

Unfair Trade

'Unfair trade is a cancer.'

Sir Leon Brittan, EC Commissioner, speaking at the World Economic Forum, reported in the *Financial Times*, 4 February 1992

1. INTRODUCTION

How near to good is what is fair!
Ben Jonson, *Love Freed from Ignorance and Folly*

Equal Exchange

Nothing distresses a child more than to feel that something is unfair and as we get older the feeling that things in the world are unfair becomes a haunting preoccupation. Whether we are among the unfortunate ones or the lucky ones we ask why this should be so. Sometimes the reason is some accident, a disablement or natural catastrophe and we feel bound to ask, 'Why me?' or 'Why my child?' But we know that there is nothing to be done about it, except to learn to live with the disadvantage and somehow to overcome it. Sometimes, however, the unfair situation is of our own creation or at least is something that could be corrected by human action. Many of us are well aware that the inequality of incomes and living conditions throughout the world is grossly unfair and are not convinced that it is 'just one of those things' that we can do nothing about. If we are among the fortunate ones, we feel that there must be something that we could do to make amends. We do not need to labour under a sense of guilt but only to wish to do whatever is in our power to set things right. Ben Jonson, the seventeenth-century playwright, was almost certainly referring to a fair lady in the quotation at the head of this chapter, but it is apt in the context of this book. Love of our fellow human beings is our greatest endowment; but it has to be freed from ignorance and folly, and then to make things fairer is halfway to goodness.

One of the unfairest things in the world is the system of trade by which we receive many of the things we enjoy — sugar, chocolate, coffee, nuts, bananas, tobacco — and many of the minerals which go into making the machines and vehicles upon which we rely in our daily lives, from people who receive a bare pittance for their work and enjoy (if that is the word) a standard of living that is a bare twentieth of our own. We may know this, but do not know how it has come about nor what we might do to alter this unequal exchange. Understanding how it all happened is complicated and some of the explanations in this book may seem to be very far from our immediate concerns and some of the proposals for correcting all the unfairness to be far above our heads. Nonetheless some of the things which it is suggested that we could do are quite simple. If we really want to be fair, we could begin by changing some of our choices when we are shopping.

Here is an example. I have in front of me a glass jar of honey — it does not appear at first sight to be anything unusual, although this is a rich, dark-coloured honey and boldly labelled DARK TROPICAL MEXICAN HONEY PRODUCED BY COOPERATIVES. This is slightly unusual, but what is really surprising is that the label carries the name of no big supermarket chain, but the imprint of Equal Exchange, which is an alternative trading organisation in Scotland. Even more interesting is that the label is decorated with drawings of two Mexican peasant women, and in the small print on the side it tells the story of where the honey comes from and how the proceeds from the sales are used. There won't be time to read it in the shop, but it's worth reading when you get home.

BOX 1. EQUAL EXCHANGE

THIS HONEY IS IMPORTED directly from peasant cooperatives along the coast of the state of Guerrero in Mexico. The cooperatives are organised into the Union 'Alfredo V. Bonfil', a coalition of collectively organised workers who fish and produce coffee, honey and maize. Export earnings are used to fund women's groups, child care support, shops selling goods at basic prices, technical support groups and alternative sources of emergency and contingency credit.

These autonomous unions have a history of struggle in pre-revolutionary times against the large landowners of the region, a struggle continuing today in an area marginalised by the state.

The exotic flavour of this honey comes from a mixture of coconut flowers and bougainvillaea blossom.

On the other side of the label I read:

Use your bargaining power for positive change. Equal Exchange means more justice in trading. We buy products under fair terms of trade from countries and organisations committed to promoting equality in areas such as health care, landownership and education and who provide fair wages for those working in the production process. Trade positively!

Equal Exchange, 29 Nicholson Square, Edinburgh.

This is just one of the many products which an organisation like TWIN (Third World Information Network) and its associate Twin Trading Company have been identifying, developing and bringing into the European market with the aim of establishing fairer terms of trade, that is the Equal Exchange, to which the Edinburgh company is committed.

What is fair? And why should trade be unfair? What has happened in the past that should make it necessary now to promote some sort of Equal Exchange between Britain and the countries of the Third World? Does it really help the situation if we buy Mexican honey direct from peasant cooperatives?

Can we, even should we, use our bargaining power for positive change? Is it our business that export earnings should be used to promote equality and pay fair wages, to fund women's groups, child care and technical support? If it is, should we then think about such things when we do our regular shopping in the supermarkets and find out if they are trading fairly? What does it mean to trade positively? How could any small change in our purchasing habits affect the whole world trading system? Should we in fact suffer any deprivation if we did help to trade more fairly? Would it just be the very rich who lost some of their advantages or would all of us in the industrialised world have to go without something that we now enjoy? These are the questions we have to answer.

Why a Third World?

We have begun to speak of the Third World, following the widely accepted usage for describing the non-industrialised countries. The so-called First World then consists of the industrialised countries of Western Europe, North America, Japan and Australasia. The Second World was supposedly the countries with planned economies — the USSR and Eastern Europe. But, although their planning got them some way towards industrialisation, they are no longer recognisable as a separate bloc; and China always insisted that it was a part of the Third World — indeed a leading force in it. For the Chinese the concept of First and Second Worlds distinguished the super-powers — the USA and the USSR — from the other industrialised countries. The Third World comprised the rest. There was always some objection to the idea: Third World suggested a sort of inferior status like third class on the railways. The origin of the term lay in the French *tiers monde*, on the analogy of *tiers état* — the third estate, like the House of Commons to be distinguished from the Lords, temporal and spiritual, and having no derogatory connotation. The term caught on and has stayed as a convenient simplification, although there are great differences in size and wealth between the many different Third World countries. The alternative distinction of North and South is far from accurate: nearly all of China, much of India and Mexico, the Middle East and North Africa lying north of the tropics, and Australia, New Zealand and South Africa all in the southern hemisphere. A further possible distinction can be made between developed and developing, undeveloped or underdeveloped countries. This is equally unsatisfactory because it implies a single path of development for all to follow which may be inappropriate or even damaging for some. Industrialised and non-industrialised is probably the best distinction, but it is long-winded; and so we are left with the popular usage of the Third World.

What do we know of this Third World? We are constantly hearing and seeing on our TV screens stories from the Third World of famines, floods, droughts, earthquakes, hurricanes and plagues of locusts. We feel naturally concerned to make our contribution to appeals for emergency aid and for assistance to rehabilitation and development projects. We are bound to begin to wonder why these things should happen apart from those that are obvious 'Acts of God'. But why especially should we think of trading with the Third World? We can, of course, think of the people who make some of the things we buy every day, and prefer to buy goods which carry with them the message of solidarity with countries which are beleaguered and with groups of men and women who are trying to make a living in the most cruel environment. But, where so many of the goods we buy come from those who have suffered in order to produce them, is there no more that we can do? We are often asked to consider whether we should be buying anything at all which can be eaten or worn when it comes from some of the poorest people in the world? Are we helping them when we encourage them to grow cash crops for our consumption? Should they not perhaps put their food first?

There are no simple answers to such questions. But, if we know more about the problems involved in trading and in achieving fairer trade relations, we can make more informed decisions for ourselves. Our bargaining might be used for positive change. Our small actions could be joined with those of others to lead to quite big results. It is the aim of this book to assist that process. So we shall start by looking more closely at our Mexican honey-producing cooperatives to find out how they have been struggling, why they should be marginalised by the state and what difference it really makes to them to find opportunities for equal exchange. We can start with this single case, but we shall have to go on to ask whether it can be generalised. Is their experience typical and can the answers they have found to some of their problems, particularly in their search for development through trade, have a much wider application? What alternatives are there, which others have tried, in attempting to redress the inequalities of the world market? To try to answer such questions will take us deep into the complexities of the chain of commercialisation that leads from the original producer to the ultimate consumer. Let us start, then, at the beginning with the peasants of the high mountains of the Mexican Sierra Madre.

Campesinos of the Mexican Sierra Madre

High in the mountains of Guerrero in Southern Mexico the campesinos of the Sierra Madre on the Costa Grande have organised themselves into a regional alliance of cooperatives and have begun to manage their own export trade in coffee and honey. These cooperatives are primarily concerned with production and local sales — of fish, maize, beans, coffee, cocoa, bananas and honey; but they are involved also in communal health work, education, housing and political activity. They are cut off from Mexico City in their mountain ranges, although the city is no more than 150 miles away, isolated in small communities without proper roads or communications.

This is guerrilla country. This was the base for Zapata's revolution in 1914 against United States intervention. The campesinos look back on a long history of struggle against oppressors, first against the Spanish conquerors, then against the big local landowners. Coffee was introduced here in 1882 by Spanish planters and the campesinos were held in peonage suffering the most cruel exploitation. After the revolution of 1910 the campesinos could rent small parcels of land, but they were permitted to grow only the annual local grain crops. Production of the perennial crops — coffee and cocoa — remained in the hands of the landowners, since the growing of these crops carried ownership rights to the land.

Campesino struggles have continued ever since, peaking in the early 1930s and again in the 1940s when they won their land and the right to organise. But their troubles were not over. A massacre of coffee growers in the late 1960s generated a guerilla movement which was savagely repressed. In the early 1980s a new cooperative movement sprang up. The modern movement combines struggle against the landlords, against the traders, whom they call the 'coyotes', and against the state, as it is embodied both in the official peasant unions and in the state marketing organisations. Between them these state organisations control prices, credit, export permits and the legal status of all private bodies — and these are major concerns of the campesino cooperatives.

The campesino movement thus has the aim of strengthening the position of rural producers in every stage of the production process — in storing, transport, distribution, including exportation, and in finance, commercial and industrial development. They mean to diversify the economic base, run their own basic food stores, improve their roads and comunications. To achieve these ends they believe in encouraging and developing the participation of the people through local autonomy, educational provision and decision making by representative bodies, eschewing all authoritarian and opportunist leadership. They have joined up with other similar organisations in Mexico. Nearly 50 organisations from all over the country came together in August 1988 for a second meeting of UNORCA (the National Union of Regional Campesino Organisations). A feature of the new movement is the role of women in it. *Machismo* is a Spanish word and not at all unknown among Mexicans. Women do most of the work, especially the hand grinding of grain for their tortillas. In their struggle for mechanical grinders, women's organisations have grown up rapidly in the last few years. In the Guerrero cooperatives the women play a full part in the decision-making assemblies. They have altogether nine local branches and publish their own paper, *The Grinder: Women against Ignorance and Oppression*.

Coffee is the main cash crop of the Guerrero campesinos. They have had in the past to sell this crop either through the state marketing organisations or through the 'coyotes'. Either way, they get at best 45 per cent of the price when delivered at the city stores or free on board at the ports. For the cooperatives to improve on this proportion, they are now performing all the processes themselves — scraping, cleaning, drying, hulling, sorting, grading, packing, transporting, marketing and now exporting also, through their joint venture with Twin Trading Ltd, the commercial arm of the London-based charity, Third World Information Network (TWIN). Their main problem is that the campesinos need payment as soon as possible after the crop is gathered, but the cooperative does not normally get paid until the beans are sold. They have the same problem with their corn crop; they cannot hold it off the market when the price is lowest — just after the harvest. When the campesinos are getting hungry, the 'coyotes' descend and the campesinos must accept a poor price if they are not to starve. Somehow the cooperatives have to forestall this eventuality, but with little or no capital, and credit available only at exorbitant rates, they need outside aid. This is what the independent Mexican support agency, ANADEGES, has been helping them to find over the last few years. It is only one of many similar organisations, but we can take it as an example of non-governmental grass-roots support organisations.

Autonomy and Development

ANADEGES stands for Autonomy, Development and Self-Management. It is an umbrella organisation that provides financial and technical assistance to campesino associations throughout Mexico and to urban migrants who want to return to their villages. ANADEGES has made contact with European aid agencies, like Twin Trading, which are prepared to put money up-front and share profits with Third World peasant associations and cooperatives. There is much else that organisations like TWIN have to do in helping such associations — to improve the packaging, control the quality and then arrange the shipping and insurance, find the markets in Europe or North America and organise delivery. Getting the containers onto a ship is still the job of the cooperatives and, as they are not a state organisation and not prepared to bribe the port officials, this may be the hardest part.

It is unwise, however, for the campesinos to rely on just one crop. Prices rise and fall and in the 1980s prices of tropical foods have been falling steadily. They need to diversify. In Guerrero they produce honey. Though the season is short high up in the mountains and the bees have to be fed in the winter, nectar is plentiful and the honey is of excellent quality as the bees take the nectar from the many flowering trees, none of which has been sprayed with insecticides. There are problems with 'raiders' bringing in their hives from other districts and the ever present 'coyotes' waiting to pounce. But quite large quantities of honey are produced. Several thousand hives each producing 30kg to 40kg make over a hundred tonnes. Sold locally by the kilo, the honey fetches no more than a few cents, but selected and packed in barrels it can be exported at three times the price. Containers of 18 to 20 tonnes filled with barrels of honey have been successfully imported into the UK for bottling and sale in Europe's alternative trade shops, and also in the commercial market, including shops like Fortnum and Mason. In addition to coffee and honey there are peasant craft products for which Third World agencies like Oxfam Trading and Traidcraft have found a ready market.

In many countries of the Third World, collective work organisations, cooperatives and producers associations, have joined together to strengthen their position not only in their local economies but in the world economy. We shall take an example again from Latin America and the Caribbean. After a long period of contact and discussion among popular producer associations in Chile, Cuba, Mexico, Nicaragua and Peru, an organisation called FENLACES was established in March 1991. FENLACES is the acronym for the Spanish translation of Latin American and Caribbean Federation for Trade in the Social Economy Sector, and *enlace* is the Spanish word for a link or connection. In its Declaration of Principles, FENLACES states *inter alia*:

BOX 2: A THIRD WORLD ALTERNATIVE TRADING ORGANISATION'S PRINCIPLES

Fair trade allows all national efforts in each country to be integrated. FENLACES is constitutionally based on this integration in such a way that, by integrating in a spirit of democracy and solidarity the commercial effort of organised producers, for whom solidarity is of primary importance in decision-making and acting, they integrate the sector of popular economy in the business sector of each country.

FENLACES is autonomous, in so far as it determines its orientation and course of action with full independence and sovereignty, in each country, in the Latin American/International arena. Nevertheless, it declares its internationalist aims of integration of world-wide efforts for fair trade as an alternative to the present world order.

FENLACES is inspired with the idea of contributing to the establishment of a new Economic International Order, based on an economy of a human scale in which the human being may be a producer and beneficiary of this economy.

⟶

FENLACES contributes to this new economic order by establishing and instituting fair trade relations at a national, regional and world level.

FENLACES considers Popular Economy to be that which is formed on the basis of collective work organisations operating on the basis of the interests and democratic control of their members . . . . We want to promote and strengthen a social economic sector based upon fair trade.

FENLACES believes that our economy and our reality will undergo a greater development, to the extent that fair and equitable relations of exchange with developed countries exist. In this we take into consideration our own development, and a certain responsibility of the rich countries to contribute to the qualitative change in our reality.

FENLACES affirms its support for the struggles of humanity for peace, for the clear respect of human rights, the rights of the woman, of the youth and of the children. It condemns every form of discrimination and racial or social oppression. As scientific and technical advances are incorporated, FENLACES looks at this from the point of view of improving the quality of life and preserving the environment

The commitment to autonomy, development and collective work organisation are here combined with the belief in fair trade as a means to wider ends. FENLACES has established a regional office in Chile and has begun to organise trade exchanges between its several members and to establish links with alternative trade organisations in Europe and North America. What FEN-LACES is looking for, like so many other small-scale producer organisations in the Third World, is a wider framework for fair trading, an alternative market within which to operate.

A Framework for Fair Trading

All the efforts of such producer organisations in the Third World to develop exchanges between themselves and to expand their sales through alternative trade organisations in the First World, in Europe and North America, Australasia and Japan, pale into insignificance by the side of the four or five giant trading companies in each commodity who market 90 per cent of the world's production. Alternative trade amounts to perhaps some $50 million worth of exchanges a year. The sales of coffee alone by just three giant companies exceed $50 billion. The 'coyotes' and the state trading organisations in Mexico are small cogs in the gigantic wheels of international trade that bring together the production of literally millions of peasant coffee growers to fill your jars of Nescafe or sachets of Kenco. If you buy your coffee from Nicaragua or from the 'front line states' of Southern Africa, your conscience may rest more easily and a few campesino villages looking for an alternative to the old ways of trade exploitation will have gained a new confidence in cooperative effort. But, world-wide the effect will be almost negligible.

What then would be the nature of a 'fair trading' system in the world? What has to be changed? And to answer that question onc has to ask first how the world economy has come to this condition where millions of peasants are subject to such gross exploitation, so that we should enjoy our coffee, cocoa or tea, our tobacco and cane sugar, pineapple and other tropical fruits, our cotton, natural rubber and forest products. We could ask the same question about those who produce most of the minerals we use — from oil to tin and phosphates, gold and copper, iron ore, nickel and bauxite. Is it fair that most of them live so poorly and most of us live so well? What caused this great rift in the earth's population that leaves on the one side, mostly in the North, the developed industrialised countries and on the other, mainly in the South, the underdeveloped lands of food and raw material production? This is where this book must start; but our story of the campesinos of Guerrero has given us some clues and a picture quite different from the tragic stories of earthquakes, hurricanes, drought and floods that seem to ascribe solely to natural causes the disasters of the Third World. We shall have to look back at the period of colonial rule, and at the continuous interventions of imperial powers in the Third World, to discover how this great rift occurred and how it can be healed. It is a long and terrible story, but we need not approach it with a sense of overwhelming guilt. The people in the First World in the North have suffered from many of the same forces at work, from exploitation by the same companies, as their brothers and sisters in the Third World of the South. There are rich and poor, exploiters and exploited, in the undeveloped South as there are in the developed North. We have seen that there are producer organisations in the Third World working together to make changes in their trading relations. We know that there are alternative trade organisations in the First World committed to the same ends. What we should seek is a framework within which all peoples of the North and South, the East and the West, can trade together fairly without oppression or exploitation. For we all share one world, the planet earth.

Notes

This chapter is partly based on a report entitled *Estrategias de Accion y Programa de Trabajo 1988* of the Coalicion de Ejidos y Comunidades Caficulturas de la Costa Grande de Guerrero, Atoyas de Alvares, Gro., Enero, 1988. The Mexican story is supplemented by readings in American history and especially in W. E. Woodward, *A New American History*, Faber, 1938, Chapter 6 of Part I. The address of FENLACES is P.O. Box 2373, Managua, Nicaragua.

2. THE WORLD DIVISION OF LABOUR IN HISTORICAL PERSPECTIVE

Why go back into history to explain unfair trade? Isn't it enough to see that some countries are rich and powerful and others poor and weak? But why, then, are the rich mainly in the North and the poor mainly in the South, the rich mainly white and the poor mainly black? It was not always so. The first great civilisations emerged in Egypt and Central Asia, in India and China, long before there was any similar development in Europe or North America. Like so many others the Mexican people have a long history of civilisation, predating most of Europe's cities by several centuries. The Spaniards who conquered Mexico in 1519 and Peru in 1532 came upon the heirs to the great empires of the Mayas, Aztecs and Incas in Middle America, dating back to the time of Christ and before. When Columbus, seeking a western route to the spice islands of the East Indies on behalf of the King and Queen of Spain, made his landfall on the Bahamas in 1492 and named the Caribbean Islands the West Indies, he opened up the way not just to a new continent but to societies of immense wealth and high culture. As they marched into the interior of Mexico and down into Peru, the Spanish *conquistadores* found a population alienated from their rulers, formed popular alliances with them and then laid waste their cities by fire and sword. They melted down the ornaments and monuments of gold and silver that they seized, to send home as bullion. To add to this rich haul they turned on the local population which had at first supported them and set the men to work in the gold and silver mines. Between 1521 and 1660 the Spanish government fleet alone brought back from the Americas as much as 200 tons of gold and 18,000 tons of silver.

The Slave Trade

There was worse to follow. The decimation of the indigenous population in battle and in the mines and from European diseases, and the subsequent flight of many of the people into the forests and mountains, left a large gap in the labour force working the mines and plantations. As early as 1505 the King of Spain dispatched 17 black slaves with mining equipment from Sevilla. In 1551 the first consignment of black slaves was sold in the West Indies and five years later the first importation of slave-grown sugar came back from the Caribbean to Europe. The shipments of slaves built up slowly to about 6,000 a year by the year 1600. Black slave revolts made the King of Spain move cautiously. Soon the English joined in the trade. Drake's capture of gold and silver which he brought back to Queen Elizabeth in the

Golden Hinde amounted to more than a ton. J.M.Keynes once calculated that, cumulatively reinvested overseas for three centuries, this could account for the whole of British foreign investment by 1900. Slaves were for many years the main channel of investment. Sir John Hawkins took 300 slaves to the West Indies in 1567, slaves which he had received from one African king for his help in defeating a rival. The slaves went to work on plantations.

Sir Walter Raleigh is best known for introducing tobacco into Europe from the Americas. The American Indians had learned over many years to cultivate maize, potatoes, tomatoes, cane sugar, cocoa, tobacco, cotton, rubber, sisal and many root crops like ginger and turmeric. Some of these could be transferred to Europe's temperate climates, but others — above all sugar, tobacco and cotton — had to be cultivated in sub-tropical lands. Production was developed on large plantations managed by Europeans using African slave labour, not only in the Caribbean Islands, in Mexico and Brazil but in the southern states of Britain's North American colonies. The first boat-load of Africans was landed at Jamestown, Virginia in 1619.

As the demand in Europe rose for sugar and tobacco and then for cotton, so the need for slaves grew apace. By 1700 1.3 million had been transported. In the next century another six million crossed the Atlantic. At the peak of the trade in 1750 some 65,000 slaves were being taken every year. This trade in African slaves had become part of what was called 'the triangular trade'. It laid the foundation of Britain's industrialisation. On the first leg manufactured goods were exported from Britain to the west coast of Africa — mainly guns (100,000 a year by 1750), but also pots and pans, knives and tools and trinkets from Birmingham. These were sold to African chiefs in exchange for slaves. The next leg was the voyage across the Atlantic to the Caribbean colonies of Britain, Spain, France and Holland, and to Brazil and the southern states of North America. Here those who had survived the crossing were sold to work on the plantations. On the final leg, sugar, tobacco, cotton and other plantation crops were transported for sale in Europe. The mainly British shipowners made a profit on each leg of the trip. By the Treaty of Utrecht in 1714 Britain had gained the monopoly of supplying the Spanish colonies, as well as her own, with slaves. It was not, however, only Britain and the other European colonial powers who gained from the slave trade. Despite the veto of the British, by the time of the American War of Independence, for every 100 slave ships sailing from Liverpool there were 60 to 70 slavers sailing out of Rhode Island. They took rum to Africa and exchanged it for slaves to be transported to the West Indies, where the slaves were sold for molasses for the ships to bring back to the North American distilleries.

CHART 1. MAP OF TRIANGULAR TRADE, 18TH CENTURY

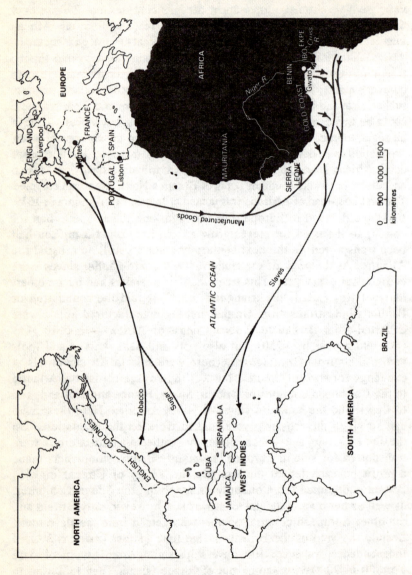

Source: Basil Davidson, *The 'Triangular Trade'*.

The results both for Africa and for America south of what became the United States were equally disastrous. Africa lost the strongest and healthiest of her young men and women. The harsh rule of the chiefs was imposed with foreign guns upon the people who remained. Local handicrafts were destroyed by the competition of cheaper factory products. Middle America suffered from the destruction both of the people and of their native products. The land was turned over to production for export, each island or territory assigned to one or two crops or minerals. Spanish or other European settlers became managers and governors of colonial territories. The picture was perfectly drawn by Daniel Defoe in 1719 in the character of Crusoe in his famous novel. Crusoe is carrying £40 of 'toys and trifles' to exchange for slaves when he is shipwrecked. With his gun and tools saved from the wreck, and by the power of religion, Crusoe initiates Man Friday into servitude. More natives are captured and rescued from cannibalism. A Spaniard is put in charge of this labour on the island plantations and after returning to England Crusoe finds himself 'master of an estate . . . above a thousand pounds a year'.

The world had been divided into developed and undeveloped, rich and poor, producers of manufactured goods and primary producers, north and south, white and black. And something else had happened in the process. In 1609 when the Flemish painter, Peter Paul Rubens, painted his great canvas of the Adoration of the Magi, he followed an ancient European tradition in depicting one of the wise men from the East, one of the kings of Orient, who came to worship the infant Jesus, as a splendidly bejewelled black African. But this was the last time. Rubens became the Flemish ambassador at the Spanish court and when he painted the same scene again in 1624 the beautiful African has become a furious turbanned Moor with cutlass and stereotypical rolling black eyes. There is a copy of this picture above the altar in Kings College chapel in Cambridge. Thereafter, the black kings in all the pictures of the adoration are replaced by white figures. The worship of Saint Maurice, the black crusader, whose pictures in shining armour graced the ikons of Central Europe for so long, are found no longer; the black St. Georges in the stained glass windows of English parish churches disappear. What had happened was the slave trade. Before the sixteenth century white and black people had met and traded on equal terms. Herodotus, the Greek historian, assumed that black people were intellectually the superiors of white people, and it seems that he was right. For we now know that Greek civilisation had its roots in Africa, transmitted down the Nile and across the Mediterranean via Crete to Attica. But once black people had been enslaved, they had to be believed to be inferior.

The deception had begun with the forged letters of the Florentine traveller, Amerigo Vespucci, whose name was given to the whole continent,

Amerigo's land. Amerigo was supposed to have preceded Columbus; he had indeed voyaged twice across the Atlantic, but after Columbus. The letters were a cruel forgery, imputing lasciviousness to the native Indian women, laziness to the men, cannibalism to both, an imputation that was repeated by Defoe. The forgery suited the bankers who disseminated it to seek to justify their involvement in the flow of stolen gold throughout Europe. If they were Jews it might also help them to defend themselves against the Inquisition, which was the instrument of Spain's unification under Ferdinand and Isabella, designed to rid the country of its Muslim and Jewish populations.

But how did it happen that Europeans should move out to bring the whole world under their dominion? Why us and not them? Why did they not colonise us? In fact Mongol peoples had ruled over much of Eastern Russia until the fourteenth century and the Moors had ruled over most of Spain for 700 years before 1492. It was in the very year that Columbus landed in the Americas that the last Moorish stronghold in Granada was defeated by the Catholic monarchs. Thereafter, European conquests were continuous — the Americas, Asia, Africa, Australasia were brought under European rule. Trade, first the slave trade and then an unequal exchange of manufactures for raw materials, was the instrument. But it cannot have been the cause, although it is widely argued that it was Europe's opening up of trade, first through internal markets and then overseas, which gave to Europeans their advantage over other peoples. There were of course markets outside Europe in all the great towns and cities of the East and the South; the argument is that the markets were restricted outside Europe by centralised state power, as they had been in mediaeval Europe by feudal power. Only in Europe were restraints on the free working of markets successfully challenged by the bourgeoisie. Elsewhere this did not happen. To take but one example, but an important one, in China the emperor in 1521 had all the ocean-going junks destroyed and trade outside Chinese territorial waters forbidden. The merchants with their wealth based upon world-wide trade were becoming a challenge to the imperial power based on tribute from the land. But why only in Europe? It could be just because the Europeans got in first, and then by many means held on to what they had.

Colonial Rule

Once the gap was opened up between Europe and the rest of the world, the rift between developed and undeveloped, between black and white, between north and south, was deepened and widened by all that was to follow. The stages of plunder and slavery were succeeded by colonisation, the seizure of land and a great expansion of trade. Some of the colonies became lands for European settlement — in North and South America, in Australasia and in Southern Africa. But most had begun as plantations and fortresses for the triangular trade and the extension of this trade into Asia. As Britain established her industrial superiority, the whole world was opened up by British traders to provide markets for her manufactures and sources of raw materials for her industry. Britain's imperial expansion was determined by this division of labour and ensured by the British navy's mastery over the high seas. Settlement of Europeans in Asia and in many parts of Africa was prevented by the dangers from the sun and from tropical diseases for white-skinned people. Europe's expansion overseas, which had begun with purely trading relationships, became an extension of the capitalist system of production as it developed at home.

Empire was only at first an instrument of merchant capital, merchant traders buying cheap and selling dear. It soon involved truly productive capital, local people being set to work to produce for the European and North American market, with all the processing and transporting being kept in European or North American hands. This is the relationship of exploitation and dependence from which the Mexican campesinos, like so many others, are struggling to escape. The most extensive example of this relationship was in Britain's Indian Empire, where cotton and jute, coir and timber, tea and tropical fruits were grown for export, often at the expense of food crops for the people. India, which became the jewel in the imperial diadem, offered the largest market for Britain's manufactures and largest source of raw materials, but also a steady supply of tribute in gold and silver and of soldiers for the imperial armies.

What the British Empire established world-wide, and where French, Dutch, Portuguese and Belgian empires followed suit, the United States established by expanding her frontiers. This was described by one of her Presidents as her 'manifest destiny'. The main target was Mexico. Between 1845 and 1848, by war and purchase, the United States acquired one half of Mexico's domain, including all the territory that now comprises the North American states of Texas, California, New Mexico, Arizona, Nevada, Utah and part of Colorado. Mexicans, who had thrown off Spanish rule in 1821, had failed to create a truly united people of Spanish and Indian blood. Their cavalry was no match for United States artillery. Their white-skinned leaders, even the arrogant but heroic Santa Anna, won only limited loyalty from the Indian masses. They were divided and conquered. Mexico was left truncated and pillaged, shorn of her richest lands, a semi-colony of the United States, the despair of her people to fuel a succession of ill-fated rebellions and revolts, the one hope of her starving masses to swim the width of the Rio Grande and find work as outlaws in the lands to the north that had once been their own.

National economic development has always been made possible only with strong state support; the later the nation entered the development stakes the greater the support that was needed. Even British manufacturing industry at the end of the eighteenth century required a 100 per cent tariff on imports of Indian textiles. Until then India had supplied Europe with its calicos and muslins, as China had supplied the silks and satins. When the machine-made cloths supplanted the products of handlooms first in Europe and then in their own lands, the ancient village industries of the East were one by one destroyed and their populations rendered destitute. The cotton towns of Surat, Dacca and Murishabad, in the centre of what is now the poorest land in the world, the state of Bangladesh, were described by Robert Clive in 1757 as just 'as extensive, popular and rich as the city of London'. These manufacturing centres of Bengal exported millions of pounds worth of cotton goods each year. Yet, within 60 years their exports had ceased and India was importing cloth from British factories using increasingly as their raw material raw cotton from India. Clive himself and his fellow officers in the East India Company were in large part responsible for this destruction. It was in that same year of 1757 that Clive had defeated the armies of the Nawab of Bengal at the battle of Plassey. Under the treaties that followed, treasure valued at £4 million (perhaps £200 million of our currency) was taken. Clive himself took a quarter of a million and an estate yielding £27,000 a year. For 50 years the annual tribute taken by the Company and its servants amounted to at least £5 million and in some years to as much as £15 million. How important such a flow of tribute was for financing the industrial revolution in Britain is a matter for argument but, while little of this wealth went directly into industry, a richer home market must have encouraged economic development. In India the effect of the destruction of native industries was worse even than the flow of tribute. The first famines were reported in 1770. 'The bones of the weavers were bleaching the plains of India . . . . The jungle and malaria are fast encroaching upon the towns . . . . One third of the company's territory in Hindustan is now a jungle inhabited only by wild beasts.' And these were the reports of an English governor general.

What happened to the Indian textile industry was repeated in other industries and in other lands. The native iron smelting industry of India that could produce the six-ton 24-foot steel pillar at Qtb Minar 1,500 years ago and the steel for the famous Damascus blades was wiped out by cheap imported iron and steel. When I once claimed in a lecture in Sheffield that the rust-free quality of the Qtb Minar pillar was a tribute to Indian steel forging, I was told in all seriousness by a local steel-maker in the audience that the steel had been preserved by the oily film which millions of Indian worshippers had given it with their hands as they passed by. I had to say that I had not met any 20-foot Indians on my travels. This is just one example among many of the inability of Europeans to recognise the accomplishments of other races, like the myth that the great walls of Zimbabwe must have been built by a lost white race, by Phoenicians or by the Queen of Sheba, by anyone in fact but Africans; or the belief that the three great discoveries singled out by Francis Bacon as those which have 'changed the whole face and state of things throughout the world' in the sixteenth century were European, when all three — printing, gunpowder and the compass — were invented by the Chinese a thousand years earlier and brought to Europe by the Arabs. Bacon knew because he had learnt Arabic in order to study mathematics. We call our letters Roman and our languages Aryan, but all came from Asia or Africa.

Why Europe advanced and Asia and Africa fell behind is a question that cannot be answered properly here. I have tried to do this elsewhere. It must suffice to say that the freedom of towns and cities and the emergence of individual landowning and of merchant ventures from European feudalism was not paralleled in the great river valley civilisations of Africa and Asia. There the irrigation systems required central control and this authority was reinforced by the need for defence against nomadic invaders from the north. This central power could prevent the emergence of a dominant merchant class, which could itself make way for industrial capitalism. By contrast, in Europe the centralising power of feudalism was much weaker. Capitalism could grow up in the town guilds, around the water mills and harbours of all the little rain-fed rivers. From these initial bases their very lack of resources sent the Europeans scurrying out across the oceans to bring lands and peoples and natural resources under their dominion. In this they were encouraged by their religion. For they believed that God created man and gave him 'dominion', as Genesis has it, 'over all the fish of the sea, the birds of the heaven, all the wild beasts and all the reptiles that crawl upon the earth'. No other religion except perhaps Islam grants to men — and I mean men — such a blessing 'to increase and multiply and fill the earth and subdue it'. There were so many ways in which Europe was different from Asia or Africa or the Americas, not better, not worse, but different in its history, resulting from different climate, geographical structure and merging of peoples. The traditional societies, from which writers like W.W. Rostow in his influential book published in 1960, *The Stages of Economic Growth: A Non-communist Manifesto*, believed that all societies could 'take off' into development, were in fact quite different in their traditions — religious, social, economic, political and cultural. It is a wholly Eurocentric view to suppose that all 'development' must follow the European way.

Free Trade

What happened was a very uneven development. Once European conquerors had spread across the world and lands were 'opened up' to foreign trade and kept open by the British navy, the cheaper factory goods drove out the handicrafts in every part of the world except the most inaccesssible mountain ranges and the most isolated islands. The craft products of these remote areas may today be in great demand in the most advanced industrial centres both for themselves and as models for modern designs; but they are all that is left of an immensely rich variety of traditions of popular art and craft work which could each have developed its own road to industrialisation. Those outside Europe and outside the lands of European settlement who were caught up in the capitalist system of world trade were assigned the role of producing the primary raw materials for Europeans to process and refine and make up into finished goods. Even when they were not set to work as slaves in mines and on plantations, the peoples of the Third World became dependent for their tools and their markets on colonial and foreign powers that were beyond their control. This was the essence of what came to be called 'free trade'.

In the lands of European settlement overseas, and particularly in North America, the colonists succeeded in breaking out of this dependent relationship. The origins of the revolt of Britain's American colonies lay in the monopoly exercised, by the home country, on the trade between them. 'It was the intention in settling our plantations in America,' wrote the Commissioner for Trade and Plantations in 1699, 'that the people there should be only employed in such things as are not the produce of England, to which they belong.' Thus iron was produced in New England but exported to old England for developing into manufactures. The famous Boston Tea Party, in which the East India Company's teas were thrown into Boston harbour, was a protest by smugglers in the colonies at the monopoly which the Company had on the shipping of tea to America. Even before the North American colonies had won their independence, they had joined in the slave trade, and their economic development undoubtedly benefited from it. There was one European people which took no part in this trade, and achieved a certain measure of economic advance. Russia not only fought off colonisation herself, both from the East and the West, but went on to colonise her Asiatic neighbours and thus took in vast resources of land and minerals, which were to become the basis for Soviet economic development.

Some lands of European settlement, however, failed to break out of the dependent relationship. The colonies of Spanish settlers in Latin America freed themselves from Spanish rule even before the British colonies in Canada, Australasia and South Africa freed themselves from British rule. But they fell under the economic power of the capital of the United States and Britain, which was being invested in their countries, and invested entirely in primary production — ranching, plantations and mining — and not at all in manufacturing. The difference between the destiny of the Spanish and the early British colonies lay mainly in the origin of the settlers: the Spanish from a country that was still largely agrarian, the British from one that was rapidly industrialising. The recent economic development of Argentina, Brazil or Mexico has been retarded by this central difference, but even more by the subsequent economic distortion from the influence of United States and British capital. The massive current debts of these countries to United States and British banks are a sorry reminder of this continuing dependence.

Only one non-European people, the Japanese, the furthest away from Europe, succeeded in avoiding colonisation, thus keeping out European influence during its most destructive stages. When Commodore Perry of the United States navy sailed into Tokyo harbour in 1853 to open up the Japanese market, the United States was not interested in annexing more territory, and the businessmen of the United States, Britain, France and Germany were by then more concerned to sell their railway equipment, ship-building and textile machinery than their textiles and pots and pans. Japanese feudalism had permitted the development of a merchant class. The religious authority of the Emperor was copied from China, but his power was nominal. Japan had no great rivers requiring centrally controlled irrigation. Her islands provided protection from Mongol invasion, and upon their rain-fed hills and valleys a feudal system not dissimilar from Europe's could flourish. The apparent exception to the rule that capitalism only emerged from European feudalism proves to be no exception. A Japanese merchant class could combine with an ancient warrior class to create a military regime which was able to carry through an extremely rapid industrialisation with borrowed European machinery, and then build up a powerful army and navy to defend its island empire and launch its attack on mainland China.

By the outbreak of the first World War, aside from the Japanese empire, the world was divided up between great European empires — some 300 million Europeans in the North ruling directly over nearly 1 billion non-Europeans in the South. The British Empire was by far the largest with 600 million inhabitants, 400 million of them on the Indian continent. The United States effectively controlled most of Central and South America. Russia had expanded her frontiers to the borders of Persia in the south, Sweden in the north and China and the Sea of Japan to the east. Japan held

Korea and Taiwan, Fukien, Dairen and Tsingtao on the Chinese mainland. Africa was divided up between France, Portugal, Belgium and Germany as well as Britain. The Dutch held the East Indies and Guiana and the French Indo-China. In seven Chinese ports, besides Hong Kong and Shanghai, European powers had concessionary treaties. Marx had spoken of a 'rejuvenating role' as well as a 'destructive role' for English rule in India; was there no plus sign then on the balance sheet of imperial trade and colonisation?

The Spread of Capitalism

There were very bad years for the colonial peoples in the nineteenth century and again in the 1930s, and these were repeated for most of the ex-colonies in the 1980s. Was there no benefit from European rule? Was the spread of capitalism across the whole world, from its heartlands in Europe, not an engine of growth and economic development? This is the view which we have been criticising of those who see in the market the key to the development of productive forces. The argument was that some time after the early years of the seventeenth century, first in Britain and then elsewhere in Europe and the lands of European settlement overseas, a merchant capitalist class began to loosen markets from the restrictions of royal and feudal government. From that moment competitive enterprise was released and these economies leapt forward to generate more productive forces in the next three centuries than had been created in previous millenia. Any nation, like Japan which freed the market in this way, could follow suit. Those countries which retained centralised restraints on the free working of market forces failed to advance, and this was the fate of what we now call the Third World. This is the story as it is told, and thus it was that these countries continued with ups and downs of good and bad harvests to enjoy no more than creeping growth to a level little above that which all peoples of the world had achieved by 1600.

We have seen that what actually happened around 1600 was the irruption of European armies from the north into Africa, America and Asia, the genocide of indigenous peoples, the slave trade, colonial rule and the displacement of handcraft production by factory goods, relegating the Third World in the south to primary production. It could still be the case that European world conquest had to do with the release of market forces and that this was the key to unlocking economic development which all peoples must grasp. What is sure is that European and Japanese feudalism proved to be more fertile soil for generating capitalism than the great centralised hydraulic civilisations of the Nile, the Tigris and Euphrates, the Indus and the Ganges, the Yangtse, the Yellow River and Mekong or the water tank systems of Peru and Sri Lanka. But the scale of the setback from European destruction cannot be denied. Almost all that these civilisations had created, except their monumental buildings, was either destroyed or distorted into a form that Europeans could exploit. The most serious distortion for the future development of the Third World was that an elite of landowners, princes, merchants and agents were encouraged and then left behind like a Trojan horse when colonial rule ended. This elite was totally tied into the world system of trade exchanges — of European and North American manufactures for Third World primary produce. The emergence of a national bourgeoisie with interests opposed to the metropolitan powers' commercial agents, themselves generally linked to the local landowning class, has proved to be both unusual and extremely difficult. Merchant capital does not evolve naturally into industrial capital. A new class of industrial capitalists had to challenge the old merchant capitalists for supremacy even in Britain, the first capitalist nation. It is only in Hong Kong, Taiwan and South Korea that we have seen any sizeable proportion of native capitalists coming into existence in the Third World.

It still has to be recognised that some economic development has occurred in the Third World, some industrialisation has taken place, some local enterprise was encouraged. Even some Marxists have seen 'imperialism as the pioneer of capitalism' — the title of a book by Bill Warren. The claim cannot just be dismissed out of hand. North America, Oceania and South Africa were once colonial territories and they have largely succeeded in all-round economic development. Japanese development we have already recognised and to this outstanding success must be added the achievements of the so-called 'Four Little Dragons' — Hong Kong, South Korea, Singapore and Taiwan. These lands contain some 60 million people and there is no doubt about the rapid pace of their economic growth since the 1950s or about their continued growth even after the collapse of the rest of the Third World in the debt crisis of the 1980s. There were other countries with similar rapid rates of growth up till then, not only the oil-producing countries but other countries of the South — the Philippines, Mexico, Brazil and even India. In the 1960s and 1970s the average growth rate of national incomes in the Third World exceeded even that in the northern First World. Before the debt crisis there was talk of the Third World catching up in some 300 years, but after the collapse of the 1980s that now looks much less likely.

It is nonetheless often claimed that the people of the Third World are today infinitely better off than they were 40 years ago. It is certainly possible to point to statistics of longer life expectations and lower infant mortality rates, to the eradication of smallpox and a huge reduction in deaths from malaria, typhus, cholera, bilharzia and tuberculosis. The result has been a massive population explosion in societies which traditionally looked to large families to ensure racial survival, to provide household labour and to procure protection in old age. Does this not mean that the world simply has more poor people? There is much evidence that the first stages of growth are associated with more unequal income distribution. It was so in the English industrial revolution. Inequalities are markedly even greater in the Third World than they are in the First World. The highest fifth of income-earners in most Third World countries enjoys over a half of all the income; in Brazil it is two-thirds. By contrast, the lowest fifth has between two per cent (Brazil) and five per cent (Philippines). In the United Kingdom and the USA the corresponding proportions are 40 per cent for the highest and six per cent for the lowest.

There has undoubtedly been some growth in incomes in the last 40 years in the Third World as a whole, but the fact is that it has been very unevenly distributed. What has been happening has been development in enclaves, similar to the 'Four Little Dragons'. In enterprise zones — in Manila, Mexico City, São Paolo, Greater Colombo or Bombay — industrial development was leading to a small elite growing much richer, able to buy the cars and other consumer goods of modern capitalism. At the same time, the great majority in the surrounding country was involved only as cheap labour, as an unemployed reserve army of labour that kept industrial wages low, as suppliers of food and raw materials for the towns or simply as small farming households where a worker's wife or husband or family could live and make it possible for the worker to survive on a wage that was inadequate alone to support a family. Within the entrerprise zones there is work for young women at sewing machines and electronics assembly lines within the complex division of labour of the giant transnational companies of Europe, North America and Japan; but this is not a basis for independent development. Something more is required which we shall look for in later chapters. Capitalism has indeed continuously extended its rule but very unevenly. The great inequalities of North and South, of white and black remain unchanged.

Notes

A full statement of facts and references to support the argument of this chapter can be found in my *After Imperialism*, Heinemann, 1963 and Merlin Press, 1970, the first chapters of which are reproduced in the Open University, *Third World Studies*, Block 2, Part B, 1983. W. W. Rostow's book, *The Stages of Economic Growth*, was published in 1960 by the Cambridge University Press. The most influential book to succeed Rostow's as a critique of a Marxist view of capitalist world development is Peter L. Berger's *The Capitalist Revolution*, Wildwood House, 1987. Bill Warren's *Imperialism: Pioneer of Capitalism* was published by Verso in 1980.

3. THE DIVISION OF WORLD RESOURCES BETWEEN RICH AND POOR

It is an unequal world, then, that we have inherited. We have seen how the divide between North and South came about, by conquest and trade, so that we now have rich industrialised lands in the North, today's so-called First World, and poor underdeveloped primary producers in the South, the so-called Third World. Given this historical division, the question is how far the trading relations that exist today can be expected to change in the future. When it is now a major issue whether the earth's resources can be conserved and the environment protected for future generations, we have to ask what resources are still available in these different worlds. For, the fact is that it is the economic development of the First World which has plundered the whole globe and most particularly the non- renewable resources of the Third World — oil and gas and minerals and forests. And it is now revealed that much the same kind of economic development has been taking place under the centrally planned economies, those we call the Second World, which were committed to building what they called socialism. Table 1 gives rough figures for the distribution of population and resources and their employment between the three worlds.

It appears that there are about five billion people on our planet, and there could be double that number in 30 years. Three-quarters are in the Third World. More than half are in Asia. This includes China's 22 per cent, but not Japan's 2.5 per cent. Another quarter live in Africa and in Central and South America. The developed capitalist countries in the North account for little more than one-sixth (17 per cent), the former Soviet Union and Eastern Europe for another eight per cent. But land is quite differently distributed. Because of the land grabs made by Europeans in North America, Oceania, South Africa and what became the Soviet Union (which alone contained a fifth of all the land), the three-quarters of the world's people in the Third World occupy not much more than half of the world's cultivable land. It is perhaps not then very surprising that they are poor, discounting the distortions of their economies which we have been looking at.

It is sometimes suggested that the Third World's troubles arise from the fact that they have allowed their populations to grow too fast for the land area. This is true in some places, but in terms of world-wide proportions, they are only just regaining the shares they had in the eighteenth century before the Europeans had their great population boom as they spread out from Europe to other lands. In 1650 Europeans comprised 19 per cent of the

TABLE 1. THE THREE WORLDS' RESOURCES IN THE LATE 1980s (annual totals and percentages)

Resource	Totals	First	Second**	China	Third
Population	5000m	17%	8%	22%	53%
Cultivable land	1500m. ha	25	22	9	44
Agricultural Output					
Wheat	550mt.	36	22	5	37
Rice	480mt.	2	1	7	90
Maize	480mt.	58	10	4	38
Total agri. output %		*38*	*26*	*10*	*26*
Energy					
Oil reserves	141btce.	12	13	5	70
output	4btce.	31	28	3	38
Coal reserves	7800btce.	21	63	6	10
output	3btce.	40	26	6	28
Gas reserves	67btce.				
output	2btce.	35	40	2	23
Minerals output					
Iron ore	524mt.	26	28	6	40
Bauxite	88mt.	41	10	3	46
Phosphates	150mt.	35	22	—	43
Tin	6.2mt.	8	10	5	77
Copper	9.2mt.	33	17	2	48
Gold	1.5mt.	16 + 45*	20	1	18
Silver	14mt.	34	14	—	52
Uranium	0.4mt.	70 + 12*	—	—	18
Industrial output					
Steel	700mt.	49	30	2	19
Motor cars	32m.	90	6	—	4
total in use	400m.	80	8	1	11
Air travel passenger km.	600b	82	9	1	8
Paper	180mt.	78	7	—	15
Cement	1000mt.	41	18	3	38
TV sets	90m.	54	13	—	33
Total %		*64*	*23*	*1*	*12*

Source: United Nations Statistical Yearbooks.

Note: m. = million; mt. = million tonnes; b. = billion; btce. = billion tonnes of coal equivalent; km. = kilometres; ha. = hectares.; — = not available.

* Output of Republic of South Africa; ** These figures relate to before the collapse of the Soviet and East European state socialist systems.

world's peoples. By 1940 they peaked at 34 per cent and it is from this peak that the European proportion has declined to 25 per cent in 50 years, and is expected to decline further, to 15 per cent in the next 30 years, perhaps to only 12.5 per cent in another 100 years. By adding in people of European origin in Latin America and in South Africa, the figures would be increased by a percentage point or two, but no more.

Population and Land

It's a hungry world for many and, as the twenty-first century unfolds, the contrast between numbers of people and the cultivable land they live on seems set to worsen. Calculations of potentially arable land suggest that, while the area available to the Europeans could possibly be doubled by taking in marginal land, that available elsewhere could only be increased by at most 75 per cent and that of even more doubtful value; and all the time we are losing land to desert and salt marsh. As populations grow, we could have a situation early in the twenty-first century in the Third World whereby 85 per cent of the people have rather less than 50 per cent of the cultivable land. What is more, the Europeans' land would be the best land with the best climate for growing food. Already, the rich First World with only half as much land produces, with the aid of machines and fertilisers, as great a value of agricultural output as the Third World, including China, although this figure is somewhat exaggerated by the subsidised prices in the First World.

The tragic position today is that land hunger and debt are driving peoples in tropical lands to cut down the rain forests. These are equivalent in area to half of all their cultivable land, but the cleared forests cannot be used for cultivation after two or three seasons. As they are now, the forests serve to absorb the tropical rains and without them the land becomes a desert in the dry season and is flooded in the wet season allowing the top soil to be washed down the rivers. This not only results in loss of fertility but in silting up the great reservoirs, which have been created by damming the rivers for generating hydro-electricity. Of course, the Europeans cut down their forests and those of North America long ago, but the effect was not quite so serious for the global eco-system.

The increasing pressure on the land in Third World countries is aggravated by the artificial division of labour in the world between manufacturing in the First World and primary production in the Third World. There is a complication here which we need to sort out at once. It is only in certain minerals and fuels and tropical fruits and beverages that the Third World is the major supplier, and in a very few of these that the Third World has a monopoly, as we shall see. The First World in fact provides most of the food and raw materials entering world trade in addition to most of the manufactures — over two-thirds of all manufactures, around 85 per cent in the case of chemicals, machinery and transport equipment. The problem for most Third World countries is that they have nothing else to offer on the world market except products of the land, including minerals, and often only one product from each country.

Most Third World countries rely for over 60 per cent of their export earnings on agricultural products. This is true for all the Central American and Caribbean states, for all of East Africa and West Africa (except Nigeria), for Egypt, Turkey and Syria and all Southern Asia and the Philippines. Until the 1970s, when oil deposits were discovered, Nigeria could have been added to this list and also Malaysia and Indonesia. For many of these countries the proportion of agricultural products in their exports was over 80 per cent and only one crop was involved — sugar from Cuba, Jamaica, Mauritius; coffee from Ecuador; tea from Sri Lanka; cotton from Sudan; cocoa from Ghana; beef from Paraguay and Botswana; bananas from Honduras. As a result there are countries where over a third of the cultivated land is devoted to export crops.

This is true of Costa Rica, Cuba, Ghana, Guatemala, Haiti, Côte d'Ivoire, Jamaica, Malaysia, Paraguay, Sri Lanka. Some people argue that the only hope for such countries is to end completely their dependence on cash cropping for export. We shall see later that this is not so easy, nor is it totally necessary or desirable. It is the quite excessive allocation of land to export crops in certain countries that is the problem, particularly where it is the most productive land, often the irrigated land, which is given up to these crops. And export crops have frequently been grown without thought for the condition of the soil. Natural bush cover has been removed which protected the soil from desertification by the wind, or artificial fertilisers have been used together with herbicides and pesticides which have poisoned the land and the rivers.

Food Imports and Exports

The fact that all the tropical lands are in the Third World means that most tropical food products are exported, since they find a ready market in the First World. Some of these products, like coffee, tea and cocoa, have no food value, but foods like bananas, palm oil, coconuts, ground-nuts, cane sugar, soya and many tropical fish are important sources of both calories and protein. It is mainly bread grains that are imported in exchange from the First World. The exchange is thus very often of high-protein exports from the Third World — nuts, vegetable oils, pulses, meat, fish — for high-calorie imports — grains and flour. This results in serious protein shortages in the diets of many Third World people: 60 per cent were said in 1967 to be short of protein, 20 per cent to be short of calories, while the rich in the First (and equally in the Third World) eat too much of both. Some 40 countries have inadequate supplies for their own peoples' calorific requirements, let alone protein needs, and yet they are net exporters of food. Table 2 shows lists of countries according to their status as net food importers or exporters, having or not having sufficient food to feed their people.

The figures in Table 2 for net food exports are a monetary calculation, and it cannot be said that, if exports ceased or were reduced, food supplies would be adequate. This is because export crops have higher monetary values than staple foods. The fact remains that a third of the countries which are net food exporters have nonetheless experienced famines since 1950. Other countries have insufficient food for their people despite being net importers of food. China is the main country in this category, but there are others, as the Table shows. Of course, many countries which are net food importers have more than enough food thanks to their imports. Most of Western and Eastern Europe are in this category, together with Japan and South Korea, and even the Soviet Union relies on imports of food, despite its extensive lands. The main countries which export food from a surplus over and above what they need to feed their people are in the grain-producing regions of the First World — North America, Australia, South America. There are some other net food exporters in the First World, mainly in Europe; and there are even a few in the Third World in this happy situation.

The varying positions of different countries in the Third World in relation to self-sufficiency in food reveals the danger of making generalisations. Even in Africa and India there has possibly never been a year when there was not adequate food for all — if supplies could have been moved to the famine areas, if distribution had been more equal and if net exports had been reduced. Populations have risen sharply in recent years, especially in Africa, but world production of food has, nonetheless, continued to grow faster than the rate of population increase, so that output of food per head has been growing on average throughout the world as a whole at just over half a per cent per year in the 1960s, 1970s and 1980s. Even the Third World countries have shared in this increase, but at a slightly lower rate — about a quarter of a per cent a year. This overall average figure conceals some actual decline in the 1980s in Africa and stagnation in Latin America and in Central and Southern Asia including India.

Enough Food but Badly Shared Out

The implications of this picture are that the food produced is simply not

TABLE 2. WORLD TRADE IN FOOD AND SELF-SUFFICIENCY

Countries having enough food and being net food exporters		Countries having enough food due to net imports		Countries having insufficient food despite net imports		Countries having insufficient food despite net exports	
First & Second World	Third World	First & Second World	Third World	First & Second World	Third World	First & Second World	Third World
Australia	Argentina	Austria	Chile	NIL	Algeria	NIL	Afghanistan	Kenya
Bulgaria	Costa Rica	Czechoslovakia	Egypt		Bangladesh		Angola	Liberia
Canada	Madagascar	France	Israel		China		Bostwana	Mozambique
Denmark	Malaysia	Germany*	Jamaica		Haiti		Burma	Namibia
Eire	Mongolia	Italy	Korea		Iraq		Cameroon	P. New Guinea
Greece	Nicaragua	Japan	Libya		Iran		Chad	Philippines
Hungary	Panama	Norway	Morocco		Kampuchea		Dominican Rep.	Senegal
Netherlands	Paraguay	Poland	Saudi Arabia		Laos		El Salvador	Sierra Leone
New Zealand	Thailand	Portugal	Syria		Mauretania		Ethiopia	Somalia
South Africa	Uruguay	Romania	Vietnam		Niger		Ghana	Sri Lanka
Turkey	Zimbabwe	Spain			Pakistan		Guinea	Sudan
USA		Sweden			Venezuela		Guatemala	Tanzania
		Switzerland			Zanbia		Honduras	Uganda
		UK					India	Zaire
		USSR**					Indonesia	
		Yugoslavia**					Ivory Coast	

Source: Open University, *Third World Atlas*, derived from FAO statistics.
* Prior to unification
** Prior to its disintegration

getting to those who most need it; even farmers in the Third World are going hungry. There are several reasons for this apparent paradox:

(a) speculators in the Third World are sitting on stocks of food and waiting for the prices to rise;

(b) peasant farmers have lost their land to big farmers and to plantations for export crops;

(c) farm policies in the First World are pushing up prices and leading to large stocks of food accumulating, like those held in Europe under the Common Agricultural Policy. This makes food imports too dear for many poor countries unless they come as aid or at subsidised prices;

(d) at the same time, when these stocks are dumped at low prices in the Third World, Third World farmers are put out of business;

(e) incentives and mechanisms for increasing trade and transport of food within Third World countries and between them are lacking.

All these things are undoubtedly happening, but correcting them is not so easy. There are political obstacles: in the First World, governments protect their farmers to gain votes; in the Third World, ironically, governments choose to win votes in the urban areas by food aid from abroad; votes in the countryside are literally disposable, either by terror or by throwing the ballot boxes away. There are economic obstacles: food is exported or stored because this is profitable for the middlemen involved, and the small producers do not have the money for storage or to hold their crops off the market. There are, of course, physical obstacles as well in the Third World: there is no railway system in Africa or in South America connecting north and south or east and west. But sea transport and air transport are possible. In Britain we can buy sweet corn from Zimbabwe, while next door in Mozambique people are starving.

We shall look for answers to these political and economic problems in the next chapters, but we shall have to take into account the awful fact that, in the words of former US Senator Hubert Humphrey, 'Food is a new form of power . . . an extra dimension to our diplomacy.' As an example, the US Food Aid Programme, PL 480, requires recipients to 'take self-help measures'; and these include 'creating a favourable environment for private enterprise and investment', 'using available technical know-how', 'developing agricultural, chemical, farm machinery and equipment industries' and setting aside counterpart funds for 'common defence', i.e. imports of military equipment from the USA. Furthermore, countries entitled to PL 480 aid in 1974 'actually paid out at least three times as much for United States commercial agricultural exports as they received from aid supplies under PL 480', according to Susan George in her book, *A Fate Worse than Debt*. No wonder that many Third World governments are beginning to prefer trade of their choice to such tied aid, and that organisations in Third World countries are looking for alternative trade channels.

Much of the land in the Third World is taken up by forests and by non-food tropical and semi-tropical crops — jute, sisal, rubber, tobacco, coca, derris — as well as by crops with dual use, like cotton, coconut, palm and hemp — and by the beverages, tea, cocoa and coffee. All these crops may be grown on large plantations, which in some cases — cotton and tobacco in the Sahel, for instance — have opened land up to the wind and tropical rains and led directly to erosion and the making of deserts. It may appear unimportant that only a small part of the land — under 10 per cent — is devoted in any country to export crops, but this can be the best land, the irrigated land, or the land that should be broken up into smaller plots to prevent soil erosion. The use of artificial fertilisers, and of herbicides and pesticides, on these plantations is even more serious in poisoning the soil and the rivers. But worst of all is the spread of commercial practices into lands which have provided self-sufficiency during thousands of years for millions of Third World people. Especially destructive is the introduction of wage labour on estates, since this disturbs the cooperative village system of food production without supplying an alternative source of basic foods. Furthermore, cutting down the indigenous forests for grazing beef cattle and for planting gum trees to make paper and scaffolding all yield a quick profit, but this destroys the peasants' sources of firewood and of other forest products and causes erosion and disturbance to underground water-courses which feed the ancient terrace irrigation systems.

Minerals and Industry

If the Third World is short of land in relation to its population, it is generally assumed to be rich in mineral resources. This is certainly true of the energy fuels and particularly of oil. It is less true of the key minerals. Only in a few cases does the Third World provide more than half of world production, but Third World countries are responsible for much larger shares of the international trade in minerals. This is because Third World countries export nearly all of the minerals they produce, while First and Second World countries use the greater part of their production in their own industrial undertakings.

TABLE 3. THIRD WORLD'S SHARE IN WORLD MINERAL PRODUCTION (percentages)

Mineral	Third World Share (including China)	Main Third World Producing Countries
Iron Ore	45	Brazil (15), India (5), Liberia (2), Venezuela (2), China (15), South Africa (3)
Bauxite	46	Guinea (15), Brazil (7), Jamaica (8), Surinam (4), India (3)
Phosphates	45	Morocco (15), Tunisia (4), Jordan (4), Brazil (3), China (8), South Africa (2)
Silver	50	Mexico (16), Peru (15)
Gold	25	Papua (3), Philippines (3), Brazil (3), Colombia (3), Ghana (1), Zimbabwe (1), China (5), South Africa (40)
Uranium	20	Namibia (10), Niger (10), Gabon (3), South Africa (12)
Copper	40	Chile (15), Zambia (6), Zaire (5), Peru (5), Papua (2), Philippines (2), China (3)
Tin	70	Malaysia (15), Brazil (12), Indonesia (12), Thailand (8), China (12)
Zinc	25	Peru (8), Korea (3), Mexico (3), Brazil (2), Zaire (1), China (3)
Lead	25	Peru (8), Mexico (3), Korea (3), Zaire (1), China (3)
Diamonds	85	Zaire (26), Botswana (15), Namibia (11), Brazil (7), Ghana (6), Tanzania (2)
Nickel	35	New Caledonia (9), Indonesia (9), Cuba (5), Dominican Republic (3), South Africa (2)
Manganese	45	Brazil (12), Gabon (11), India (5), China (8), South Africa (15)
Tungsten	60	Korea (7), Bolivia (3), China (35)
Chrome	20	India (6), Zimbabwe (5), Philippines (2), Brazil (2), South Africa (20)
Cobalt	85	Zaire (50), Zambia (15), New Caledonia (6), Cuba (5)

Source: British Geological Survey, *World Mineral Statistics, 1982-6*, BGS, 1988.

It can be seen that the industrial countries of the North would be in some difficulty in sourcing the essential minerals for their industries and would certainly face a major rise in prices without supplies from the Third World. This is true in the case of iron ore, bauxite, phosphates, silver, copper and manganese, and particularly true for tin, diamonds, tungsten and cobalt. The future of South Africa is uncertain, but its mineral resources, not only of gold but also of the platinum group of metals, in which it has a near monopoly, make this a crucial question for the industrialised countries.

For many minerals Third World output forms a much larger proportion of world exports than of world production. This gap between mineral production and mineral use in the Third World is a reflection of the very small proportion of industrial production that takes place in the Third World — only about 13 per cent, of which the oil states account for half. The contribution of the Third World countries to trade in industrial products is rather larger — 20 per cent, of which the oil states' contribution is five per cent. Taking manufactured goods exports alone, the Third World in the mid-1980s was supplying only about 16 per cent of the total. This was, however, twice the proportion which they supplied in the 1970s. The increase is the result of expanding exports in what are termed 'other manufactures', that is excluding machinery, chemicals and transport equipment. These came mainly from the new industrialising countries — Hong Kong, South Korea, Singapore and Taiwan — the so-called 'Four Little Dragons' and from enterprise zones in the Philippines and Sri Lanka, but also from the much faster growth of industry in Brazil, Mexico and India. Much of all this development has taken place within the operations of giant transnational companies; we shall look at them in the next chapter as potential agents of increased trade between the First and Third Worlds.

New Exchanges in World Trade

Between 1976 and 1986, the Soviet Union and Eastern Europe greatly increased their share of world industrial production — from 20 per cent of the world total to 26 per cent; but their share of world trade in manufactures hardly rose over the same period — from five per cent to six per cent. Likewise, from a lower base, China in these years doubled her industrial output — from two per cent of the the world total to four per cent, but raised her share of trade in manufactures only from one per cent to 1.5 per cent. The shares of the three worlds in international trade seem to change very little even over the long run. If we think of the Soviet Union and Eastern Europe in 1913 as part of the Third World of non-industrialised countries, and emerging thereafter to form a Second World of centrally planned states oriented towards building socialism, then there has been no change in the pattern of flows of world trade between the three worlds over the last century. Table 4 shows that the First World of industrialised countries has always provided two-thirds of the value of the world's trade, rising sometimes, as today, to 70 per cent, falling sometimes, as during the oil price hike, nearer to 60 per cent. About half of world trade has consisted of exchanges within the First World. The Second World, as it emerged, followed suit; most of its trade consisted of exchanges between the centrally planned economies themselves.

The major change in world trade over the years has been that the importance of primary products has steadily declined, with a particularly sharp drop in recent years. The change is considerable — from two-thirds of the total at the beginning of the century to less than a third today. The reasons are many and diverse. There is first the entry of Japan and of the Second World into the pattern of exchanges of manufactured goods. Secondly, there is the Engels curve effect — that households spend a smaller proportion of their income on food and fuel as their incomes rise. But the main contributory factors in the most recent changes are the increased substitution of synthetic or temperate products for natural, tropical products — nylon and rayon for cotton and wool, artificial for natural rubber, beet sugar and corn syrup for cane — and the greater amount of working up in relation to materials used in the manufacture of goods. Bio-technology is increasing the range of substitutes. There are already coffee substitutes and a cocoa substitute on the way, not to mention the cloning of many tropical fruits that might be grown in temperate lands under glass. There have been no corresponding scientific advances which would advantage the Third World producers. The First World countries, because of their relatively large land area and their dominance in food exports as well as in manufactures, continue to supply not only 80 per cent of all the manufactured goods but also 40 per cent of all the primary products entering world trade; excluding fuels the proportion is 60 per cent.

Trade and Development

Why should Third World countries try to improve their position in such an unequal struggle? Some economists have indeed concluded from the recent experience in world trade of Third World products that the countries of the Third World would now do better if they ended their exports of minerals and other raw materials to the First World altogether, held on to their remaining resources to use for themselves and expanded the trade exchanges between each other. This view is strongly supported by those who believe that Third World countries should reduce their exports not only of non-renewable resources but also of cash crops, since these, it is said, have taken too much of the best land, so that Third World countries have had to import food. They would do better to put 'food first' and become self-reliant. In the next chapter we shall look at the way the world market works and the advantages as well as disadvantages of continuing world trade exchanges. Here we need only notice that world trade has grown at a rate consistently faster than world production. For this reason, a second and more traditional school of economists has argued that foreign trade is an 'engine' of economic growth. Their critics would question the benefits of this growth and draw attention to its unevenness and to the squandering of non-renewable resources and the destruction of the global eco-system.

If it seems to governments in some Third World countries that they should concentrate on developing their trade between each other, there is as yet little evidence of this happening. There has been much talk of common markets in South America and in Africa and there have been proposals for developing them within the framework of the United Nations Regional Economic Commissions. But little seems to change and the reason is not far to seek. The Third World is still locked into the artificial division of labour that we saw earlier had marked the relations of these two worlds since the eighteenth century, and that now operates within the giant transnational companies themselves.

The First World continues to act as an irresistible magnet pulling in products from the rest of the world which it needs for its growth. From time to time, in periods of slump, the current is turned off. Behind the consistencies which we have noted in the pattern of world trade, there have been major fluctuations in both volume and prices. It would seem to reveal a contradiction if the volume of goods moving between the different worlds should show much less consistency than the proportions of the total for which each of the worlds is responsible. The explanation is that when the volume of any group of products rises their prices generally fall, and vice versa. When oil prices rose in the 1970s, for example, volumes were cut back, but in this case the rise was so great that for a time the Third World's share of international trade rose; the share of fuels in world trade rose from eight per cent in 1970 to peak at 24 per cent in 1980 only to fall back to 13 per cent in 1986.

World prices of manufactured goods have risen fairly consistently over the last 100 years to a level eight times that prevailing at the beginning of the period. Primary product prices have also risen roughly in line, but they have moved up and down in great waves during the century. This is shown in Table 4 in the figures for the terms of trade between manufactured goods and primary products. In the 1930s the primary producers' terms dropped down to 73 per cent of the manufacturers'; today they are only 65 per cent and the Third World primary producers' terms are down to 54 per cent. At

TABLE 4. PATTERNS OF WORLD TRADE, 1880s TO 1980s (percentages)

Region	1880	1913	1937	1953	1967	1977	1981	1987	1990
	slump end	boom end	slump end	boom	slump	oil price end	slump end	boom	slump
First World Total	71	67	60	65	70	64	67	70	72
to First	45	43	35	44	53	46	45	54	56
to Third	26	24	25	20	14	15	15	13	14
to Second				1	3	3	3	2.5	2
Third World Total	29	33	33	26	19	26	24	20	23
to First	25	28	24	19	14	19	20	13	15
to Third	4	5	9	6	4	6	7	5	7
to Second				1	1	1	1	1.5	1
Second World Total			7	10	12	10	9	10	5
to First			5	2	2	3	3	2.5	
to Third			2	1	3	1	1	2	
to Second			0	7	7	6	5	5	
Total World Trade									
in %	100	100	100	100	100	100	100	100	100
in $billions	13	28	25	82	214	1,150	2,000	2,500	3400
Primary products									
% of total trade	64	64	63	52	36	42	41	30	28
First World Share of									
pp. exports	42	55	36	40	45	38	40	44	48
mfg. exports	100	98	96	88	87	77	72	70	75
Index of World Trade									
pp. volume	32	100	118	133	272	425	760	860	1080
mfg. volume	32	100	92	170	460	1,117	1,500	1,900	2400
Index of Prices									
pp.	121	100	71	230	193	730	750	500	590
mfgs.	103	100	114	212	245	500	750	797	995
Terms of Trade									
pps./mfgs.	107	100	73	110	88	146	100	65	59

Source: P. Lamartine Yates, *Fifty Years of Foreign Trade*, 1959. United Nations, *Satistical Yearbooks*

Notes : (1) pp. = primary products ; mfg. = manufactured exports. (2) In 1982 world trade totalled $36 billion. (3) In 1937 Second World countries comprise all Second World in 1953. In 1967 oil exports were 2%, in 1977 14%, in 1980 24%, in 1987 12%. Non-oil Third World exports were respectively: 17%, 12%, 12%, 15%. (4) Terms of trade = pp. prices as % of mfg. prices, based on 1913 = 100. (5) In 1987, for Third World only, pp. prices = 430; terms of trade = 54.

the height of the oil price hike, the Third World's terms of trade were up to 146. What this means is that in the 1930s, and again today, Third World producers have had to supply twice the volume of primary products for the same volume of manufactured goods. The measurement of volume, or in American terms of quantum, is the changing value over a period of time adjusted for price changes. It is not the same as the quantity, because you can't meaningfully add quantities of different products together. But comparing two particular commodities, you could say, for example, that a Senegalese farmer today has to supply many times more peanuts to get a bicycle than his father did. This is only partly because bicycles are now made with much more capital equipment and much less labour than they were a generation earlier while the peanut farmer's tools have hardly changed. It is mainly because the bargaining power of the Senegalese farmer is much weaker and we shall see why in the next chapter.

It seems that time and again the Third World improves its position through better terms of trade for its primary products in relation to manufactured goods, when world trade is booming, only to fall back in times of slump as the terms of trade for primary products deteriorate again. This is a striking fact — that there is no aggregate advantage, even for the First World, in getting Third World products on the cheap because this tends to happen primarily in times of global recession. How are we to explain the swings in the terms of trade? Which way round is it? Does the boom raise Third World prices or do Third World rising prices cause the boom? The answer is that prices and volumes follow the booms and slumps of the capitalist trade cycles in the First World. These are above all investment cycles, that is ups and downs of investment in capital equipment for industry. Their effect on the Third World is obvious from Chart 2.

As First World capitalist industry booms, it draws in primary products, their prices rise, their producers can buy more industrial goods, the boom accelerates and primary producers are encouraged to expand their capacity in line with growing industrial capacity. But crisis comes and slump follows as the unequal distribution of incomes has raised the profits available for investment far ahead of the earnings of those for whose consumption the extra investment is intended. Prices collapse, especially the prices of primary products since, as we saw earlier, the millions of primary producers are less able to hold their prices than the few big manufacturing companies. Then, the falling demand of the primary producers world-wide pulls down still further the whole level of world trade and industrial activity. The cycle starts up again when old industrial plant has been written off and the new and more efficient equipment of the more competitive industrial producers in the First World has enabled them to reduce costs and expand sales.

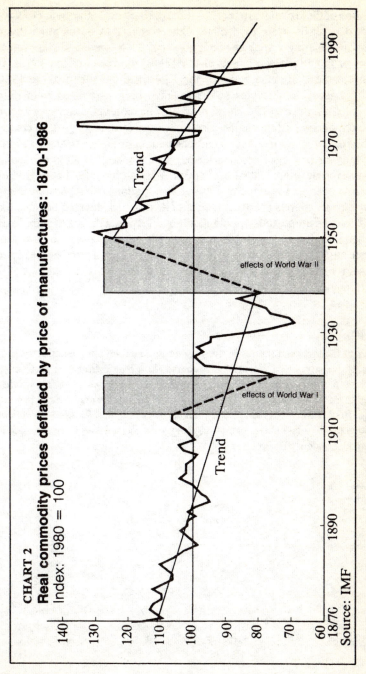

CHART 2
Real commodity prices deflated by price of manufactures: 1870-1986
Index: 1980 = 100

Source: Overseas Development Institute Briefing Paper, March 1988.

Source: IMF

Some of these cycles are short — three or four years of upswing followed by two or three years of decline. Others appear to be of much longer duration, covering a span of about 50 years. Thus, we can distinguish the boom of the 1860s, the slump of the 1880s, the boom of the 1910s, the slump of the 1930s, the boom of the 1960s and the slump of the 1980s. Each of these long cycles seems to have been associated with major technological advances — steam power for locomotion, electric power and the internal combustion engine, electronics and computers — each creating high profits for the innovators and encouraging new investment and new demands for raw materials, but leading to unequal generation of incomes and uneven development of economies. With each cycle, a new group of countries reaches the stage of full industrialisation. After Western Europe came North America and Australia; after them Japan; then the Soviet Union and Eastern Europe; today South Korea and Taiwan with Brazil and Mexico on their way. It is a slow and uneven progress and, as populations rise, more people are left out than before. How might they all get a piece of the action? To answer that question we must look more deeply into the workings of the world market.

Notes

Many of the facts and figures in this chapter will be found in greater detail in the Open University, Third World Studies course *Third World Atlas*. The argument on the terms of trade can be found in M. Barratt Brown, *The Economics of Imperialism*, Penguin Books, 1974, especially Chapters 5 and 10. For the argument in favour of 'food first' and self-reliance, see Paul Ekins et al. in *The Living Economy*, Routledge, 1986 and Clive Robinson, *Hungry Farmers*, 1989, Christian Aid, PO Box 100, London, SE1 7RT.

4. THE WORLD MARKET

One World, One Market

The long history of international trade has made the whole world into one market. Whatever governments have done to try to protect their infant industries and markets and to substitute local production for imports, they have had in the end to come back into the world market or fall behind in their economic development and technological advance. The most recent and most striking example of this has been the re-entry of the Second World — of the Soviet Union, Eastern Europe and China — into the capitalist world market. These countries were more successful in achieving all-round industrialisation than any of those (apart from South Korea and Taiwan) which were still industrially undeveloped 60 years ago. They still relied chiefly on their exports of primary products — fuels and minerals and food products — for their share of world trade, just like the Third World countries. Their failure to achieve competitiveness with the advanced industrial countries in modern technology, however, left them at a grave disadvantage. Why should dependence on primary product exports have been a disadvantage? We have seen already that primary products form a decreasing proportion of world trade and noted some of the reasons for the falling demand for these products. But why should the bargaining position of Third World producers be so weak, why should their prices always collapse while manufacturers' prices stay up or, at worst, drop only slightly in a slump?

According to classical economic theory there should be no disadvantage to either party in a division of labour in world trade between producers of manufactured goods and primary producers; rather the contrary should be the case. Each should benefit. Ricardo's Law of Comparative Advantage rules that, if each country concentrates on producing what it is best at, then output is optimised with existing resources. This may well be true, although there are many questions to be asked about the historical distribution of capital and labour at any particular time and about future possibilities of capital and labour mobility. But the most important question to ask is how the results of this optimisation are distributed between the different parties to the deal. Ricardo took the example of port wine from Portugal and woollen cloth from England, and showed that both countries benefited from the exchange. Neither in fact could have produced the other's product. Portugal had the sun for ripening the grapes and England the rain for grazing the sheep. He accepted that some countries like the USA might be best at producing everything in different parts of their vast territories. It would still, he argued, be making the most of existing resources for each country to concentrate on its very best product or products. This seemed like a powerful argument in favour of the division of labour between producers of manufactured goods in the North and primary producers in the South which we found has been established by European conquest and continued by the trading relationship.

Unequal Exchange

Unfortunately for the South, and for the theory, there are major differences in the bargaining position of manufacturers and of primary producers in the world market. In the first place, many food products are perishable and cannot, therefore, be held off the market, as manufactured goods can, to prevent a fall in price. Secondly, and what is more serious for the Third World producers, they do not have the facilities for processing, packaging and storing, so as to get a better price and add value to their basic product. It is either the local middlemen from the towns or, more often, agents of companies from the First World who benefit from the added value at all the stages of processing, packaging, transporting and marketing the product from producer to consumer.

Thirdly, as we saw earlier, many of the smaller European colonies were allocated the production of a single crop or at most two or three crops — sugar and tobacco in Cuba, for example, bananas and tobacco in Jamaica — or just one or two materials — as with tin and rubber in Malaya, iron and oil in Venezuela. This meant that they became totally dependent on the swings in demand for their one or two products. The many islands whose lands were devoted to growing cane sugar, like Cuba, Jamaica, Haiti, Mauritius, Trinidad and the Philippines, have been devastated by the encouragement of beet sugar production in Europe, especially under the Common Agricultural Policy of the European Community. Fourthly, while the number of manufacturing companies in the world can be counted in their thousands, and the number is reduced with every year that goes by, there are millions, literally tens, even hundreds of millions, of peasant households engaged in primary production. The manufacturers can and do form combines and cartels to keep up prices. For the primary producers to reach commodity agreements is very difficult indeed, as we shall see.

The fifth problem facing primary producers is that, compared with manufacturers, the application of machinery to the production process has been relatively slow. As a result, output per person (labour productivity) has hardly risen over centuries in the case of many crops, while productivity increases in manufacturing have taken place at annual rates of three per cent to four per cent. This is a doubling every 20 years. That is why we saw that the peasant in Senegal growing ground-nuts needs to perform as much as half a year's work to buy a bicycle which a Nottingham worker produces in a few hours. This has led to the concept of 'unequal exchange' and to much talk about the 'imperialism of trade'. At first sight, of course, it is clear that the Senegalese peasant and the Nottingham worker are involved in an unequal exchange of labour. But if we compare levels of productivity and wages per hour in the two countries, we find that the two levels are very closely related. In fact, wages are on average higher among workers in the poorest countries than net output per head would suggest. The real inequality lies in the capital equipment — almost nil — available to the Senegalese peasant and the huge range of equipment available to the Nottingham worker. Of course, there are big differences in the capitalisation of labour even inside a country like Britain, but the differences between Britain's situation and that of a Third World country, as a result of its colonial history, are immeasurably greater.

All this leads to a sixth explanation for the relative weakness of primary producers in relation to manufacturers. This is that the very machinery and the new technology, together with the capital available for investment to increase productivity, are in the hands of the capitalists in the developed First World economies. Third World industrialists must find their capital and equipment mainly from outside their frontiers and pay for both at First World prices or borrow at First World interest rates. There was much argument among economists in the 1960s and 1970s about the so-called 'dependency effect' of such relations, but the growing burden of Third World debt has tended to settle the argument. From 1983 onward for the rest of the decade the flow of capital was once more reversed, as it was in the 1930s, moving from the Third World to the First, from the poor to the rich, instead of the other way. Between the mid-1950s and 1980 the annual flow of funds into the Third World had averaged about $40 billion. After 1982 the flow of funds *out of* the Third World averaged about $35 billion a year, amounting to nearly 10 per cent of the value of the Third World's total exports. For some of the Third World countries the flow of debt payments took as much as 50 per cent of the earnings from their annual exports. Out of the $1,200 billion which the Third World owed in 1990, only $400 billions constituted the original borrowing. The rest consisted of accrued interest and capital liabilities.

These unequal trading relations between manufacturers and primary producers have become incorporated in the operations of the large transnational company, whose size and importance have steadily increased over many years and most rapidly in the last decade. The dominant position of these companies throughout the Third World, with their control over both buying and selling of the goods entering international trade, provides the final explanation for the weakness of the millions of small Third World producers in the world market. Large, vertically integrated companies first began as primary producers in the colonies of First World countries. Apart from the plantations and mines of early nineteenth-century European companies, the first truly international company was established in the 1890s, when Lever Bros. built up its wide interests in African plantations. The oil companies were from the start based on the integration of all the stages of production and distribution from the oil well to the petrol station. Imperial Tobacco, Dunlop, Brooke Bond, Tate & Lyle all offer other examples of the vertical integration that was at first quite specific to colonial products. As the field of production dominated by giant transnational companies has widened, and the size of the companies has grown, so more and more of the world's trade has been taking place inside these big companies through their own internal transfers.

The Holders of Big Capital

The strength of the large transnational companies, and the reason for their growth, lies in their control over sources of capital. For the Third World countries, this involves a vicious circle even without the circle of indebtedness which now surrounds them. Since capital is supplied from the First World, the profits flow back to the First World, and it is there and not in the Third World that capital accumulates. 'Unto him that hath shall be given . . . and from him that hath not shall be taken away even that which he hath.' Even though in good years funds will flow out into the Third World faster than they flow back, come the bad years and the flow is reversed, as we saw in looking at the current Third World debt crisis. It is the banks who lend the money, but the money they have to lend comes from the accumulated profits of the giant companies.

The giant transnational companies not only have the capital; they also have the latest technology. This gives them a competitive edge over all others and determines the whole growth path of production. The big manufacturing companies will want to extend both the production and marketing of the products of their more advanced technology. This generally means either armaments or the goods which rich consumers can afford, such as motor cars, *par excellence*. These companies have, therefore, begun to look to the Third World, not only for their raw materials and for cheap labour, but for an expanding market among those who can afford their consumer goods. In their world-wide operations these companies need to achieve a very difficult balance — a rich market on the one hand and cheap labour on the other. Obviously the same people cannot provide both. So, the transnational companies look round the world to find good markets in one place and cheap labour in another. But this need not be in different countries; they can find both in the same country. Even in the First World there are great inequalities, and these have grown greater in recent years, as the rich grew richer and some of the poor became poorer still. Many of the poor in First World countries in fact came as immigrants from the Third World — in Britain from Asia and the Caribbean; in the USA from Mexico and Puerto Rico; on the European continent from Turkey and Algeria. In this way the Third World continues to supply a reserve of cheap labour. In the First World the ratio of rich consumers to such poor producers will be quite high, at least two to one in the total population. It will be the other way round in Third World countries. At most, one-quarter of the population will be able to consume the products of the giant companies while the great majority will be available as cheap labour. We saw earlier that there are even wider inequalities between rich and poor in the Third World than there are in the First World. In most Third World countries the top fifth of income earners enjoys more than half of the total income (we saw earlier that in Brazil it is two-thirds). This situation in fact suits the giant companies quite well — rich consumers at one end of the scale and a vast reserve of cheap labour at the other.

Much of the new industrial production in the Third World is being developed by transnational companies in enclaves — special so-called 'enterprise zones' in Manila or Greater Colombo or in territories like Hong Kong and Singapore. In advertising these enterprise zones the authorities give the game away. They offer to international companies, which are considering a new site for their plants, a package of concessions: cheap labour — young, educated and English speaking — tax exemptions and reductions, free trade for imports and exports, with assistance for establishment, political stability and restrictions on trade union activity, good geographic location along major air and sea routes. The enterprise zone in some cases — in Greater Colombo, for example, which was advertising all these benefits in the financial press in the First World in the late 1970s — is surrounded by high fences with barbed wire on the landward side. Port facilities are constructed along the shore. It is expected that most of the raw materials will be brought in by ship and the finished products exported by sea or air. The workers are bussed in from the surrounding countryside or housed in barracks. The companies which are attracted to respond to such offers will be transnational companies with a world-wide synergy of operations: raw material production in one place, refining and processing in another, manufacture of components where labour is skilled for some of the processes, where labour is cheap for others, assembly near to the market, the design, research and development and the overall management held firmly at the centre, in Europe, Japan or North America.

Uneven Development

The implications of this international synergy for the trade and development of Third World countries should not be exaggerated. There is much loose talk of the New International Division of Labour and the Globalisation of Production, with goods and capital supposedly buzzing round the world at ever-increasing velocities. The fact is that, while the transnational companies continue to dominate the marketing of Third World primary products, their investment in industrial production in the Third World is concentrated on a very few areas. Half of all manufactured exports from United States-based transnational companies in the 1970s came from only four countries — Brazil, Mexico, Singapore and Hong Kong. Three-quarters of total employment in the 'export promotion zones' in the late 1970s was located in seven countries — Brazil, Mexico, South Korea, Singapore, Malaysia, the Philippines and Hong Kong. The Third World's share of world manufacturing output rose from six per cent to nine per cent in the decade of the 1970s and to 11 per cent towards the end of the 1980s. The proportion of the manufactured goods entering export markets from the Third World was somewhat higher — at 15 per cent excluding oil. The increases in shares of world output and exports of manufactured goods coming from the newly industrialising countries and enterprise zones was, however, being offset by a fall in the share of other Third World countries. To put this in perspective, the First World's imports of manufactured goods from the Third World rose during these two decades from one to two per cent of the First World's total consumption.

If we look at the effects of the development of new industrial countries and enterprise zones from the point of view of the people in the Third World, the results are even smaller and often negative. The establishment of enterprise zones makes a few building contractors rich and ruins the eyesight of the young women who etch or assemble the micro-chips or work all day at the sewing machines. Many of the sub-contracting plants in the enterprise zones have been closed down as higher technology — in chip integration for example — reduces the amount of assembly required in electronics production. By the time they are closed down the country concerned had received little. The government had conceded most of the taxes and the profits had flowed back into the First World. To look at the situation in another way, we can compare the proportion of the population which has a TV, motor car or telephone. This is on average 0.1 per cent in Asia (excluding Japan), one per cent in Africa, six per cent in Latin America, but it is 60 per cent in North America, 50 per cent in Japan, 33 per cent in Western Europe and Oceania and 10 per cent in the Soviet Union. Remembering that there are at least three or four persons to the average household the figures look better for the Third World. As averages they appear quite crazy in the First; but it is far from true that every household has a car. Some have two or three, others have none. In the UK as many as 40 per cent of all households have no car.

There is at least one major exception (and possibly two) to this picture of the failure of Third World development through trade in the world market. This is the success of South Korea and Taiwan, which we shall have to look at more closely in considering ways for Third World countries to emerge from the grip of the giant companies based in the already industrialised countries. In South Korea, and to a lesser extent in Taiwan, a local capitalist class has emerged controlling giant conglomerate companies which are competing in world markets alongside Japanese and United States companies. They have broken into the manufacture of products of advanced technology — motor cars, ships, machine tools, electronic equipment, TVs, videos and telecommunications. There are special circumstances in the high level of Korean development in the nineteenth century and in the Japanese occupation of Korea up to the end of the Second World War. Unlike the British in Africa, the Japanese at once proceeded to set up refining and processing industries in their colonies. It is also evident that the South Koreans and Taiwanese learned important lessons from their Japanese neighbours without becoming dependent on them. The main lessons we can note at this point are that they had to begin their industrialisation behind protective tariff walls, but once begun they could open up to the world market to find their own niche in it. This meant state involvement not only in managing the market but in developing the product so as to coordinate the operations of their own competing companies. World Bank reports recognise this as the basis of Korea's success, but still recommend that African governments stimulate growth by opening up their markets to the industrialised countries.

The Korean story serves to emphasise the uneven nature of capitalist development. The experience of continuing and even widening inequalities, repeated within nation states, both rich and poor, and between rich states and poor states, demonstrates that those economists are wrong who suppose that the market provides a kind of escalator by which the poor are carried up behind the rich to equal levels at different stages of the ascent. Somehow it happens that at each landing the rich have started up again ahead of the poor. We have seen that some do catch up, though not many. New centres of capitalist development have emerged since the first industrial revolution

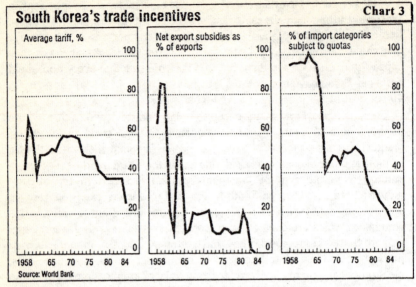

South Korea's trade incentives   Chart 3

Average tariff, %

Net export subsidies as % of exports

% of import categories subject to quotas

1958 65 70 75 80 84
Source: World Bank

Source: The Economist Third World Survey, 23 September 1989, p.27

in Britain — initially in Western Europe, then in North America, Oceania and South Africa, finally in Japan and in South Korea and Taiwan and the enclaves which we have been examining. This proves that the world capitalist trading system does not just polarise wealth and poverty. Marx has long been ridiculed for predicting the increasing misery of the mass of workers at one pole in the capitalist system while capital accumulated at the other. He was in fact cautious enough to add that 'the workers' wages might be high or low'. In other words, growth of incomes and wealth would be generated by capitalism, but very unequally; and it is this uneven development that we have seen. Those Marxists of the American *Monthly Review* school who have descried development at the centre of capitalism in the United States, continuously pumping wealth from the Third World pool, are evidently wrong. Had they been right, the pool would soon have dried up. It is because of the real development in the lands of European settlement and in Japan and elsewhere in the Far East that the system has expanded. Had all the gold in the world continued to accumulate in Fort Knox, the United States would have perished like Midas, surrounded by piles of gold that he could not eat.

At the same time, the anti-Marxists like W. W. Rostow and Peter L. Berger are not right because some Marxists are wrong. Rostow called his book *The Stages of Economic Growth: A Non-Communist Manifesto* and Berger sub-titled his book, *The Capitalist Revolution*, a 'critique of Marxist theories'. So they knew what they were doing. The fact is that the stages of economic growth have not taken all the peoples of the world to the top of the escalator as a result of the capitalist revolution. Moreover, the chances of this happening in a world which is increasingly dominated by giant transnational companies are indeed remote. For it is central to the working of these companies that they are not just trading companies, through whose hands move the exchanges of goods and services between all parts of the world, not least between the North and the South. They are above all production companies, setting labour to work all over the world to produce goods and services. Just as it was a mistake to see the imperialism of British capitalists as some kind of merchanting and commercial venture, rather than as an extension of the direct exploitation of labour, slave or free, indentured or waged, into mines and plantations in lands overseas, so it is a mistake today to see the transnational company, as it is now, simply as a trading company. Some economists draw comfort from this and expect the transnational operations of these production companies to ensure the transfer of technology from the centres of innovation to all parts of the world in ways that trading alone could not achieve. This possibility of converting the traditional trade between manufacturers and primary producers into a genuine transfer of technology for sustained development in the Third World is the subject of later chapters. It is clear from what we have seen so far that to ensure such decentralised development will need something different from the internal transfers of giant transnational companies which retain the key controls at the centre.

Notes

The several theories referred to in this chapter are comprehensively reviewed by Rhys Jenkins in his book *International Corporations and Uneven Development: The Internationalisation of Capital and the Third World,* Methuen, 1987. A historical review of these theories will be found in my book, *The Economics of Imperialism*, Penguin Books 1974. An excellent summary of the state of development of the New Industrial Countries and of their contribution to world trade is to be found in David Gordon, 'The Global Economy' in *New Left Review*, No. 168, March-April 1988. W.W. Rostow's book, *The Stages of Economic Growth*, was published by Cambridge University Press in 1960 and Peter L. Berger's *The Capitalist Revolution* by Wildwood House in 1987. The World Bank report on South Korea, *Capital Accumulation and Economic Growth: The Korean Paradigm*, is by Shahid Yusuf and R. Kyle Peters, World Bank Staff Working Papers, No. 712, 1985.

5. THE ROLE OF THE MARKET

A few giant transnational companies now dominate the world market, moving goods from country to country by internal transfers, for which they fix their own prices. What then is the role of the market? Producers have become traders; and traders, even retailers like Marks and Spencer or fast food chains like McDonald's, have come to control production either directly or through sub-contractors. What is the point of a market when production and distribution are in the same hands and controlled by companies operating on a global scale? A study by UNCTAD officials has shown that for major commodities entering world trade in 1980, the proportion of the total which was marketed by the 15 largest transnational companies ranged between 70 per cent and 90 per cent, and that in most cases only three to six transnational companies accounted for nearly the whole of the market. The figures in Table 5 give the details. Why do such companies bother with the markets? Of course, so long as there are three or more companies they can make a market, but the possibilities of collusion and price-fixing cartels are obvious. We all know how the petrol companies move their prices religiously in line with one another. One answer might be that there is still a part of world trade that does not go through the transnational companies, even if it is the lesser part. It may be that the big companies, which have not yet ceased to compete with each other, still need a market to set a price. A Soviet economist once told me that the communists needed capitalism to tell them how to fix their prices. The most obvious answer is that they can make money out of the markets by manipulation and speculation and can at the same time manage the prices of exchanges which they do not directly control.

What Markets Do

We need then to ask what the market does in normal trading. We are all familiar enough with the idea of a market, with our local market and market days and with the supermarkets which have grown bigger and bigger over the last few years. But these markets for goods are not the only markets. The whole market system, which is sometimes just called 'the market', comprises many other markets — for the three factors of production: for labour, the job centre or labour exchange as it used to be called; for capital, the stock exchange and the money markets and foreign exchange markets operated by the big banks; for land, the auction rooms and property market; for the products of the land, the commodity exchanges; and for intermediate products, all the other wholesale markets. The central principle of a market

TABLE 5. CORPORATE CONTROL OF GLOBAL COMMODITY TRADE, 1983

Commodity	World exports ($ million)	% marketed by 3-6 largest transnationals*
Food		
Wheat	17,851	85-90
Sugar	10,636	60
Corn	9,833	85-90
Coffee	9,636	85-90
Rice	3,613	70
Cocoa beans	2051	85
Tea	1,844	80
Bananas	1,324	70-75
Pineapples (fresh)	74	90
Agricultural raw materials		
Forest products	47,255	90
Cotton	6,567	85-90
Tobacco	4,239	85-90
Hides and skins	4,047	25
Natural rubber	3,321	70-75
Jute	135	85-90
Ores, minerals and metals		
Mineral fuels	382,685	75
Copper	8,287	80-85
Iron ore	6,231	90-95
Tin	2,320	75-80
Phosphates	1,588	50-60
Bauxite	833	80-85

* in a few cases up to 15 transnational traders account for the bulk of the market.

Source: UNCTAD Secretariat estimates, based on extensive research and interviews with trade and marketing specialists. The figures represent figures of magnitude only. Also, FAO *Trade Yearbook*, 1983, FAO, *Yearbook of Forest Products 1983*, UN Monthly Bulletin of Statistic, National Statistics. The author gratefully acknowledges this table which is taken from J. Cavanagh and F. Clairmonte, *Merchants of Drink* (Penang: Third World Network), p.59.

is that it indicates what people want and how much this would cost. As a result of supply and demand a price is arrived at that clears the market. If the supplier loses money he goes out of business or switches to some other product. If the supplier makes a profit he thrives and can expand production. If he fails and goes out of business, labour and capital and plant can be used elsewhere. So, the market not only brings buyers and sellers together and establishes a price; it also allocates resources of labour, capital, land and raw materials where demand is strongest.

This capacity of the market to indicate to suppliers how and where to provide the goods that people need has given it the great reputation that it enjoys. Buyers are offered a choice of suppliers. The efficient are rewarded, the inefficient are penalised. We need to note that a market does not necessarily imply the private ownership of capital or the employment of labour. The suppliers and traders could all be either self-employed individuals or cooperatives or state enterprises. All that is necessary is that there should be several suppliers and traders in competition in every line of business. Capitalism could not operate without markets, but markets do not require capitalism. Some would say that they would not work very well, because it is the profit motive, the aim to accumulate capital, that provides the driving force of all capitalist markets. If people start with different amounts of capital there will always be some element of capitalism in a market. Those that are born rich will have an advantage which becomes cumulative. They can live just by lending money at interest to others. The market does, moreover, tend to be skewed towards the rich. Demand in the market is the pull of money and not of people. The rich will get what they want; the poor will remain deprived and, as we have seen, the gap can easily widen as wealth attracts and poverty repels.

There is another weakness in all markets apart from the tendency towards inequality. This is the element of uncertainty. Strangely enough, this is not made any less by the instantaneous communication across the whole world made possible by modern information technology. Information is the most valuable commodity in all trading. It is said that the Rothschilds made their first fortune as a result of establishing communication between the major capitals of Europe by pigeon post, and having news of the result of the Battle of Trafalgar before anyone else. Radio, telephone, fax, telex, electronic mail, all mean that the communication of information today is extremely rapid and enables the central direction of even the largest corporations to decentralise production while retaining total control of overall strategic decisions. This technology is, however, available to anyone who has the necessary equipment. This, as we shall see, has brought a whole new range of actors into the market as speculators. The fact, however, that the equipment is no longer beyond the range of any small producer is an important point for future reference, since this means that any cooperative or peasant association which wants to can plug into all the information that exists in the public domain.

Not all information is in the public domain. Private traders and privately owned companies will try to keep some of their information secret, but most information about supplies and markets and ruling prices has to be public to serve its purpose in trading. Chat over meals and drinks in the City of London means that the markets are often referred to as leaky buckets. 'Insider' trading, as it is called when a trader uses the inside knowledge he has to buy or sell his own product on the market, is outlawed. This is not to say that it does not occur, but when it does there is a scandal. If someone important has suffered from such unfair trading then there is an inquiry, like the recent inquiry into the Guinness take-over of Distillers in the UK and into Mr Boesky's evidently quite literally 'informed' predictions of price movements in United States markets.

This use of information is more concerned with speculation about price movements than with finding a price that clears the market. Even with all the information available about markets and all the modern aids of market research, suppliers cannot know in advance what will sell well, although the bigger ones may do all in their power by advertising to persuade buyers that what is on supply is just what the buyer wants. It is only too easy for suppliers to overproduce or to cut back too far, since they are all getting the same messages from the market. This is particularly serious in the case of primary products since, for many such products, whether they are crops or minerals, it takes some time for production to be increased and cutting back entails costly waste of land and investment. It is little better where changes in production can be readily made, as in the case of annual crops like potatoes. Excess demand over supply one year will lead to high prices which encourage farmers to sow more land to potatoes the following year. As all farmers do the same, a famine is followed by a glut and prices swing up and down from year to year. It is partly the result of these uncertainties that giant transnational companies have become more and more involved in trading as well as in production. We shall look at the nature of this involvement in the next chapter. Here we need to discover more about the workings of the commodity markets, which even the giant transnational companies evidently need to work through.

The London Commodity Markets

Many of the commodity markets are in London and have for long provided the foundation of the City of London's wealth, but there are extensive commodity markets in New York and Tokyo and many narrower markets in Chicago, Singapore, Rio de Janeiro and elsewhere. These markets are not like most markets where products are offered for sale and buyers choose according to taste and price. Someone once said that most dealers in the soya market wouldn't recognise a soya bean plant if you brought one onto the trading floor. You will see no tin in the London tin market, nor copper in the copper market, not even tea or coffee or cocoa in their respective markets. Although there will have been much tasting of samples by expert assayers and tasters, this will not be done in the market, but the results will be fully detailed in the offers of lots for auctioning. Standards have been established for all produce as have standardised weights and measures and qualities, so that the commodity dealers in the markets can know that what they are dealing in, coming though it does from different sources, is a comparable product. The quantities dealt in tend to be large — minimum contracts of 30,000 lbs for example in the cocoa market. Often the product has not yet even been mined or harvested but is to be exported to be available by a certain date and to comply with well-defined specifications. On any day the brokers who are actually dealing on the floor of one of the exchanges are making hundreds of deals, although their principals will have been cancelling out in advance any orders to buy and sell the same quantities of the same commodity.

There are several different kinds of principals operating in the London commodity markets. The first are called 'physical traders'. They do really buy and sell commodities, keep them in stock if they expect prices to rise, and sell stock if they expect them to fall. Both buyers and sellers represent the very big companies, but the sellers are generally selling the products of many producers, even millions, while the buyers are generally buying for one or two powerful companies. These physical buyers and sellers in fact set the parameters for the market price. Their forward buying or selling sets the market trend. By playing the market the big companies can insure themselves against sudden changes in price. Without them the big companies would simply transfer products within their operations at their own transfer prices or fix prices between themselves. There are in fact many commodities for which there is no market. Magnesium is an example. The two United States producers, the Norwegian producer and the Canadian producer, and also the Russian producer, sell directly to the fabricators. Prices only move occasionally when costs rise or demand changes significantly, a quite different picture from the sharp ups and downs of prices in the commodity markets. There is some evidence that the price of magnesium is relatively high in relation to costs, compared, say, with the price of aluminium, taking into account the relative ease of producing magnesium from seawater or from mineral salts. The metal has a narrow range of uses — mainly in aeroplane manufacture — but for these purposes there are no substitutes. The quantities involved are not large, and demand does not rise or fall with the price. The demand for the product is termed 'price inelastic', and it is probably because of the lack of response to price changes that there is no true market. Spices offer another example. But, from these examples of price setting where there is no true market, it should not be assumed that the commodity markets in fact ensure that there is no exercise of monopoly power.

By far the largest number of operators in the commodity markets are not really trading in commodities but in futures — in paper titles to commodities. Some of these operators are called 'fundamental traders'. This is because they consider all the factors involved in present and future demand, existing stocks, future supplies and market sentiment. These traders may include the agents or employees of large companies who are 'hedging', that is securing their purchases or sales against losses from adverse price movements by a compensating transaction, e.g. buying forward at the same time as selling today or the reverse. To operate in this way they need liquidity, to find money or supplies at any time. They may also be trading in options, that is again not actual commodities but options to buy or to sell at any time. Thus, there is a market in options and also markets in currency differences in commodity prices, taking into account the existence of commodity markets all over the world. It is a very complicated picture.

Trading in Futures

The major complication in the market is the trade in futures. In the balancing of demand and supply, the expectations of supplies available or expected to be available at future dates are set against the demands placed for supplies now and in the future. As a result of the interest charged for borrowing money or the interest on capital forgone in purchasing and storing commodities, there are, depending on the rate of interest ruling at any time, different prices for any product — a price today (the spot price) for delivery today, a price for delivery in one month, three months, six months and even longer (futures or forward prices). Any two parties can agree to a price for forward delivery, i.e. delivery in a few weeks or months. Futures prices, however, are the result of the influence of a whole range of dealers outside the markets who are in effect speculating on changes in the prices of commodities. Depending on whether there are shortages or surpluses at the time or expected in the future, prices can rise and fall not just by a few percentage points but in great booms and slumps. There are fortunes to be made out of gambling on these changes. In part, the speculative element arises from the desire of dealers and their customers to insure against violent changes. The dealer who is hedging is bearing the risk, but if he is successful he will be taking a profit, sometimes a very large one. So, the main reason for speculation is the money that is to be made out of it, on top of the market price of the commodity. When for a time in the 1970s the price of copper was held fairly steady many dealers went out of business. There was nothing to speculate on in that market.

Let us see how it works. Suppose that a dealer needs tin for a customer in three months time and the price is low but is expected to rise. He will buy the tin and hold it in stock. Of course that costs money, i.e. the cost of borrowing or forgoing interest, so that he will have to take that into account in his calculations. He may buy more than he needs, expecting to find a buyer at the better price later. If, instead of expecting the price to rise, he expects it to fall and he needs to have the tin in three months, he will sell tin now if he has stocks of it, that is at the higher price, and will agree to buy at the expected lower futures price, or he may sell futures expecting the price to continue to fall until the time he has to make delivery. Of course, if all the other dealers do the same the price may go down even further as a result of their sales. Alternatively, contrary to expectations, the price may rise and our buyer who has sold the tin he had, and even tin he didn't have, has to find tin for delivery at a higher price than he bargained on. Other dealers evidently had different expectations. Our dealer who bought at a futures price that he comes to think will turn out to be higher than he anticipated may wish to cover himself by buying more at a later futures price still, and so on and so on.

In some markets there are just two or three giant firms dominating the market (see Table 5). It is in that case obviously quite easy for them to act in collusion, even while not actually employing inside knowledge. They can therefore manipulate the market, 'squeezing' it by withholding supplies to raise the price or flooding the market to lower the price. In the coffee market, for example, Cargill of Minneapolis, Volkart of Winterthur, Goldman Sachs and its subsidiary J. Aron of New York and the *sogo shoshas* of Japan are the dominant traders. In the cocoa market, Cargill and Volkart are to be found again, but two British companies, Gill & Duffus/Dalgety and S & W Berisford, have appropriated almost three-quarters of the global market. What this means for Third World countries is shown by the fact that, for example, a third of Guatemala's coffee crop is exported by J. Aron to the United States and Duffus/Dalgety controls Ghana's exports of cocoa to the UK. The giant manufacturing companies are also involved. General Foods, for example, which along with Nestlé controls three-quarters of the soluble coffee market (one-sixth of total coffee consumption) takes a half of all the Côte d'Ivoire's coffee exports to the United States. A report from the Congressional Research

Service of the United States in 1983 stated that there were two ways of manipulating prices: one was to spread false information, the second was to corner the market. 'All that this requires,' observed a former vice-chairman of the Chicago Mercantile Exchange, 'is a great deal of money and brokers who are willing to look the other way.' He was testifying at the hearings into widespread speculation and manipulation which had led to a jump in soya bean futures prices from $3.31 to $12.90 in the course of one month in 1973, of which the vice-chairman opined that 'the last $5 or $6 . . . was the result of manipulative practices.'

In other markets, the metal exchange for example, there are for most commodities at least 12 and often more companies involved. The largest companies exercise a form of price leadership. In what is called 'the mating season', around October or November, the largest buyers and traders agree a price or price range for the next year. This sets the parameters for trading thereafter. A big dealer may still renege on the agreement if he can see a profitable opportunity. There is plenty of rivalry even among the giants. There are other ways of fixing the market. The six giant Japanese financial and industrial groups have begun to operate in the world's commodity markets, but no one other than the representatives of the six groups can operate on the Tokyo exchanges. This could of course be said to be because of the language barrier, since all the dealing on the floor is done by screaming and shouting.

The final complicating factor is that because of the money to be made from speculating in commodities, by far the largest number of commodity traders are not physical traders or even fundamental traders. They know absolutely nothing about the commodities or future trends in demand and supply. They are called 'technical traders'. Anybody can be one. They may work for banks or big institutions. They may be rich individuals. Sometimes, they may be Muslims because the Koran forbids usury and speculation is not usury. They may represent specialist companies and consortia of companies or individuals. Some are called 'dentists' houses', because groups of rich professional people with cash at their disposal have formed syndicates to put their money in the hands of a technical dealer.

Sometimes people with money go into commodity speculation because they are paid in cash which they do not wish to declare to the tax collector, sometimes in order to practise what is called 'tax-straddling', which is deferring taxable trading income over a period of years. Commodity speculation is a risky business like any other form of gambling and requires a fair amount of money to start with. The technical dealers employ 'systems' like casino addicts on the basis of which they buy or sell different commodities. The systems are constructed on past and current movements of prices extrapolated into the future. These are built into computer programmes and, as new information is fed in, the computer signals whether and when to buy or sell a particular commodity. These instructions are then passed to brokers on the floor of the exchanges. Many people regard these systems as no better than astrology for all the technical complexity of the equations and graphs that go into them.

TABLE 6. FUTURES CONTRACTS TRADED IN THE UNITED STATES, BY COMMODITY GROUPS, 1982

Rank	Commodity group	Number of contracts	Per cent
1	Agricultural commodities of which:	46,310,209	41.21
	Soybean complex	15,528,665	13.82
	Grain	14,263,908	12.69
	Livestock, products & poultry	11,702,487	10.41
	Imported agricultural commodities	3,276,512	2.92
	Other agricultural commodities	1,538,637	1.37
2	Financial instruments	28,825,112	25.64
3	Precious metals	18,809,458	16.73
4	Foreign currency	8,690,285	7.73
5	Stock indexes	4,911,121	4.37
6	Non-precious metals	2,362,625	2.10
7	Petroleum products	1,875,414	1.67
8	Lumber products	616,655	.55
	Total	*112,400,879*	*100.00*

Source: Futures Industry Association, Washington D.C. as quoted in the *Financial Times*, 24 February 1982.

TABLE 7. VALUE OF FUTURES CONTRACTS TRADED IN LONDON, BY COMMODITY GROUPS, 1982

Rank	Commodity group	Value (£million)	Per cent
1	Metals of which	63,222	67
	Non-precious metals	55,430	59
	Silver and gold	7,792	8
2	Soft markets* of which	31,362	33
	Tropical beverages	12,321	13
	Gas oil	10,069	11
	Other	8,972	9
3	Soft market options**	209	–
	Total	94,793	100

Source: International Chamber of Commerce, *Futures Trading in Commodity Markets*, Paris, 1983
* Includes options
** Double options counted twice

In the USA it is agricultural commodities that mainly enter the futures markets. Together with financial instruments — that is speculation on the value of money, i.e. interest rates — these account for two-thirds of the total. By contrast, in the UK it is metals market that accounts for two-thirds of the futures contracts. The scale of futures trading has rocketed in the last two decades. In the United States alone the volume of trading in futures rose from 13.6 million contract lots in 1970 to 158.7 million lots in 1985. This was in a period when the volume of international trade in commodities barely doubled. The increasing activity in the markets today of the technical dealers has meant that the prices that emerge are only in part the result of any kind of rational estimate of future trends. By hedging and other operations, the dealers may take some of the risk out of the business on behalf of the buyers and producers, although as we have seen the dealers are often big producers themselves. But, far from having a smoothing effect, as it is sometimes claimed, the futures market can easily exaggerate the up and down swings. Chart 4 shows how prices moved just in the two decades of the 1970s and 1980s. And this chart conceals much of the volatility of prices. Statisticians at UNCTAD have calculated an 'instability index', which relates monthly variations around a long-term trend. In these two decades the percentage variations for more than half of the commodities covered exceeded 20 per cent. For some they were over 40 per cent. And again these monthly figures are averaging out even wider daily fluctuations. In the week of writing the price of nickel has fallen by over 10 per cent, cocoa and coffee by five per cent.

It is the growers, especially the small growers, who suffer most from these swings, gaining little from the upswings and often losing heavily on the downswings. Coffee prices in 1989 had to fall by over a fifth before Nestlé reduced its soluble coffee price by a tenth, but the grower's price was cut at once. We shall look at the grower's share of the final price of coffee and other primary commodities in the next chapter. It is worth noting here that the grower's share in the green coffee price in the United States swung from 35 per cent in 1972 to 50 per cent in 1976 and right down to 16 per cent in 1977. In general it is clear that with the growth of the role of the giant transnational companies and the manipulation of the commodity markets, the share of the grower has steadily declined over the past four decades. In 1941 it was estimated that the grower received a third of the US retail price of Brazilian coffee. Today, the grower's share is rarely more than a tenth, and coffee workers on estates receive no more than four cents in the dollar of the retail price for coffee. Family labour is almost always unpaid and not even counted in calculating the grower's price.

It is, of course, true that dealers can also lose money as well as making profits. As in any other form of gambling, there are winners and losers. When the price trend changes many dealers are caught. In the tin crash of 1987 dealers had bought large quantities of tin in the expectation of rising prices. At that time, there was a tin agreement between producer and consumer governments, which we shall discuss in the next chapter, and the buffer stock manager had borrowed money from brokers in order to continue buying. When the price dropped and stayed down, the dealers were holding tin claims for which they had paid far above the spot price in the expectation of continued rising prices. The tin agreeement collapsed and many people lost money. It is easy to see why only the giant companies have been able to survive in this casino. They not only have the resources but, by the sheer scale of their deals, they can influence the price. Apart from them, the successful dealers are those who have enjoyed a mixture of luck and good information. The luck largely concerns the date when they entered the market and the date when they left it. The best days were after the 1930s when there was a steady rise in prices for 20 years and in the early 1970s when there was another boom running. The time to get out was just before the slump began in the years that followed the booms. But timing is of the essence. The Rowntree's cocoa buyer in 1973 sold forward cocoa that he did not have because he was sure the price would turn down. When it continued to rise (to peak at four times the 1972 price by 1974) Rowntree panicked and closed its futures contracts, losing £32 million in the process. The information needed mainly concerns the likely actions and reactions of

CHART 4. MONTHLY INDEX OF FREE MARKET EXPORT COMMODITY PRICES, 1970-88

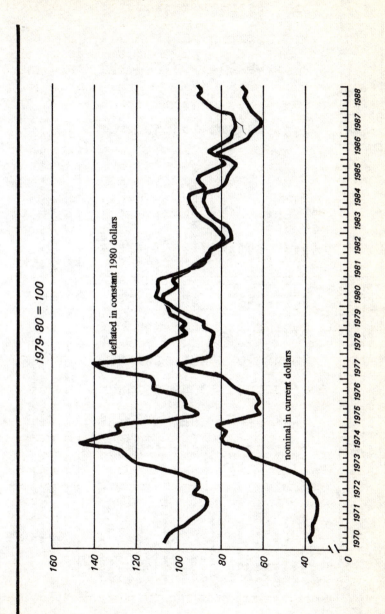

Source: This chart is taken from UNCTAD *Statistical Pocket Book,* 1989.

TABLE 8. TRENDS IN MONTHLY MARKET PRICES OF PRIMARY PRODUCTS

Commodity	In current dollars			In constant dollars [1]		
	1960-1971	1972-1980	1981-1988	1960-1971	1972-1980	1981-1988
Food						
Wheat	-1.4	5.8	-7.7	-3.0	-5.2	-10.6
Maize	0.7	7.0	-7.4	-0.9	-4.0	-10.4
Rice (free market)	1.0	5.7	-11.0	-0.6	-5.3	-14.0
Bovine meat	8.1	7.2	-1.8	6.5	-3.8	-4.8
Sugar (free market)	-4.4	3.3	-14.3	-5.9	-7.6	-17.3
Bananas (free market)	-1.3	10.5	-1.2	-2.9	-0.5	-4.2
Pepper	4.5	8.2	22.6	2.9	-2.8	19.5
Soybean meal	1.5	5.0	-4.9	-0.1	-6.0	-7.9
Fish meal	0.9	5.5	-4.5	-0.6	-5.5	-7.5
Tropical beverages						
Coffee	1.5	17.6	1.0	-0.1	6.5	-1.9
Cocoa	4.9	19.4	1.0	3.3	8.3	-2.0
Tea	-3.3	11.0	-2.5	-4.8	0.0	-5.5
Vegetable oilseeds and oils						
Soybeans	1.0	5.3	-5.0	-0.5	-5.6	-8.0
Soybean oil	1.4	7.5	-6.1	-0.2	-3.5	-9.0
Sunflower oil	2.6	5.4	-8.4	1.0	-5.5	-11.4
Groundnuts	3.4	6.6	-9.9	1.8	-4.4	-12.9
Groundnut oil	3.6	7.9	-6.8	2.0	-3.1	-9.8
Copra	0.7	10.9	-6.5	-0.8	-0.2	-9.5
Coconut oil	2.9	9.5	-6.8	1.3	-1.5	-9.7
Palm kernels	-0.2	10.5	-11.3	-1.7	-0.5	-14.2
Palm kernel oil	3.0	11.6	-7.7	1.4	0.6	-10.7
Palm oil	-0.3	9.5	-9.5	-1.8	-1.5	-12.4
Linseed oil	-0.9	6.1	-8.4	-2.4	-4.8	-11.4
Agricultural raw materials						
Cotton	1.6	8.5	-4.7	0.0	-2.5	-7.7
Wool	-8.5	7.1	-0.2	-10.1	-3.9	-3.2
Sisal	-10.7	6.6	-3.8	-12.2	-4.4	-6.7
Jute	-0.3	2.4	-0.2	-1.8	-8.5	-3.2
Hides and skins	2.5	8.5	1.2	1.0	-2.5	-1.8
Tropical timber	0.4	10.8	1.4	-1.2	-0.2	-1.6
Minerals, ores and metals						
Rubber	-4.4	14.6	-2.5	-5.9	3.6	-5.5
Phosphate rock	0.4	11.6	-6.3	-1.2	0.6	-9.2
Manganese ore	-3.5	10.2	-4.3	-5.0	-0.8	-7.3
Aluminium	2.6	14.5	2.1	1.1	3.4	-0.9
Iron ore	1.5	7.9	-1.6	-0.1	-3.1	-4.5
Copper	5.4	4.1	-0.9	3.9	-6.9	-3.9
Lead	2.6	13.4	-4.5	1.1	2.4	-7.4
Zinc	1.8	1.9	-1.0	0.2	-9.1	-4.0
Tin	2.1	18.2	-12.2	0.5	7.1	-15.1
Tungsten	21.5	17.3	-17.8	19.9	6.2	-20.8

Sources: UNCTAD, *Monthly Commodity Price Bulletin;* United Nations, *Monthly Bulletin of Statistics,* various issues.

Notes: The percentages are derived from a semilogarithmic regression equation, calculated on a monthly basis.

1   Constant 1980 dollars (current dollars divided by the United Nations index of export unit value of manufactured goods exported by developed market-economy countries).

other dealers as they respond to changing news about demand and supply for different products. The combination of luck and good information can make fortunes, when a dealer comes upon a new piece of information which no one else has. As a result of the activities of the technical dealers there are real dangers of runs on the market, and when the computers themselves are instructed to sell or buy at certain pre-set moments, these runs cannot then be easily controlled by human agency.

All this is a game, albeit a risky one, which may be fun for the players, but it is hardly a serious way of doing business. The famous words of John Maynard Keynes are worth recalling, as even more relevant today than when they were written in his *The General Theory* in 1936:

> Speculators may do no harm as bubbles on a steady stream of enterprise. But the position is serious when enterprise becomes the bubble on a whirlpool of speculation. When the capital development of a country becomes a by-product of the activities of a casino, the job is likely to be ill-done.

The reader may well be thinking that there must be some more effective method than a casino for linking buyers and sellers of commodities. To find alternatives, we shall have to look at all the many stages involved in the import-export relations of international trade, from the labour of farmers and miners right through to the display of the finished products on the shop counter. So long as there are people who want to speculate in commodities, and there are markets for commodities, speculators will find ways of doing this and a place to do it, so that no good can come of simply taxing speculators out of existence in London or New York. They will just appear somewhere else, as gambling dens appear where there are no regulations to forbid them. We have to find alternatives to the commodity markets that not only bring traders and producers together without eliminating freedom of choice, but also bring the final consumer more closely into touch with the producers themselves.

Notes

There is a simple introduction to markets in Joan Robinson and John Eatwell, *An Introduction to Modern Economics*, 1973, Chapter 5, McGraw Hill. Stuart Holland, *The Market Economy*, Weidenfeld, 1987, Part 2 offers a comprehensive critique of the working of markets today. A more technical introduction to commodity markets may be found in *Futures Trading in Commodity Markets*, International Chamber of Commerce, Paris, 1981. Many of the examples in this chapter have been taken from Frederick Clairmonte and John Cavanagh, *Merchants of Drink: Transnational Control of World Beverages*, Third World Network, 1988.

6. THE MIDDLEMEN

Middlemen have got a bad name. In Australia they are called sharks, referring originally to the press gangs; in Mexico, coyotes after the prairie wolves; in Peru, piranhas from the man-eating fish of the Amazon. They play many roles — money-lender, merchant, trader, agent, packer, storer, carrier, shipper, insurer, dealer, wholesaler, distributor. They are the indispensable linkmen between the producer and the consumer. When the command economies of the Soviet Union and Eastern Europe collapsed, and their new governments sought to establish markets in place of the orders and allocations issued by ministries to enterprises, they had to look for middlemen. They could only find such people in the black markets, which were promptly legalised. It should not be assumed that middlemen are necessarily wicked or wholly rapacious. Their standing varies very much from one society to another and from what angle they are viewed. Their considerable power in the Third World does not make them loved; but attitudes in the First World have varied over time according to the general ethos of society.

In producer societies, generally, the middlemen are hated because they seem to take all the profit without doing any of the real work. In consumer societies, by contrast, they are admired because they quite literally deliver the goods. In agrarian England trade was despised but in the towns and cities it came to be respected. In our consumer society the City of London is honoured. In the transition, trade came to embrace all forms of industrial activity where one's hands might be dirtied. As a result there is deep confusion about the proper definitions, at least in Britain, of commerce and industry. The authority of Marx has come to be sought and, despite much argument about marginal cases, his distinction between productive industrial capital and merchant, commercial capital, does seem to be based on a real life difference. With productive capital, profit is made primarily in production — whether in industry or agriculture — by setting labour to work and paying less in wages than the value that is added by the work. With merchant capital, profit is made by buying commodities at one price and selling them at another (better) price. The goods may be transported half way across the world, but the merchant's profit is not made primarily from the labour of the transport workers. The profits which banks make by borrowing funds at one rate of interest and lending at a higher rate reveal them to be merchant capitalists.

The importance for us of the distinction is that, while it is true that great wealth may come to individuals and even to whole societies from successful application of merchant capital, by extending its use and establishing monopoly positions, real economic growth can only come from increasing the productivity of labour. The increase of output per person, whether in agriculture or in industry, has been the dynamic of industrial capital and the explanation for the meteoric rise of capitalism. All other modes of production, we saw earlier, were sucked in behind this whirlwind — slavery, peonage, indentured labour, sharecroppers, peasants, contract workers and then all the landlords and their agents and the middlemen. It is these last which must be our concern in this chapter. They are not by any means all nationals of the Third World producer country, and if they are they may well be agents for a First World company. By far the greater number of intermediaries in international trade in fact operate in the First World. We can set them out in order of their appearance, distinguishing them according to the different functions they perform.

BOX 3. FROM CROP TO SHOP

The Chain of Individuals and CompaniesInvolved in Trading

Production — Individual peasant household, small farmer, craftworker, bee-keeper, nut-gatherer; Sharecropper, peon, contract worker; Cooperative or Producers association; Plantation workers, out growers, miners, working for local companies or for large transnational companies from the First World.

Technical consultancy — specialist firms usually from the First World, occasionally from the Third World.

Storing and processing — *first stage*: generally by production workers; *second stage*: on local estate by local private company or by big company, often from the First World.

Finance for purchase — private banks, often from the First World, sometimes Third World state banks, or cooperatives.

Preserving and packaging — roasting, refrigeration, vacuum packing, quality control etc., by local company or transnational.

Transporting — by specialist local company or transnational.

Marketing — *home market*: local company or state organisation or agent, occasionally a cooperative; *overseas*: local trader, big company or state marketing board.

Exporting — Third World company agent or First World transnational.

→

Shipping and insurance — agents for First World importers or big company, occasionally Third World exporters;

Importing, inspection and documentation — merchants or big company from the First World;

Commodity dealing — First World dealers and big companies;

Finance for trading — First World banks and Government department (credit guarantees);

Legal and accountancy services — specialist firms from the First World;

Manufacturing — big company or specialist firm from the First World;

Wholesaling — wholesalers,wholesale markets, big companies, Cooperatives;

Advertising and promotion — First World agencies;

Distribution and transport — specialist firms, big companies, sometimes cooperatives — all First World companies.

Retailing — Chain stores, retail cooperatives, small shops, mail order.

From Box 3 we can see that the big company — one of the giant transnational companies — frequently performs all the functions distinguished here, from direct production to the final sale in the shops. Yet, there is room for an enormous number of middlemen in the business. It is also evident from the box that there is much more to being a middleman than just buying and selling. The margins for merchanting and financing roles are only minor compared with the value added to the primary product in processing, preserving and packaging, transporting and marketing. What is of the greatest importance for us to discover, if we are looking for a larger piece of the action for the small producer, is where the power lies. In this respect we can recognise four or five centres of power, in each of which it might be possible to devise measures which could increase the bargaining position of the small Third World producer. These centres are respectively:

(a) producer power, where monopoly positions are established or competition is regulated;

(b) marketing or trader power, where access to markets is monopolised or effectively controlled;

(c) financial power, where access to finance is restricted to those who already have money or is available only at exorbitant rates of interest;

(d) consumer power, where market tastes and fashions are created by advertising and the promise of convenience of delivery;

(e) nation-state power, where subsidies, tariffs, levies or the activity of marketing boards manipulate the channels of trade.

Only in the case of marketing boards and other similar state trading agencies can governments be included in the list of middlemen, but there is no doubt that the nation-state remains a centre of power, however weak it may often appear in relation to the power of the giant transnational companies. It is possible to influence the policies of governments both in the First and Third Worlds with the aim of strengthening the bargaining position of the small producer, or at least of removing some of the obstacles strewn across the path of the small producer. But this will be the subject of discussion in the next chapter. Here we need to note that there are at least four centres of power which effectively corral the small producer. Power is exercised at each centre in very different ways and these must be understood if they are to be challenged.

TABLE 9. WHERE DOES THE MONEY GO? (pennies in the £)

Who gets what	Coffee (soluble)	Bananas
Staying in the producing country (some for the grower, some to the state for tax)	37.3p	11.5p
Going outside the producing country		
Transport costs and insurance	4.5p	37.5p
Ripening	—	19p
Processing and packaging		
materials and labour	13p	26p
overheads and promotion	26.6p	11.5p
manufacturer's profit and royalties	7.1p	—
Retailing	9.9p	32p
Total	100p	100p

Source: Simon Fisher & David Hicks, *World Studies 8-13. A Teacher's Handbook*, Oliver & Boyd, 1985, drawing on information from Christian Aid publication, *Show You Care*.

Note: Since the figures predate the collapse of primary commodity prices, especially of coffee after 1989, the share shown to be going to the producers is likely to be much greater than it would be today

Who Gets What?

The first thing to note is who gets what at each different stage in the make-up of the final price. Taking two examples: coffee and bananas — we can see from Table 9 that in the case of coffee 37p stays in the producing country, while in the case of bananas only 12p The average for all agricultural products is calculated to be about 15p, and of course nothing like all of this goes to the grower. He or she generally gets 1p or perhaps 2p for what we pay £1 for in the shops.

There are two questions to ask after a glance at these charts. The first is: why is the grower's share so low compared with that of all the middlemen? The second is: why is not more of the processing and packaging done in the producing country? We have noted all the reasons that primary product prices tend to fall behind manufactured goods prices, but we are looking here at the shares within the final price, and it is by no means the case that raising the market price would necessarily help the growers or, in the case of minerals, the miners or other producers. The middlemen might get all the benefit. An example is the raising of the oil price by OPEC. This enormously increased the profits of the big oil companies and the wealth of the sheikhs and their families and entourage, but the oil workers gained little and the nomadic pastoralists who grazed their herds where the oil rigs now stand gained nothing at all.

Producer Power

We saw earlier that most people in the Third World, that is about half of all the people in the world, live and work on land that they own or rent. They are farmers, but may engage in some craft production, bee keeping, mining and gathering forest products on the side. These are the small producers we shall mainly be concerned with, although they may have many different kinds of relationship to the ownership of the land they work on. A few will be owners of the land, most will be tenants, sharecroppers, peons or contract workers. Minerals and manufactures are largely produced by wage workers, mainly in the First World. Most Third World producers are in fact extended households, engaged in subsistence farming. They feed and clothe themselves, find fuel for cooking and heating and repair their houses from what they can grow on the land or collect in the common forests. In addition, they try to produce some cash crop or crops as a surplus to their needs, which they can sell to pay off their debts and to buy salt and spices and cloth, tools and cooking equipment which they cannot make themselves. In many countries such small-holders predominate over the large estates in production for export. This is true, for example, of cocoa production in Ghana or of Ugandan coffee production.

The cash crops may be coffee or peanuts, cocoa or tapioca, tobacco or vegetables, tropical fruits or a side product like honey or nuts or rubber. If this crop harvests before their main food crop, many small producers may have to sell at once to buy food for their families. Even if they have food, they may still have to sell at once because they do not have storage facilities or refrigeration or vacuum packing to preserve perishable foods. So, the middlemen descend like the coyotes. The peasants who are all trying to sell at the same time cannot hold their crop off the market and must take a price that barely covers their costs, even excluding their labour. Their only alternative will be to sell to a big company, which may offer a better price but with strings attached — only the best-quality produce and exclusive trade deals.

Increasingly today the giant transnational companies, which we have discussed, are moving from direct production on plantations to the establishment of outgrowing contracts. In this way they obtain more flexibility and cannot be accused of paying starvation wages. The grower can even be worse off, because flexibility means that the giant company can cut back or extend its contracts according to the demand for the product, without the problems involved in sacking and re-engaging labour. Examples may be found in tea growing in Sri Lanka. The recent 'development' of Belize by Coca Cola, Nestlé and Hershey, as a result of the cutting down of one of the largest remaining tropical rain forests of Central America, consists mainly in contracting local farmers to grow cocoa and oranges for one of these transnational companies as sole buyer.

It is not only giant overseas companies which dominate production for export in Third World countries. The role of domestic landed families must not be ignored. An outstanding example was the Somoza family in Nicaragua which, before their overthrow in 1979, owned a quarter of all the land, a third of industrial and commercial capital and nearly all the mines and off-shore fishing rights. Elsewhere in Central America most coffee plantations are controlled by the nation's wealthiest families, which constitute the ruling political dynasty. Links between the great domestic landed families in the Third World and giant companies in the First World were forged in colonial times and continue to this day. The Tata family group in India, aside from its interests in steel, engineering and power generation, controls the largest tea estates in the sub-continent in a joint venture with J. Finlay, and operates several tea-packaging plants. Brooke Bond's Indian and Kenyan companies are also local national companies with local shareholders, although part of the Unilever combine.

Very occasionally the producers themselves may have combined together to form a cooperative or local growers' association to present a common front to the buyers, but such an association will need funds to give the growers a down payment of at least part of the value of the crop in order to keep the middlemen at bay. They will also need to have information about world prices in order to reassure their members that they are getting a fair deal, and should not listen to all the stories of low world prices regaled by the coyotes. They will need much more if they are to reinforce their position by taking over the storage and processing and by further adding value to their product by packaging and transport. We shall look at all this in a later chapter, but here we must simply note how much is needed to strengthen the bargaining power of the small grower.

Trader Power

Here we are at the heart of the matter. We have seen the dominant position in the world market of a quite small number of giant companies buying and selling a wide range of primary products. Their power derives from the scale of their resources, the integration of their operations from grower right through to consumer, their access to finance, their ability to manipulate the market and increasingly the freedom they enjoy to switch supplies from one source to another, and even to switch operations from plantations to outgrowing. When there was serious overproduction of orange juice in the mid-1980s, Cargill and some of the other giants survived by savagely cutting back on contracts and investing heavily in modern transport, including new terminals in Brazil and refrigerated ships and warehouses in Western Europe and the United States. We noted, however, in the last chapter that there were, at least in most of the main First World markets, a number of competing giants whose rivalry ensures that prices are not always fixed, however much technical trading may add to them. It is far different in a Third World country, where there may only be one or two giant companies offering a market for each product, even for all products. The same companies can at the same time be providing the main channel for imports from the First World, engaging in the main local manufacturing enterprises and operating the main local stores.

This position, straddling the whole range of buying and selling, shipping and manufacturing, is illustrated best by Unilever's United Africa Company in those parts of the African continent where there were British colonies, or by the CFAO where there were French colonies. Lonrho (whose name derives from London Rhodesia) not only owns a million acres in Zimbabwe and has 19 breweries in joint ventures with African governments, but also has subsidiaries operating hotels and casinos, motor distribution, engineering, textiles, printing and publishing, finance and general trade,

TABLE 10. MAJOR FOOD TRADERS AND PROCESSORS, 1980

Commodity	Leading traders	Leading processors	1980 sales (billions USD)
Sugar	Tate & Lyle (UK)	Gulf & Western (US)	5.3
	Sucres et Denrées (F)	Lonrho (UK)	5.0
	Engelhard (Philipps) (US)	Tate & Lyle (UK)	3.4
	E.D.F. Man (UK)	Amstar (US)	1.8
Coffee	J. Aron (US)	Nestlé (Switzerland)	13.8
	Volkart (Switzerland)	Proctor & Gamble (US)	11.2
	ACLI International (US)	General Foods (US)	6.4
	Socomex (US)	Coca Cola (US)	5.9
	General Foods and Proctor & Gamble (US)	Jacobs (FRG)	1.6
Corn	Continental (US)	Cargill (US)	25.0
	Louis Dreyfus (F)	CPC International (US)	4.1
	Bunge & Born (Brazil)	Standard Brands (US)	3.0
	André (Switzerland)	ADM (US)	3.2
	Cargill (US)	Bunge & Born (Brazil)	n.a.
Rice	Connell (US)	Cargill (US)	25.0
	Continental (US)	Continental (US)	n.a.
	"Six Tigers" (Thailand)		
Cocoa	ACLI International (US)	Nestlé (Switzerland)	13.8
	Volkart (Switzerland)	Cadbury-Schweppes (UK)	2.7
	Gill & Duffus (UK)	Mars, Inc. (US)	2.3
	Internatio (US/Holland)	Rowntree-Mackintosh (UK)	1.5
	J.H. Rayner (US)	Hershey Foods (US)	1.3
Tea	Allied-Lyons (UK)	Unilever (Liptons) (UK)	24.3
	Unilever (UK)	Associated British Foods (Twining) (UK)	5.8
	J. Finlay (UK)	Allied-Lyons (UK)	5.0
	Brooke Bond (UK)	Brooke Bond (UK)	1.6
	Associated British Foods (UK)	James Finlay (UK)	n.a.
Bananas	R.J. Reynolds (Del Monte)(US)	R.J. Reynolds (Del Monte)(US)	10.4
	United Brands (US)	United Brands (US)	3.9
	Castle & Cooke (US)	Castle & Cooke (US)	1.7
Pineapples	Mitsubishi (Japan)	Mitsubishi (Japan)	66.1
	R.J. Reynolds (US)	Nestlé (Libby) (US)	13.8
	Castle & Cooke (US)	R.J. Reynolds (Del Monte) (US)	10.4
		Castle & Cooke (US)	1.7

Source: Trade sources.

The author gratefully acknowledges this table which is taken from J. Cavanagh and F. Clairmonte, of UNCTAD, paper presented at a Consumers' Association of Penang Conference in May 1980.

freight and container shipping, including Kuhne and Nagel, one of the world's biggest cargo, warehousing and forwarding businesses spreading across 80 countries. On a smaller scale you could take the example of the Australian companies, Burn and Philips, and Steamships, which have a duopoly of buying and selling, shipping and supermarkets in Papua New Guinea.

Even in the markets and auctions of the larger Third World countries, there may be only two or three dealers. Brooke Bond and Lipton, both now owned by Unilever, hold 98 per cent of India's packet tea market and more than half of the total Indian tea market. They supply about a third of the world's tea in the auction sales of seven countries — the UK, India, Indonesia, Bangladesh, Sri Lanka, Malawi, Kenya. This includes 42 per cent of the UK tea market (Lyons' Tetley, Cadbury's Typhoo and the CWS contributing roughly 15 per cent each). These two Unilever companies not only have their own tea plantations, blenders and processors and packing stations, but their own brokers. In the Calcutta tea market two brokers account for 80 per cent of tea sales. In Colombo there are five, in Mombasa three and in London four. Just three companies divide up the world's banana economy — Del Monte, Castle and Cooke, and United Brands (formerly the United Fruit Company). United Fruit was said at one time to control 85 per cent of the land in the American tropics (except for Ecuador) suitable for banana cultivation. This meant control over the major export crop of Costa Rica, Honduras, Panama, Colombia and Jamaica.

Ownership or control of shipping has been an essential element in the power of First World trading companies in the economies of the Third World since colonial times. Access to cold storage and refrigeration was essential in the transport of meat and fruit across the oceans. Many plantation companies were associated with shipping companies. Examples are P & O and Booker McConnell. We have noted the recent involvement of both Cargill and Lonrho in sea transport and warehousing. The oil companies have always operated their own fleets of oil tankers, and the large ore carriers as well as refrigerator vessels have generally sailed under the colours, if not the flags, of the trading companies. Insurance is an important part of trading and transportation. Unilever/Brooke Bond and Gill & Duffus, apparent competitors in the commodities market, have a jointly owned insurance venture, named Gillbrooke Ltd. This issue leads us on into the whole area of financial power.

Financial Power

'Wealth is power' wrote Adam Smith, the father of political economy. But he went on to explain: 'The person who either acquires or succeeds to a great fortune does not necessarily acquire or succeed to any political power either civil or military . . . but the power of purchasing; a certain command over all the labour or over all the produce of labour that is then in the market.' Today we have to add that it is not necessarily the inheritance of wealth, although that greatly helps, but the capacity to make money which gives that certain command. The money may be more or less honestly come by. What matters is that those who have money — not only wealthy people but the managers of financial institutions — should be prepared to put their money into the hands of someone whom they believe to be a money-maker. This is the secret of the Bonds and Murdochs, the Goldsmiths and Hansons of our times. In other words, these men had access to money. A quite small initial sum can be 'geared up', as it is called, with loans and overdrafts to finance a very big operation.

Access to large sums of money is the secret of most of the traders whose activities we have been looking at. The funding which they require takes the form of credit. Capital for trading does not for the most part have to be sunk in plant and equipment, although we have seen the importance of owning ships and warehouses and port installations. Nor does it have to be in land or even in employing labour on plantations. What is absolutely essential is access to credit — for making purchases and holding stocks. Interest can be paid from the proceeds of sales, but the key to trading is the ability to draw upon lines of credit. Clairmonte and Cavanagh, in their book on transnational control of world beverages, report that:

> Traders' individual credit lines with a large bank can soar to as high as $200 million, a sum whose volume is determined by the size and profitability of a trader's collateral. Mega multi-commodity firms like Cargill and Philipp Brothers in the mid-1980s established as many as 40 credit lines with different banks at any one time. While on average, traders utilise between 30-70 per cent of their credit lines, in peak trading periods this can be catapulted to 100 per cent.

Clairmonte and Cavanagh make the point that up to the 1970s most trading companies were family owned. This was true of Cargill, Volkart, ACLI and J. Aron in the United States and of James Finlay, John Swire, Dalgety and S & W Berisford in the UK and many others. Family ownership makes it easier to preserve commercial secrets and to make lightning decisions involving big risks. When the great expansion of the volume of trade in commodities came to an end in the late 1970s, and prices began to fall, the pikes in the fish pond began to eat each other. Only the giants survived and these were themselves absorbed into finance houses like Goldman Sachs or became in effect, like Cargill, financial conglomerates. In the case of the corresponding Japanese groups, the *sogo shoshas,* the links between finance and trade as well as industry had always been close from the beginning of Japanese capitalism through the merchant houses of the *zaibatsu*. After the Second World War six groups emerged to establish their dominance over the whole Japanese economy, and now control overseas investments throughout the world which exceed even the stock of United States foreign investment.

No one who stands outside the giant conglomerates of Japan, the USA, the UK, Germany or any of the other centres of capital accumulation is today going to find it easy to gain access to finance from the banking system for international trading. 'To him that hath shall be given . . . .' Without adequate collateral, lines of credit are just not available. This is above all true of any Third World country which has large debts outstanding to the Western banks. A new and ugly word has entered the language — bankability — to define creditworthiness. Banks have begun to draw red lines around customers, institutions and even whole countries and ruled them out as unbankable. This does not unfortunately mean that their debts are written off, only that they will not be lent any more money or allowed any more credit. The only alternative recourse for funding outside the banking system is the nation-state. We shall look at nation-state power in both the First World and the Third World in the next chapter.

Consumer Power

Devotees of the market faithfully believe that the final consumer has the ultimate power in the market, because he, or more likely she, can choose to take or to leave what is on offer. In the last chapter we noted that she might have preferred something that was not available, and especially a public service instead of private goods, and she might not have been able to afford what was available. She has a choice of goods so long as she has the money to pay with. Public provision in a planned economy tries to relate incomes to the goods produced. It does not, however, necessarily offer either the choice or the goods, even where the shopper has the money, as we have learned from the experience of the Soviet Union and Eastern Europe. Hence the enthusiasm of Eastern Europeans for a market economy. Consumer power in a market economy is based on the very real capacity of most consumers to choose among alternatives according to taste and price. The domination of the market by a small number of giant companies, which we have been looking at, does inevitably restrict the choice and allow prices to be managed by the largest companies. When the retailers, as in the case of Marks and Spencer, Sainsbury's or AZDA, are also the producers or control the producers, not only of the finished goods but of the primary products too, we have to ask to what extent the consumer can really exercise any power over what is produced and over how it is produced through the choice they make of suppliers.

Choice between products in the market remains, but it can hardly be denied that for most people, even in the First World, choices are narrowing. It is not certain, however, whether this is regarded as a deprivation. Let us take the example of the provision of fast foods. In this market a very narrow range of products is offered, but it is immensely popular; the total value of annual sales is estimated at over $100 billion. McDonald's alone sells $100 billion worth of identical products in over 10,000 identical outlets in almost every country (155 at the last count) throughout the world, and adds another 500 outlets every year. Coca Cola products are the only drinks available in McDonald's restaurants. Pepsi Cola has a similar link with Kentucky Fried Chicken and two other fast-food chains, giving them access to 15,000 restaurants world-wide in 1986. These two soft-drink companies after recent acquisitions hold between them over 80 per cent of the world soft-drinks market and this applies equally in the Third World as in the First. It is only a tiny group of organic product enthusiasts who have begun even to question the quality of fast foods and the drinks that go with them.

Clairmonte and Cavanagh in their study of the world beverage industry list 50 top firms with total annual sales approaching $200 billion in 1985. This included not only the soft drinks, but alcoholic drinks, tea, coffee and cocoa and the fastest growing market of all, the bottled water market, which is edging up to the $10 billion per year mark. Total sales in all these markets rose five-fold in the decade from 1970 and during these years many of the largest firms merged or were taken over by rivals. We can cite Philip Morris and General Foods, Reynolds and Nabisco, Guinness and Distillers, Cadbury and Schweppes, Rowntree and Suchards. Is there no subsequent reduction in variety? Nestlé and Coca Cola are each known for what they are, but Nestlé also owns Carnation milk as well as a whole range of cosmetics; and Coca Cola owns Minute Maid fruit juices. Usually there is no way of knowing who owns the brand name you choose. Café Hag belongs to General Foods. Before Polly Peck bought it, Del Monte belonged to RJ Reynolds, which also owns Kentucky Fried Chicken, Camel cigarettes and Canada Dry ginger ale, and who now owns Polly Peck since Mr Nadir's empire collapsed? Unilever has the widest range of products of any of the giant multinationals. BAT (British American Tobacco), until it was subject to a bid from Mr James Goldsmith, was another tobacco giant, like Philip Morris, Reynolds and Imperial tobacco, seeking to diversify out of cigarettes, as the health hazards of smoking come to be more widely recognised. All of these giants — Unilever, Coca Cola, General Foods, BAT — have plantations in the Third World of the kind we have already noted, but they do not rely on these wholly for their supplies, preferring to sub-contract to smaller producers under their control.

There is, of course, still a sort of choice we can make as consumers even among the giants. Millions of dollars of advertising money are spent on trying to attach us to one brand rather than another. Often the choice lies between no more than two or three brands, but it is a choice. Choosing one rather than another generally involves choosing the store where we shop or the cafe or public house where we drink. As we have seen with Coca Cola and Pepsi Cola, it is not only the brewers who have established tied houses. It is important to note that there has been of late a definite consumers' revolt against the standardisation of food products. It took a major campaign to get real ale back into British pubs, after its displacement by carbonated, watered beer concentrate. Only a mushrooming of small wholefood shops has brought wholemeal bread back into the bakeries to replace the caramelised white loaf called brown bread. But these things have happened. Of course, you have to pay more for the real thing, but you can get it now. This demand not only for a wider choice but for a purer product, and especially for food that is organically grown, shows the way to make at least a minor challenge to the dominant power of the giant purveyors of food and drink. And this we shall take up in a later chapter.

What we have seen in reviewing the power of growers, of traders, of financiers and finally of consumers is that any challenge to the giants who dominate the whole field of commodity trade will have to be made at many points, because the power of the giants is many-sided. Even to talk about challenging such power may seem to be romantic beyond even the dreams of Don Quixote. Nothing less than a coordinated and combined strategy on a large scale can be expected to begin to increase the piece of the action which Third World producers can obtain from the commodities which, by their labour and their expertise, they now bring onto the world market. The rest of this book is devoted to considering the attempts that have been made to devise such a strategy and the successes and failures that have attended them so that we may reach some conclusions about the key elements that would be needed for any strategy to be successful.

Notes

For a picture of the situation of primary commodity growers in the Third World, readers should look for Clive Robinson's *Hungry Farmers* published by Christian Aid, PO Box 100, London SE1 7RT, in 1989. For the description of trader power this chapter relies heavily on Frederick Clairmonte and John Cavanagh, *Merchants of Drink: Transnational Control of World Beverages*, (Third World Network, 1988) and on these authors' earlier paper 'Transnational Corporations and Services: The Final Frontier', UNCTAD *Trade and Development Review*, No. 5.

Part Two

Making Trade Fairer

'Fair trade guarantees a better deal for Third World producers'

Slogan of the British Fair Trade Mark,
backed by Oxfam, Christian Aid, and other leading UK Third World
agencies

7. REGULATING THE MARKET

It is one of the myths of history that there was ever a free and wholly unregulated market or a *laissez-faire* economy and a 'night watchman' role for the state, even in Britain in the nineteenth century. Markets have always been regulated, generally by those with most power — rulers, property owners, large companies — and just sometimes by those trying to limit monopoly power and discourage swindling. Property law, company law, contract law, labour law, together make up the greater part of the work of lawyers and judges, and these all reflect the legislative acts of governments. At the height of the supposed *laissez-faire* economy in Britain the government was raising taxes not only for the basic administration of law and for the defence of the realm, but also for education and health and public services, which no individual employer would meet without ensuring that his competitors were bearing equal costs. It is sometimes said that the British economy in the nineteenth century was distinguished by the limited role of government. In fact central government expenditure in Britain was more than double per head of population than that of any other great power over the period from 1860 to 1914. As for the 'night watchman' state, it was ruling over the greatest colonial empire the world has ever seen and deploying a navy across the seven seas to protect the markets for British exporters and the mines and plantations for British investors overseas. Other nation-states — the USA, Germany, France, Italy, Japan — which sought to industrialise did so by protecting their markets until they were strong enough to compete with Britain. But they tended to retain this protection over their own spheres of influence for much longer.

Protection of the First World's Markets

Protection in trade has nearly always been protection by those who are already strong. Nation-states with the power to do so have used many different protective devices — import controls, tariffs, levies, quotas, preferences and other restrictive practices — to safeguard their own producers, both agricultural and industrial, against foreign suppliers. Many of these were retained long after they were needed to give infant industries the chance to survive against established competitors. United States, German, Japanese and Korean industries were all built up behind protective walls, but thereafter such protection was used by those already well placed to prevent others from becoming established. Thus, nearly all industrialised states operate an escalating system of tariff rates — generally nil for raw materials rising by steps, according to the stage of production, to the highest rate for completely finished products. This can be as high as 50 per cent added to the value (*ad valorem*). Take the example of soya beans entering the European Community. Raw beans pay no duty; soymeal seven per cent; refined oil 15 per cent; margarine 25 per cent. Or take the rate for pineapples: the fresh fruit pays nine per cent; canned pineapples 32 per cent; pineapple juice 42 per cent. These are major obstacles for Third World producers to overcome in establishing their own processing plants: to add value to their primary products, and so obtain a larger piece of the action in international trade.

GATT (the General Agreement on Tariffs and Trade) has been much in the news recently. At the end of the Second World War, as part of the general post-war settlement, nearly all nation-states signed this agreement. The aim of GATT was to achieve, through a series of negotiated rounds, the ultimate reduction of all barriers to trade. The more than 100 members were to lower not only tariffs and other non-tariff barriers but each member was to treat all other members as their most-favoured nation (MFN). In the several rounds of agreement, barriers to trade have been much reduced. It remains true that many forms of protection are still retained, especially by the most advanced industrial nations. Indeed, an Indian delegate was once impelled to describe GATT as a 'one-way street'. You could drive down it from the North, but the road was blocked from the South. The fact is that most industrial products from the Third World are subject to some restriction in the First World, through quota systems and other limitations. The Multi-fibre Agreement (MFA) for example, established in 1974, limits textile imports into First World countries. The General System of Preferences, which is supposed to give preference to developing countries, has many crucial exceptions, and these affect just those industrial goods that Third World countries can produce in the early stages of industrialisation. Other non-tariff barriers include the setting of technical standards which are hard for Third World producers to achieve and the proliferation of import procedures, especially in Japan, which are impossible for all but the most experienced importers to comprehend.

The most glaring restrictions on free market trading which are exercised by First World countries are, strange as it may seem, those which protect their agriculture. The USA, Japan and the European Community have all erected high barriers against imports of food. The argument for agricultural protection has often been said to be either strategic, the defence of food supplies in time of war, or political, the farm vote — which remains a crucial marginal determinant of political power even in the most industrialised nations. And we have all seen on our TV screens the ways in which European farmers protest, with little or no interference from the authorities at their blockading of ports with their tractors and burning of imported meat products. Nonetheless, the reality is that high food prices are today protecting not the European or American farmers, certainly not the small farmers, so much as the suppliers of tractors and farm machinery, fuel, fertilisers, insecticides, herbicides — i.e. the big manufacturing, oil and chemical companies. The Common Agricultural Policy (CAP) of the European Community contributes 60 per cent to the annual gross value added by agriculture in the 12 countries, and the total cost of farm support is equal to twice the farmers' incomes in the year. Some goes to the landlords, some to the richer farmers (80 per cent of CAP support goes to 20 per cent of the farmers), most goes indirectly to the agricultural supply industries.

We may ask in particular who stands to benefit from the latest GATT round of negotiations which began in Uruguay in 1987. This was chiefly concerned with liberalising the world's trade in services to complement the liberalisation of trade in goods. But the major issue has become the liberalisation of the world food trade. Proposals were made for eliminating subsidies and reducing import levies. These came in for a storm of protest from United States farmers and from farmers throughout the European Community and led to a war of words between US and European negotiators. The governments in both North America and Western Europe seek to protect their agriculture but they do it in different ways. The Americans give a subsidy to their farmers to keep food prices down below their costs. The subsidy is supposedly unrelated to world prices. The Europeans relate their subsidy precisely to world prices, since it makes up the difference between their estimated costs and the world price at any time. The Americans say that the Europeans are providing an export subsidy and this is not fair and should be cut. The fact is that, because the USA is the dominant exporter of many food products, the price the American farmers get before receiving their subsidy becomes the world price. The difference is that the American system, if it were generalised, would keep world prices down at American levels or at the levels of the most efficient producers which are the large agri-businesses, while the Europeans would like world prices to rise nearer to their farmers' costs. They could then reduce the farm subsidy which is often as much as the world price itself and swallows up most of the Community budget.

The big question for Third World producers is whether a change in either system of subsidies for First World agriculture would do anything to help them. They are now kept out of the European and American markets by a mixture of import controls and levies, and kept out of other markets by heavily subsidised European or North American products including surpluses that are given as aid or, in effect, dumped at prices well below costs of production. If all export subsidies and all other protective measures were in fact removed, the econometric studies suggest that all countries would gain. Some would gain more than others and some groups in each country would gain while others lost. Farmers in Australia and New Zealand and in Argentina would gain most, as would some of the large-scale farmers in the richer Third World countries. The small-scale farmers in the Third World would also benefit because the price of agricultural products would rise, but they would still find difficulty in competing with the cheap products of agri-business and the possibility of food dumping through aid. The urban populations of the Third World, which are often the chief concern of Third World governments, would appear to be the losers in the short run, because food prices would rise, but in the longer run they would gain. Reciprocal trade between town and country would grow. Poor farmers offer a poor market for the produce of the towns. Hungry farmers, as one writer has called the Third World food producers, will not be able to increase their productivity and their contribution to their country's economic wealth will decline. That they are in this condition is the direct result of subsidised agriculture in the First World.

Third World countries which import basic foods would benefit only indirectly from the liberalisation of agricultural trade in so far as their food producers would be able to expand production. Their governments would still need to protect their farmers from outside competition. It is only the rich countries which should abandon the protection of their agriculture. In fact, no such total abandonment of agricultural protection seems at all likely. It is more probable that the American system of subsidy will be adopted in Europe. World food prices will be kept down to the level of American agri-business costs and small farmers will be ruined everywhere. Food aid will remain a political weapon for use by governments in both the First World and the Third World. The suppliers of farm machines and fuel, fertilisers, pesticides and herbicides will continue to be the true beneficiaries of the system. As food takes up a smaller proportion of people's incomes as they become richer, and as the numbers of food producers in the First World declines, it should be easier to end the artificial distortions of food subsidies. But agri-business will still produce the cheapest food, at least in terms of labour costs. The cost to the environment is another matter, but the destructive effects of large-scale farming are not yet widely recognised. In the long run no doubt, it will simply be impossible for food to be produced by agri-business methods because of the cost in fuel and the damage to the soil and to the environment. Those who are arguing today for organic farming have an uphill task, which we shall consider again at the end of this book.

It is not only in basic foods that European protection of agriculture has been so damaging to the Third World. In the case of other products,

European production has been developed at the expense of Third World producers. The worst effects of the Common Agricultural Policy (CAP) for many Third World countries is related to the subsidies granted to the European beet sugar industry. These are the equivalent per tonne of five times the current world sugar price. The European Community has become a net sugar exporter instead of a net importer and increased its share of world exports from five per cent in 1972 to 25 per cent in 1985. Latin American, Caribbean, Philippine and other Third World cane sugar producers have proportionately lost out. Only the Caribbean has enjoyed some protection through special arrangements made by the European Community with its ex-colonial territories under the Lomé Convention — arrangements that were to be changed after 1992.

Are there any signs that the market might be regulated so as to strengthen the weak rather than the strong? GATT seems to have failed; and indeed the new round of GATT talks, designed to free services, in effect means giving greater freedom to the big companies to move their capital and to manage markets without government restraints. One development which seems likely to become generalised is the creation of extended free trade areas, but it is not designed to help the weak; rather the contrary. The European Community was originally a Common Market of six West European states; it now embraces 12 states, has incorporated East Germany and has outstanding applications for membership from most of the other European states, both East and West. With its associated ex-colonial territories, mainly in Africa, it seems set to become one market in the 1990s not only for the 12 but for the whole of Europe outside the former Soviet Union and perhaps Switzerland (there must be somewhere for the rich to bank their money in secret!). At the same time, the USA has reached a free trade agreement with Canada and proposed the inclusion of Mexico in a Western Hemisphere zone that must ultimately incorporate the whole of Central and South America. Across the Pacific the Japanese have been building a chain of trade links around the entire Pacific rim from Vladivostock in the north to New Zealand in the south, with major connections to the Chinese mainland. What is all this but the rebuilding of old spheres of influence with the Europeans attempting to unite, and the former Soviet Union, the Indian continent and above all the Middle East with its rich oil reserves to be fought over? It is not a prospect to relish, but it must inevitably follow from the failure of world-wide international regulation of the market and the difficulties facing Third World countries in each of the regions in mounting their own free trade areas. We shall examine this possibility in a later chapter. In the meantime we will examine the history of attempts to regulate the market for particular commodities.

Commodity Control Schemes Between the World Wars

Not all market regulation is designed to strengthen the already strong. Contrary to received wisdom, Adam Smith's famous 'invisible hand' which he called upon to lead each individual 'who intends only his own gain . . . to promote an end which was no part of his intention' was not some sort of unregulated market force. It is, says Smith, the force of 'sympathy' leading the rich to advance the interest of the whole society and thus providing the social foundations for what he calls 'modern civility' (we would say civilisation). Adam Smith was at the same time realist enough to recognise the tendencies in the business community which needed to be regulated. 'People of the same trade,' he wrote, 'seldom meet together even for merriment or diversion, but the conversation ends in a conspiracy against the public or in some contrivance to raise prices.' Adam Smith's appeal to moral sentiment provided much of the regulation of markets in the past, but it has probably been less urgent in the thoughts of traders than the fear of disorder and all-round collapse. This was what led to the commodity control schemes between the wars and has been leading First World governments since the Second World War to give some aid and support to Third World countries which are suffering from the worst effects of unregulated market forces.

Any form of support by the rich for the poor may seem strangely out of keeping with the history we have studied and the market system we have explored. But, in the history of colonial rule, under which primary production was first encouraged, there was always a double intent — to exploit and to develop, not only as sources of raw materials but also as markets for industrial products.

It should be remembered that many of the 'colonials' were kith and kin of Europeans and that many of the producers who found themselves at a disadvantage in the market were not then part of giant transnational corporations but colonial companies with European foundations. They too suffered when prices collapsed, although not so miserably as their workers. Colonial governments' revenues were also affected and this became a matter of concern for the colonial powers. It should not then be a surprise to find that the first efforts to control the commodity markets occurred at the end of the First World War and in the 1920s when prices were falling heavily. There was a sharp recovery in 1921, but it was short-lived and by 1924 most prices had peaked and were falling — that is long before the crisis of the 1930s. The general cause of falling commodity prices, as we have already noted, lies in the decline of demand in the industrial countries, but several different factors can be involved: (a) an economic recession in those countries; (b) unwarranted expansion of capacity by the producers; (c) development of substitutes for primary products, particularly those which can be produced in industrial countries. Commodities which will be most affected will be those for which demand elasticities are low, i.e. for which lower prices mean lower receipts because no more is sold at the lower price, but if prices are raised there is the threat that substitutes or alternative producers will be drawn in.

Such low demand elasticities characterised all the commodities for which control schemes were establshed in the 1920s. Schemes were introduced in 1921 for copper and tin; in 1922 for rubber; in 1923 for coffee and wheat; in 1926 for sugar; and in 1929 for cotton. These were all initiated by the voluntary action of producers' organisations, but followed up by official government support. Experience had been gained by governments during the First World War in managing markets by pooling surplus stocks and restricting output when demand was interrupted by the submarine threat to shipping. The United States government had acted in the case of copper, Canada with wheat, the British and Australian governments with wool, the British colonial government in Malaya with tin and rubber, Brazil with coffee and Cuba with sugar. It was not difficult therefore for these governments to apply similar control schemes when prices fell in the 1920s.

The schemes all involved measures to restrict output combined with the building up of stockpiles in order to maintain prices and then running them down slowly when demand allowed. In addition, a further measure was applied in Brazil in relation to coffee, in the shape of a 'valorisation' scheme. The Coffee Institute, as the government buying agency was called, borrowed money from the banks, to an extent that the planters could not, and used it to pay the planters an advance against their deliveries of coffee. The banks had the backing of a British government guaranteed loan to the Brazilian government. When a planter's coffee was released and sold, the planter paid back the advance and any balance was his profit. All went well until bumper crops met a declining market and, finally, there was the crash of 1929. The Institute had to dispose of huge quantities of unwanted coffee. To keep the price up it was decided to collect in the coffee and burn it. The whole of two year's average crops were burnt over a four-year period. Of course, the price had been set too high, as were the advances to the planters. This only encouraged extra production. But the fact was that coffee formed 70 per cent of the value of Brazil's exports and the hope of managing the market when Brazil met two-thirds of the world's coffee consumption encouraged a fatal optimism.

All the other commodity control schemes of the 1920s came to a sticky end, not because of overgenerous valorisation schemes but because high prices either attracted new producers to enter the market or encouraged the development of substitutes. It is, therefore, somewhat surprising that similar schemes were introduced again in the 1930s to meet a much more serious collapse of prices. The history of these schemes has important lessons for commodity producers today when the major industrial economies are once more experiencing a period of recession if not of actual slump. One of the first commodities to be considered for control was tea, which had been subject to voluntary restriction in the 1920s. This had not, however, prevented new planting and after 1930 the price collapsed. The British government joined the Dutch government in an agreement on export quotas for their respective colonies and on a virtual ban on new planting. This kept the price fairly steady. The problem was more intractable with the two food crops — wheat and sugar. Large surpluses of both had arisen through European producers expanding their output with government support, even though many European countries relied also on imports from the Western Hemisphere and Australia. In the case of sugar, an international agreement was signed in 1931 between the main producers, fixing export quotas. This failed to keep up the price because there were non-signatories in the British Empire and also in the USA where production was expanded. In the case of wheat, an International Wheat Agreement was signed in 1933, by which importers and exporters agreed to limit their wheat acreage. But this proved hard to police. The Canadian Wheat Board continued to buy wheat to keep up the price and would have held unmanageably large stocks by 1935 if black rust had not ruined the crop. In the United States President Roosevelt introduced a new policy for agriculture which was enshrined in the Agricultural Adjustment Act of 1933. It was applied particularly both to wheat and cotton production, and consisted mainly in paying growers to plough in their crops and in guaranteeing their prices. The principle of subsidising farmers was thereby established; it became a habit and the habit spread. At first the effect was that the United States for a time ceased to be a wheat exporter and greatly reduced its cotton exports. Cotton growers in other parts of the world increased their sales, even within the United States market. Later, as we have seen, the subsidy was to be used to capture world markets.

Where prices are raised artificially new suppliers will always be attracted to enter the market. A similar switch to new producers took place in the case of rubber, following an agreement in 1934 between the British, Dutch and French governments to introduce restrictions of output on the estates in their South East Asian colonies. But when the price of rubber was raised, the result was a huge increase in non-estate production by small-scale farmers, for whom it is worthwhile at a certain price level to go into the forest, tap the wild trees and take the latex down to the local estate factories. Reclaimed and artificial rubber production was also encouraged.

Nonetheless with the approach of war, demand rose until the US slump in 1937. Stocks were built up to maintain the price, stocks which proved to be of great value when war began. Substitutes were also gaining in importance in the tin market. The International Tin Restriction Scheme was introduced in 1931 by the British and Dutch governments on the basis of proposals made by the Tin Producers Association. Production was restricted to a third of 1929 output, later raised to 40 per cent, at first in Malaysia and then elsewhere as other producers joined the scheme in 1934. Stocks were pooled and released according to a sliding scale of quantities and prices. Of course, mine workers who were laid off in the process of restriction suffered unemployment, but those in high-cost mines in Bolivia and Nigeria would not have been employed at all at lower prices.

Policies designed to keep the prices of commodities high do not expand the volumes that are traded and generally fail to increase total values. The price of tin was in fact held well above the costs of the lower-cost producers and the British government was only able to enforce the agreement on both low-cost and high-cost producers in different British colonies because of Britain's commanding position as a smelter of tin. A similar power could be exercised over copper production, because United States copper producers had both high-cost mines in the USA and low-cost mines in Peru and Chile. In 1926 the United States copper producers had established a world-wide marketing organisation — Copper Exports Inc. — to restrict output and keep some of the higher-cost mines alive for a little longer. As usual, the result was an expansion of supply elsewhere, in this case in the Belgian Congo and Rhodesia, leading in the end to a pile-up of stocks and total collapse of the organisation in 1930. When a new attempt was made to establish a control agreement in 1936, the United States and Canada stayed outside and the other producers operated a moderate regulatory control scheme through a system of quotas. It is clear that all these government-backed control schemes of the 1930s were only of limited value to small producers. While the controls kept the price up they did so only by restricting production. The total value of sales went down and with it the whole level of world trade.

International Commodity Agreements after 1950

During the Second World War much thought and many negotiations were devoted to post-war reconstruction, especially of the international economic order. The pre-war 'beggar-my-neighbour' policies between states were seen as having created many of the conditions for the rise of fascism and military aggression. What came out of the negotiations was the series of Allied agreements reached at Bretton Woods in the USA in 1944, which established the IMF, the World Bank and the GATT, and alongside these a number of international councils to study the problems associated with the main primary commodities entering world trade. J.M. Keynes, as the chief British delegate at the negotiations leading up to the Bretton Woods agreement, had made very different proposals from those which were finally adopted. To avoid the restrictionist policies of the 1930s, his proposals were designed to expand the world economy by strengthening the bargaining power of the primary producing countries, and especially the poorer ones. To this end he sought to bring the world's financial and trading policies under the management of international civil servants employed by the United Nations.

Keynes's proposals were based on the assumption of the existence after the war of a number of great powers — those which formed the permanent members of the Security Council. In the event, however, not only the defeated nations but the victorious Allies emerged from the war economically very greatly weakened, with one single exception. The United States was left holding most of the world's industrial capacity, nearly all the surplus food production and virtually all the world's stock of gold. As a result, while some of the names of Keynes's chief institutions remained the same in the Bretton Woods agreement, the World Bank and International Monetary Fund, his expansionary intentions were severely modified by restricted funding and his management proposals were altered to make way for the hegemony of the United States dollar under United States control. Keynes's plan for an International Trade Organisation was reduced to the General Agreement on Tariffs and Trade. Nevertheless, despite the rejection of most of Keynes's ideas on an expansionary role for world-wide financial and trading initiatives by the United Nations, procedures were agreed for re-establishing international commodity agreements.

Keynes had argued that agreements should not, as before the war, be based on restriction of production, but rather on the interventionary use of buffer stocks, to be built up in times of surplus and run down in periods of shortage. The assumption was that relatively short-term fluctuations of demand, caused by good or bad harvests or by economic booms or slumps, were the main problem that had to be addressed. Longer-term disequilibria were to be dealt with by aid for development and diversification, which would be supplied from national or international funds contributed by the industrial countries. Commodity agreements should be introduced (a) where a 'burdensome surplus' appeared, which would harm producers and especially small producers, and could not be eliminated by the normal working of the market, and (b) where widespread unemployment was affecting workers who had no alternative employment.

The proposals for commodity agreements were made at a meeting in

Havana, which was originally to have established an International Trade Organisation, as an executive agency to give positive support to trade development. While this was demoted to a purely monitoring agency in the GATT, the responsibility for commodity control schemes was retained. Where member states asked for them, study groups were to be established for each commodity and the United Nations was required to convene inter-governmental conferences to draw up control schemes. The rules to govern such schemes were laid down under the Havana Charter. All member states which were producers or consumers of commodities, or traders in commodities, should be invited to participate. Non-participants should get the same treatment as participants. Consumers and producers should have equal voting power on the Commodity Council set up under any agreement. The terms of an agreement must be published in full and the agreement must not last for more than five years. The aim should be to meet world demand at reasonable prices and ensure that increases in output should come from the most efficient producers. All agreements were to be subject to United Nations review.

It was not long after the end of the war before the need appeared for introducing some kind of commodity market regulation. In 1951 there began a major decline in nearly all primary commodity prices. This was after two decades in which commodity prices had risen in relation to manufactured goods prices far beyond any previous experience. This long rise was mainly the result of the war and preparation for war which reduced primary commodity production in Europe and in many other areas in the East and in Africa, where land and productive activities suffered from military operations. It was also the result of a massive expansion of United States demand as the vast economy of the USA, having exhausted its own resources, came to rely more and more on imported raw materials. The Korean War of 1950-51 added a final upward surge to prices as buyers, and particularly the United States government, scrambled to build up strategic stockpiles. Prices of wool and rubber trebled in a year, jute and sisal prices doubled, market prices of copper, lead and zinc rose by almost as much, and cotton, cocoa and sugar prices increased by 50 per cent. By 1952, however, nearly all prices were falling again — many of the metals and rubber, jute and sisal to half of their peak levels.

In the face of this collapse, the Study Groups which had been established for tin, rubber and wool were activated; the existing International Councils for cotton, sugar and wheat were reorganised; and Study Groups were created for lead and zinc, cocoa and coffee. International agreements followed for all these products except for lead and zinc, which were subject to measures of restriction introduced from time to time by the Study Group. An international tea agreement between India, Pakistan, Ceylon and

Indonesia also operated from 1950 to 1955, but this did not conform to United Nations procedure and was simply a restriction scheme with quotas for each producing country. Informal inter-government agreements were reached for sisal, abaca and jute which are all substitutable for each other as hard fibres. An agreement was worked out for cocoa. Once again the main commodities for which international agreements were firmly established were those with especially low demand elasticities — wheat, sugar, tin and coffee.

Each of these four agreements in fact worked in quite different ways. The wheat agreement was renewed continually from 1949 to 1970 after which the Wheat Council became no more than a trade clearing house. It was in effect a system for allocating supplies through multilateral contracts, prices and stocks being effectively managed by the authorities in the United States and Canada, the two largest producers. Third World countries (except Argentina) are mainly importers and not exporters of wheat, and can be said to have benefited from a smooth flow of wheat and from concessionary sales to countries with special needs as determined under the US Public Law No. 480. On the other hand, both these provisions acted to discourage poor countries from expanding their own wheat production. This situation has been aggravated by the European Community's Common Agricultural Policy which, as we saw earlier, is designed to protect European grain production and prices and to dump surpluses in the Third World when they exceed the available storage space. Much the same can be said of the International Sugar Agreement. This was established in 1954, to regulate production through a quota system, in order to maintain supplies 'at equitable and stable prices'. The largest exporter was Cuba; the main importers the UK, USA and USSR. When the USA boycotted Cuban sugar by unilateral action, the scheme collapsed. After the UK joined the European Common Market in 1975, some protection was given to Britain's old sugar colonies, but the even more protected growth of sugar beet production in the USA and in Europe, together with the USSR's preferential purchases of Cuban sugar, all served to reduce the international market for sugar and to lower the world price.

The two other major international commodity agreements — for tin and for coffee — lasted longer and came nearer to fulfilling the Havana principles. An international tin agreement finally emerged in 1956 after almost 10 years of negotiation, but without the membership of the USA or the USSR. It was based both on regulation of exports and on the creation of a buffer stock (of 25,000 tonnes), which the stock manager was required to deal with, necessarily buying at a fixed floor-price and selling at a fixed ceiling. In the tranches in between he was free to buy or sell as seemed appropriate. Agreements were remade every few years and in 1971 a production quota system was added to ensure a fairer sharing of the market among the several producers, all in relatively poor countries. This led to much divisive competition between the exporting countries without any necessary increase in their earnings. In fact, prices rose phenomenally for a decade from 1972, only to collapse in total disaster for the buffer stock manager in 1985, as we saw in an earlier chapter. Since then, the price of tin has fallen in terms of manufactured goods prices even faster than it rose in the 1970s. When demand for any commodity declines beyond a certain point, there is no remedy in carrying stocks.

The International Coffee Agreement lasted somewhat longer. It started with a Latin American Producers' Agreement on export quotas reached in 1958 following the collapse of prices as a result of huge increases in tree planting, not only in Brazil but throughout Central America and East Africa, where production had been stimulated by the high prices of the 1950s. An international agreement was signed in 1962 with the participation of all the producers and the major consumers, including the largest, the USA. The aim was to maintain the 1962 price level and thus bolster the earnings of Latin American countries which were displaying an increasingly anti-United States disposition. The price was to be held by regulating exports through quotas, which were to be checked by the importers' use of certificates of origin. Frost and drought at first raised the price far above the 1962 level, and as supplies recovered and the price fell back it did not reach that level again, although it was generally agreed by the importers to be far above the costs of the most efficient Brazilian producers. When the agreement was renewed in 1968, an interesting innovation was included, setting up a diversification fund to help with structural changes designed to prevent the recurrence of over-planting of coffee. There was a crisis in the 1973 negotiations when it appeared that the importing countries would opt out because the producers had formed a cartel, similar to that of the oil producers, to keep up the pressure for high prices. They did hold up very well in the 1970s, but widespread availability of coffee at lower prices led to the collapse of the agreement in 1989 and to a halving of prices. Brazil as the chief producer would not agree to hold back production. The United States as the chief consumer would not pay higher prices to Brazil when coffee could be bought far cheaper elsewhere.

In trying to replicate the oil price hike, the coffee producers hoped to copy by far the most effective attempt that has ever been made to manage an international commodity market. OPEC was originally formed in the 1960s, as a world-wide oil producers' association, when the Middle East Arab countries and Iran achieved their independence. It was not, however, until the oil pipeline from Iran to Syria was cut in the Yom Kippur war between Israel and Egypt in 1973, and the Arab states decided to introduce a boycott of the West for their support of Israel, that all the OPEC members succeeded in agreeing to hold back production in order to raise the price. It was raised from $1.30 a barrel in the 1960s to $7 in 1974 and $15 in 1977. When the Shah of Persia was overthrown in 1978, speculation pushed the price up for a time to $40. This was enough to stimulate exploration and new production everywhere — in Africa, in Alaska, in the North Sea — and also to encourage the introduction of measures of conservation almost everywhere. The price dropped to $27 in 1985 and as low as $10 in 1986, recovering thereafter to nearly $20 by 1989, and to higher levels still during and following the Gulf War. These high prices put immense wealth into the hands of a small Arab elite, while the mass of the people in the Middle East countries remained extremely poor. Such prices levels were a disaster for the non-oil producing countries of the Third World, whose own commodity prices were declining while the oil they needed to import cost more. The borrowings that they made to buy the oil in the 1970s led directly to the debt crisis of the 1980s.

UNCTAD

The failure of commodity agreements to increase the Third World's export earnings from their primary commodities led to the first United Nations Conference on Trade and Development in Geneva in 1964. This established UNCTAD as a forum and monitoring centre for helping to advance the interests of the 'Club of 77' (later to become 96) Third World countries in their commodity trade and general development. Resolutions were passed at the first Conference by overwhelming majorities, comprising all the Third World states' representatives, in favour of a new relationship between richer and poorer nations, whereby primary production should in effect be subsidised in place of grants of financial aid subject to IMF surveillance. 'Trade not Aid' was the slogan. On all the key issues, however, a stubborn minority of eight of the richest countries, including the USA, UK, Japan and West Germany, voted against or abstained along with the 25 neutrals and Second World representatives. The key issues all involved some transfer of power or wealth from the rich to the poor, whether by aid, compensation or fairer trade, which would have had to include the relaxation by the developed countries of their own measures of protection and restriction on developing countries' exports (General Principle No. 7). Since UNCTAD must work by consensus, little was actually done. Nonetheless, UNCTAD proved to be an important source of information about unfair trade practices and of ideas for improving the general position of all primary commodity producers in world trade.

At the 1976 UNCTAD meeting a proposal was put forward for an

Integrated Programme for Commodities (the so-called Corea Plan). The aim of this programme was to enable export diversification, to achieve stable and remunerative prices, to expand access to markets, to improve marketing systems and reduce inflationary pressures. To these ends it was proposed:

(1) that international stocks of commodities should be built up to assure adequate supplies and offset excessive price movements;

(2) that a common fund should be set up for financing such stocks and for attracting international capital;

(3) that a system of multilateral commitments from governments should be established to improve the predictability of trade requirements and encourage rational levels of investment;

(4) that compensatory finance should be arranged for commodities for which stockpiling could not assure adequate prices;

(5) that discrimination by industrial countries against non-industrial countries should be reduced where this effectively prevented the latter from developing the processing stages of primary production.

As a result of all these measures, it was hoped that it would be possible to link the price movements of primary products to those of manufactured goods.

The specific proposal for setting up a common fund was accepted in principle by the richer industrial countries, but in order that it should become operational it had to gain support from 100 countries and have pledges of finance amounting to two-thirds of the $500 million required to launch the fund. It took 13 long years to gain this support, but in 1989 the fund was enabled to come into force. The irony was that by the time the Fund, which was to serve as financial support for international commodity agreements, came into existence, there were only two international commodity organisations (ICOs) with buffer stocks left to assist, namely those for rubber and cocoa; and neither of these was in a very active state. Fortunately, the common fund has a second account, which is expected to be more active in the initial stages of the fund's operations. This 'second window', as it is called, is designed to help finance commodity measures other than stocking, such as research and development, quality and productivity improvement and market development, as well as efforts to promote local processing in non-industrial countries and to find new uses for commodities. $230 million is pledged for this second account, plus a capital base of $70 million from the directly controlled capital of the fund. It appears that measures financed from the Second Window are to go to ICOs, at least in the first instance, but the Director General of UNCTAD,

Mr Kenneth Dadzie, has stated that the fund can give 'a new impetus to producer-consumer cooperation and international policy in the field of commodities'. The first example of the use of Second Window funds has been the International Jute Agreement of 1991, which is not concerned with prices, but with diversification of demand for jute and the marketing of jute products. Some of the possibilities for further cooperation will be looked at in a later chapter.

Apart from its interest in commodity agreements, UNCTAD has devoted much attention to other means for stabilising the export earnings of poor countries. The chief of these are schemes for compensatory finance (CFS). The idea of these schemes is to compensate exporters for deviations in the price or in the output of specified commodities or of total export earnings of any commodity below agreed normal levels. The market is allowed to find its own level, so that high prices do not encourage extra capacity. Instead of raising prices artificially, compensation is paid from the importers for loss of earnings suffered by the exporters. Payments may be automatic from a permanent insurance fund or subject to agreed criteria, and they could be made by way of a direct grant or through a loan. These schemes are, therefore, in effect either a form of aid or similar to any other borrowing which Third World countries can contract. The European Community has in this context made compensatory payments for lost income (the so-called STABEX arrangement) to the Third World countries associated with it under the Lomé Convention, for which it feels a responsibility as one-time European colonies, but the sums involved have not been large and quite inadequate to cope, for example, with the 1989 collapse in coffee prices. The problems of Third World aid and of the Third World debt burden are the subject of the next chapter.

There are certain conclusions we need to draw from this study of attempts to manage the market. Compared with the success of the giant companies in managing the market, which we looked at in the last chapter, all these efforts at control must seem to be quite pathetically inadequate — except where the big companies themselves have moved in. It appears that most commodity control schemes have broken down in the end because of the impossibility of restraining an expansion of output if prices are held much above the costs of the most efficient producer. But it is also evident that control schemes are quite unable to keep prices even at that level if there is a long-term fall in demand for the product, either because of the development of substitutes or because of the generally reduced use by industry of certain agricultural materials and minerals. This has been in fact the overall trend in the last two decades, not just a short-term decline or minor instability. It suggests the need for what is now called 'structural adjustment', sometimes of whole Third World economies; but such an adjustment requires a major diversification of exports. Structural adjustments have been widely recommended by World Bank and International Monetary Fund reports, but adjusting exports is not something which Third World countries can achieve on their own without overall restructuring of international trade exchanges. That involves something more than financial compensation, something more even than economic aid. We shall need to study how both might be made to work better.

Notes

The standard work on commodity control schemes is J. W. F. Rowe's *Primary Commodities in International Trade*, Cambridge University Press, 1965. From 1964 we have the UNCTAD Conference reports and the UNCTAD annual *Trade and Development Reports*. The implications of these up to 1977 are usefully analysed by H. Singer and J. Ansari, *Rich and Poor Countries*, Allen & Unwin, 1978. Fiona Gordon-Ashworth carries the analysis up to 1983 in *International Commodity Control*, Croom Helm, 1984. For the last decade the UNCTAD bimonthly bulletins summarise the progress of the commodity economy and of the major international commodity agreements. The Third World Information Network newsletter, *The Network* , gives a regular update on GATT and Lomé Convention negotiations. For the GATT Uruguay Round, see Kevin Watkins, 'Agriculture and Food Security in the GATT Uruguay Round' in *Review of African Political Economy*, No. 50, March 1991.

8. AIDING THE MARKET

The concept of economic aid was a product of the Keynesian revolution in economic thought. To prevent unemployment and ensure continuing economic growth without slumps, the tendency in capitalism towards unequal income distribution would have to be corrected. Governments would need to employ policies of taxing the rich, and borrowing from them, in order to provide income support for the poor, including the elderly, sick and unemployed. By extension, on a world-wide scale, resource transfers would be required from rich countries to poor countries. The concept was embedded in Keynes's proposals for a World Bank and Monetary Fund, but as we have seen, his original intentions were heavily modified at Bretton Woods.

Why International Economic Aid?

Two kinds of economic aid took the place of Keynes's plans for a large-scale, internationally managed, support system. The first was the massive programme of Marshall Aid for Western Europe and Japan. The programme of post-war aid proposed by US Secretary of State Marshall remains unique in the history of inter-state relations. A transfer of over $17 billion ($200 billion in today's money) was made by the United States between 1949 and 1951. This would be enough to wipe out much of the current debt of the Least Developed Countries. Within very general advisory guidelines from the USA the aid funds were left for each country to use in its own way, so long as equivalent counterpart funds were made available by the receiving government. In fact most of the money was used to buy United States equipment, food and raw materials, since no other supplies were available. While the UK put most of the funds into repaying its sterling debts to Empire countries and thus strengthening the Sterling Area, most countries used the funds for central, state-planned industrial recovery. The plannned use of these funds, far more than the freedom for economic enterprise, was the real cause of the West German 'economic miracle' and of the Japanese, French and Italian leaps forward in competitive industrial strength. The lack of such funds, far more than the lack of freedom for economic enterprise, was the real cause of the failure of the Soviet Union and Eastern Europe to maintain competitiveness with the West.

The second form of post-war aid was the provision which had to be made by European governments for their colonies, as one by one, more or less willingly, they abandoned these possessions. Most of these colonies had had their banking and finance directed from European centres and had borrowed in the European capital market. The British colonies were tied into the Sterling Area and Britain had outstanding debts to repay for war-time expenditures. Without reserves in sterling or the backing of other European governments, the newly established banking systems of the ex-colonies had to be supported by loans and credits. What came to be called 'aid' was in effect an extension of historic spheres of influence.

TABLE 11. MAIN DONORS AND BENEFICIARIES OF INTER-NATIONAL PUBLIC AID, 1955-1969

Donor	Beneficiaries	1955-60 ($m)	1961-66 ($m)	1967-69 ($m)
USA	Total	2,300	3,200	3,260
	South Korea and South-East Asia	650	1,850	2,000
	Latin America	450	550	650
UK	Total	300	350	400
	Sterling Area – Independent	100	100	110
	– Dependent	150	225	220
France	Total	800	850	830
	Algeria and Franc Zone	600	650	550
USSR	Total	360	330	360
	Egypt	115	120	160
	India	90	150	–

Source: OECD, op. cit., United Nations, *Statistical Yearbook* and U.K. *Balance of Payments*.
Note: Figures give rough orders of magnitude only and include official loans, grants and credits but not military aid.
From M. Barratt Brown, *From Labourism to Socialism* (Nottingham, Spokesman, 1972)

While Western Europe soon recovered with United States assistance, it became clear that the gap between the developed industrial countries and the developing non-industrial Third World was growing ever wider. 'Point Four' in President Truman's inaugural speech of January 1949 had promised 'a bold new programme for improvement and growth of underdeveloped areas ... through the United Nations'. But, whereas Marshall Aid for Western Europe and Japan had been valued at over $4 billion a year for the three years of 1949-51, US economic assistance to all the developing countries throughout the 1950s was estimated at between $2 billion and $2.5 billion a year. Military assistance added another $1 billion. What this meant in terms of aid per head in the poor countries can be seen from one example. The Colombo Plan for economic assistance to South East Asia amounted to $6 billion for 1953-59 — just over a dollar a head of the 600 million population per year compared with $3 a head per year received by the 300 million people in Europe during the same period. It is sometimes argued that private investment in the Third World by industrial countries (of some $2 billion to $3 billion a year) should be added to the aid figures; but this has to be clearly distinguished from aid, both because of the often high rates of return, including debt repayments, and because it should properly be compared with investment in Europe, North America and Japan of profits made in the Third World.

The widening gap between rich and poor worlds began to arouse general concern among religious groups as well as among left-wing economists. While the war was still on, a group of Quakers and other church people in Oxford had founded a committee for famine relief for victims of the war. Soon after the war ended this committee turned its attention to the poverty of what came at that time to be called the Third World. The committee shortened its name and Oxfam was born. The World Council of Churches at about the same time began to press for a proportion of the steadily increasing wealth of Europe and North America to be set aside for aid to the less developed countries. A United Nations report in 1951 proposed that the industrially advanced nations of the world should contribute one per cent of their national income each year to provide a sum of $10 billion for a Special United Nations Fund for Economic Development (SUNFED) to raise living standards in the less developed lands by two per cent a year. About $10 billion was being made available each year in unilateral official government aid contributions in the 1950s, but the SUNFED $10 billion was to be additional. In discussion, the sum was whittled down to $150 million and the whole scheme made conditional upon the great powers reaching agreement on disarmament. The SUNFED set, never to rise again. The decade of the 1950s was marked by a massive increase in military assistance by the United States to developing countries as the depths of the Cold War were plumbed. By 1955-59 military assistance amounted to over a half of all US overseas aid, and similar proportions characterised the foreign assistance programmes of the other major capitalist states and also those of the Soviet Union.

In 1960 the United Nations declared the First Development Decade and adopted a resolution which set out that the flow of resources to developing countries should amount at least to one per cent of the national incomes of the developed countries, taking together official aid and private investment. This target was adopted at the first UNCTAD meeting in 1964 and endorsed by DAC (the Development Assistance Committee), the standing committee of donor countries. This endorsement, in fact, only confirmed what was already happening. At the next UNCTAD meeting in 1968 the target was marginally stepped up to one per cent of Gross National Product at market prices, with a demand from the Group of 77 developing countries that 0.75

per cent of GNP should consist of official aid, that is excluding private investment. This was not accepted by the Group of 10 developed countries. Only France was anywhere near to that target. The average figure for official government aid, as a percentage of GNP, was around 0.5 per cent at the beginning of the 1960s, but fell steadily to 0.36 per cent by the end. The UK figure was 0.39 per cent and that for the USA, 0.33 per cent.

The United Nations Second Development Decade opened with support from a high-powered commission, set up by the World Bank under the chairmanship of Canadian Prime Minister, Lester B. Pearson. This was the so-called Pearson Report entitled *Partners in Development*. The report recommended a target of official government aid of 0.7 per cent of GNP for all developed countries to attain by 1980, and that multilateral aid, i.e that going through United Nations' agencies (including the World Bank), should be raised to 20 per cent of the official aid total. The title of the report indicated that Cold War strategies had been abandoned for concepts of economic partnership: 'We have received the definite impression that most low-income countries would welcome a larger flow of foreign investment, sharing our belief that such flows would contribute to faster growth' (Pearson Report, p. 105). So runs the opening sentence of the chapter on private foreign investment, and the report went on to recommend to the governments of underdeveloped countries that they provide tax concessions and investment incentives and remove balance of payments restrictions and other barriers to free entry of private capital. With official aid and private investment an economic growth rate of six per cent was calculated by the Commission to be achievable. The underdeveloped countries could then expect by the year 2000 to be in a position to earn their own keep through their export earnings.

Looking back we can see that from 1970 to 1980 aid of all kinds in fact grew in real terms by just over four per cent a year gross, but after interest payments and profit remittances are taken into account this amounted to less than a one per cent net. During the 1980s aid in real terms was actually steadily reduced while interest charges increased, resulting in an annual net reverse flow from the developing to the developed countries amounting to a net decline of 1.5 per cent a year. During the 1960s and 1970s the growth rate of the national incomes of developing countries almost achieved the hoped-for six per cent. This was actually faster than the growth achieved by the developed countries, but the difference disappears when we look at growth per capita; half the economic growth was absorbed in faster population growth. In the 1980s growth has been slower in the developing countries than in the developed, and after taking into account population growth, the per capita figure shows an actual decline, with all regions affected except for East Asia. Only a part of this is due to the fall in oil

TABLE 12. REAL GDP, TOTAL & PER CAPITA GROWTH RATE, SHARE IN WORLD GDP & POPULATION (%)

Sector Country group	Average annual growth of GDP Total			Per capita			Share in world GDP			Share in world population			Growth rate of population	
	1960-1970	1970-1980	1980-1987	1960-1970	1970-1980	1980-1987	1960-1970	1970-1980	1980-1987	1960-1970	1970-1980	1980-1987	1960-1980	1980-1987
World	5.3	3.7	2.9	3.2	1.8	1.2	100.0	100.0	100.0	100.0	100.0	100.0	2.0	1.6
Developed market-economy	5.1	3.1	2.7	4.0	2.2	2.1	74.3	70.0	69.1	19.0	17.2	16.0	1.0	0.6
Developing countries	5.8	5.5	2.2	3.2	3.0	-0.2	16.1	18.9	18.1	47.6	50.5	52.9	2.5	2.3
By major category														
Oil exporters	7.2	6.0	-0.3	4.3	2.9	-2.9	6.1	7.4	6.0	8.7	9.7	10.4	2.9	2.7
Manufactures exporters	5.7	6.4	3.5	3.3	4.3	1.6	4.1	5.3	5.5	5.2	5.3	5.3	2.2	1.8
Remaining countries	4.6	4.4	3.7	2.1	1.9	1.4	5.9	6.2	6.6	33.8	35.5	37.1	2.4	2.3
By region														
America	5.3	5.4	1.3	2.5	2.9	-0.9	6.1	7.3	6.6	7.6	8.1	8.4	2.6	2.3
Africa	5.9	4.1	1.3	3.2	1.1	-1.7	2.9	2.9	2.6	9.1	10.1	11.1	2.8	3.1
West Asia	7.8	6.4	-0.4	4.7	3.2	-3.2	2.8	3.4	2.8	2.7	3.0	3.3	3.0	2.9
Other Asia	5.1	6.1	5.4	2.7	3.8	3.3	3.9	4.7	5.7	27.6	28.7	29.4	2.4	2.0
By income group														
High income	6.8	6.0	1.4	4.0	3.4	-0.8	9.7	11.8	10.8	9.7	10.3	10.7	2.5	2.3
Middle income	5.3	5.4	2.1	2.4	2.5	-0.5	3.1	3.6	3.5	8.4	9.2	9.9	2.8	2.7
Low income	3.7	4.3	4.4	1.3	1.9	2.1	3.3	3.4	3.8	29.5	31.0	32.3	2.4	2.2
Least developed countries	3.4	3.2	2.4	1.0	0.5	-0.2	0.7	0.7	0.7	7.0	7.6	8.1	2.5	2.6

Source: This table is taken from UNCTAD, *Statistical Pocket Book*, 1989.

TABLE 13. GROWTH OF GDP BY KIND OF ECONOMIC ACTIVITY (AVERAGE ANNUAL GROWTH RATE IN PERCENTAGE), 1965-86

| Sector | Total GDP | | Agriculture | | Industry | | | | Services, etc. | |
| | | | | | Total | | Manufacturing | | | |
Country group	1965-1980	1980-1986	1965-1980	1980-1986	1965-1980	1980-1986	1965-1980	1980-1986	1965-1980	1980-1986
Developed market economy countries	3.1	2.2	0.9	3.2	2.7	1.2	3.2	1.9	3.4	2.7
Developing countries	5.7	2.0	2.7	2.2	6.9	0.7	6.8	3.1	6.1	2.9
By major category										
Oil exporters	6.4	0.1	2.4	1.9	7.8	-2.4	8.1	2.1	6.4	2.0
Manufactures exporters	6.2	2.5	2.4	2.7	7.1	2.2	7.0	2.2	6.7	2.8
Remaining countries	4.4	3.6	3.0	2.2	5.2	4.2	5.6	5.1	5.1	4.1
By region										
America	5.5	1.2	2.8	1.8	5.6	0.3	6.3	0.5	6.1	1.6
Africa	4.7	1.0	1.5	1.1	8.0	-0.4	8.9	2.2	4.9	2.2
West Asia	8.3	-1.1	3.5	3.5	9.5	-5.6	7.2	6.9	8.2	4.0
Other Asia	5.4	4.8	3.2	2.8	7.4	5.5	7.3	6.9	5.9	5.7
By income group										
High income	6.3	1.2	2.7	2.7	7.0	-0.4	7.1	1.9	6.5	2.3
Middle income	5.4	1.8	2.4	1.9	7.5	0.7	7.5	3.0	5.9	2.5
Low income	4.3	4.2	2.9	2.1	5.7	4.9	5.1	7.2	4.8	5.6
Least developed countries	3.0	3.2	1.2	2.7	4.7	4.1	6.0	1.6	4.3	3.3

Sources: This table is taken from UNCTAD, *Statistical Pocket Book*, 1989.

prices after the hike of the 1970s; all commodity prices were falling, as we have already seen, and the least developed countries suffered worst. Table 12 shows the detail, but the general picture is clear. What has happened in the 30 years since 1960 is that, with a much larger share of world population, the developing countries have hardly increased their share of the world's income and in the 1980s actually fell back. (To make up the totals in the Table for world shares to 100, you have to add in figures for the Second World of centrally planned economies.)

What, then, happened to all those brave hopes of the United Nations' Development Decade? Even at the time, the Pearson Commission was subjected to much criticism at a conference on international development held in Columbia in 1970 and attended by a wide range of economists from many different countries and different schools of thought. Both the view that the proposed aid would necessarily achieve a six per cent annual growth rate for the developing countries and the expectation that the gap would close between the developed and developing countries by the end of the century were regarded as being very far off the mark. Even if the six per cent growth rate were achieved by the developing countries, it was calculated that, at current growth rates for the developed countries, the gap would in fact be between three and four times wider by the year 2000 than it was in 1970. At the conference in Bogota it was proposed as an alternative scenario that aid targets should be related to income per head in the developing countries and that aid should be continually raised up to the end of the century to reach a figure of $400 per head for the receiving countries. It should, moreover, be concentrated on countries with per capita incomes of less than $300 per annum, what came to be called the Least Developed Countries (LDCs). Aid, it was argued, could not be regarded as a self-liquidating stop-gap, to be replaced within a relatively short period by trade exchanges. The inequality in bargaining power between the rich and the poor was too great. Keynes had always insisted that there was a continuing tendency for capitalism to generate inequality, which would have continually to be offset by transfer payments.

Who Benefits from Aid?

What advantage was there to be had from providing aid? Economic aid provided by one country to another, whether funded by governments or by private charity, has always been a contentious issue. We can look at the reasoning behind the Marshall Plan, by far the largest transfer of resources from any government to the citizens of other countries. On the one hand, it was a gift of a generous people, who had not suffered the privations or devastation of war in their own lands, to those who had. On the other hand, it was a calculated move by the United States government to restore Western Europe and Japan as bulwarks respectively against Soviet and Chinese communism. It was, moreover, strongly supported by United States industry as the only way to finance markets for its products after the demands of war had abated and before major new military programmes could be justified. United States economic aid has in fact always been closely associated with military aid; and military aid has, of course, been designed to cement political alliances and support private investment.

Political, as much as economic, considerations inevitably enter into the motivations of all governments in providing economic as well as military aid. It is only necessary to look at the list of recipients of such aid in the 1960s from capitalist and communist governments (see Table 11, page 97). Even aid which is distributed by multilateral donations through international bodies generally shares the same motives, as we shall see. This is not surprising in view of the close connection between political and economic spheres of interest which we have noted among the great powers. Beyond this there is a general capitalist interest in development, but not for any individual capitalist to contribute more than his competitors. The great contradiction for capitalist accumulation is that profit from productive assets is made by reducing the cost of labour, but the goods produced have to be sold mainly to those who labour. Without some income transference from the rich to the poor, wealth tends to accumulate at one pole while the other stagnates in poverty. The result is not only inequality but economic and political instability. The threat to stability began to dominate the thinking of governments of the industrial countries as the decade of the 1970s came to an end. This was very obvious in the next high-powered report on international aid, which followed the Pearson Report.

This new report prepared under the chairmanship of the ex-Federal Chancellor of Germany, Willy Brandt, was entitled *North-South: A Programme for Survival.* The report came from an independent commission on international development issues and included no less than five ex-prime ministers from developed industrial countries. The report called for the establishment of a new 'world monetary order' to strengthen the position of the developing countries and for 'massive transfers of resources' to non-oil-producing developing countries. At the same time, it gave much more attention than the Pearson Report to the need for encouraging rather than discouraging structural changes in Third World countries which would allow the aid to reach those who most needed it and could make best use of it, particularly in the very poorest countries. The chairman made no bones about the fact that ending mass poverty was the only way to end the threat of a new war which would destroy all that human beings had created on the earth in the last million years.

The Brandt Report, published in 1980, in fact followed a decade of some improvement in the economic growth of the developing countries, associated with better prices for their primary products, but at a time when, as we have seen, these prices were once more collapsing. That economic growth in the developing countries had been running at higher rates than those in the developed countries had been claimed by some to be due to aid and investment, but the main cause was the better terms of trade. Official aid had been steadily falling as a proportion of the developed countries' GNPs. Its place had been taken by bank loans, which were in effect recycling the huge increases in the oil-producing countries' earnings after the oil price hike. Without these loans the non-oil-producing developing countries could not have continued to import the oil supplies they needed; but it was these loans that created the burden of indebtedness under which the Third World was to suffer right through the second half of the 1980s and into the 1990s.

The first Brandt report was followed by a second one in 1985, entitled *Common Crisis: North-South Cooperation for World Recovery*. The world economic crisis was by then regarded as extremely serious. The report took up a proposal from UNCTAD that the special needs of the Least Developed Countries should be guaranteed an annual transfer of at least 0.15 per cent of the developed countries' GNP and argued that the worsening world economic situation, and particularly the crisis of Third World indebtedness, required emergency action. This could not be allowed to wait for the longer-term reorganisation of the global economic system. In particular, measures were needed to compensate for the losses being sustained by the developing countries in their trade relations with the developed countries. This would imply not only financial compensation for the falling prices of primary commodities but a general opening up of the markets in the developed countries to the products, including the manufactured goods, of the developing countries. The steps being taken at that time to raise protective barriers around markets were regarded as counter-productive and against the long-term interests of the rich as well as the poor.

The failure of the governments of the world's richer industrialised countries to take any notice of these high-minded reports from ex-prime ministers, and to open up their markets to the products of the Third World other than primary commodities, suggested an alternative option for Third World countries: to increase trade among themselves. Such an expansion of South-South trade was the recommendation of the South Commission report of July 1990, the first and only Third World commission to study Third World development issues. There is an obvious attraction in the idea of developing more trade between equals where the exploitation of the weak by the strong must be less pronounced. The problem remains that much of the plant and equipment which Third World countries need for their economic development can only be obtained from the First World and has to be paid for by exports of commodities which the First World needs, or funded by aid. The rich industrialised countries have an obvious interest in raising the purchasing power of the peoples of the Third World as well as in obtaining raw materials from them on the cheap. Is there then a true common interest in aid for development?

Common Crisis: Common Interest?

In determining a common interest between the North and the South, the developed and the developing, the rich and the poor, there has been an ongoing argument about what should rightly be included as genuine economic assistance. Figures for the 'flow of financial resources in the course of economic development' published regularly by the Organisation for Economic Cooperation and Development (OECD), the industrial countries' forum, include three main categories of aid:

(a) bilateral public, i.e. government to government, official contributions, including grants, credits and loans;

(b) bilateral private, i.e. company to company, lending and new investment, but including also bank loans to developing country governments and government guarantees from the developed countries for private export credits;

(c) multilateral government contributions to international agencies like the World Bank and its soft loan agency, the International Development Association.

If we are trying to distinguish true gifts from those with a *quid pro quo,* however, these categories are not entirely helpful. Grants may be tied to supplies from the donor country. It is estimated that tied aid is worth on average 20 per cent less to the recipient than untied aid. Technical assistance, for example, could often be bought in cheaper from elsewhere. Grants of food aid may raise the price of non-grant food imports for an aid-receiving country by more than the benefit of the grant. Of course, if all donor countries would agree to untie their aid, none of them would be much the worse, since their mutual restrictions must largely cancel out. There are questions also about loans. Official loans may be made at commercial rates of interest, and thus be no more advantageous to the recipient than loans which could have been obtained elsewhere. As for private investment, this generally leaves the ownership in the hands of the investor and, while in some cases a transfer of technology may take place, the return on the investment goes to the investor and may not necessarily be reinvested in the Third World country. The offer by Third World governments to foreign companies of tax holidays and free movement of profits out of the country are often preconditions of the investment. Military assistance is generally excluded from bilateral aid statistics, but the United States has developed a concept of 'military support aid', which enables an ally to carry the cost of a larger military establishment than it could otherwise afford.

In the light of these considerations, it is not surprising that developing countries have preferred the prospect of expanding trade to that of increased levels of aid. What we saw in the last chapter, however, was that the developing countries, as mainly exporters of primary products, had in the 1980s begun to suffer very seriously from the declining prices of their products. In these circumstances the idea of financial compensation for such losses became extremely attractive. We have already seen that compensatory finance schemes (CFS) had been discussed in the 1950s to cover short-term deviations in price from an agreed norm. Compensatory arrangements for commodities for which stocking mechanisms could not assure price protection had been included in the recommendations of the so-called Corea Plan for an integrated programme for commodities put forward at the UNCTAD 1975 conference. The idea was that the compensation should operate automatically either from *ad hoc* payments or from an insurance fund or interest-bearing loans. The objection from rich industrial countries was that the commodity exporters might be tempted to deliberately restrict output in order to take maximum advantage of the compensation available. When the International Monetary Fund (IMF) therefore inaugurated a CFS in 1963, payments from the IMF quota could be called upon by a country experiencing a decline in export earnings, only so long as this decline was not deliberately created. Payments were limited to 25 per cent of the country's quota. This was later increased by another 25 per cent at the instigation of UNCTAD, but this second drawing was conditional on the IMF being satisfied that the country was strictly following the IMF's recommendations for countries facing balance of payments difficulties. We shall look at the problems created by the IMF's rules of conditionality later in this chapter.

We saw earlier that schemes for compensatory finance were introduced into the Lomé convention signed in 1975 between the European Community and the 46 territories in Asia, the Caribbean and the Pacific (the so-called ACP states) which had all been European colonies. A number of concessions were made to allow privileged entry to European Community markets for these countries in exchange for open entry for European Community goods into their markets. At the same time, three systems for stabilising export earnings were established. The first was known as STABEX and covered ground-nuts, cocoa, coffee, cotton, coconuts, palm and palm kernel products, hides and skins, wood products, bananas, tea, raw sisal and iron ore. The producers of these commodities are guaranteed a minimum level of earnings, provided the commodity concerned represents a certain proportion of the total export earnings of the producer country. Payments are made if export earnings fall by 7.5 per cent compared with a moving average of earnings from the product over the preceding four years. To the original STABEX scheme a further scheme called SYMEX has been introduced to cover mineral earnings, and most recently a scheme called COMPEX to assist non-ACP countries categorised as Least Developed Countries. The sums transferred are not very large, amounting, for example, to some 234 million SDRs (see below) under the STABEX scheme in 1986 and 5.2 million SDRs under the COMPEX scheme in 1987. By 1986 drawings from the IMF compensatory fund totalled over 1 billion SDRs, but only eight per cent of this had gone to the Least Developed Countries. In that year these countries' export earnings fell by over $500 million and their combined deficits exceeded $7 billion.

What then is an SDR? The letters stand for Special Drawing Rights. This is the nearest the international monetary authorities have got to embracing Keynes's ideas for a world currency. They were first introduced in 1970, to increase the money available for financing international trade when the value of trade exchanges continued to rise faster than the supply of gold and other reserves. Whereas in 1948 the reserves held by trading countries in the capitalist world would have financed 12 months trading, by 1970 they would have covered only three months trading. So the richer trading nations had agreed to make available some of their own currencies as a special reserve; the ratio of SDRs to the US dollar was at that time not far off 1:1. The amounts added in 1970 and 1971 to the sums available through the International Monetary Fund were quite small — less than five per cent of the world's reserves — and fell far short of meeting the real needs of the world's traders and especially of those in the the Third World.

There was worse to come. In 1971 the United States government ceased to offer gold in exchange for its dollars and for the next two decades the USA ran a mounting deficit on its foreign trade, buying more than it sold and paying with dollars. So long as the rest of the world was prepared to accept dollars in payment, all went well and what came to be called the Eurodollar market — that is to say a market for dollars used for payment outside the United States — steadily expanded to finance the world's trade. Credit grew far ahead of the actual volume of goods traded. As the United States deficit grew, doubts arose about the continuing value of the dollar; the German mark, the Japanese yen and the Swiss franc became increasingly preferred. It became more and more important for countries wishing to hold their place in world trade to earn one of these hard currencies. As the products of the Third World, apart from oil, declined in value, the Third World's need for aid increased. What was happening now to the multilateral aid which the World Bank and International Monetary Fund were set up to provide from the contributions of the whole world community? In the 1980s the world economy was in common crisis. Where was the common interest?

Multilateral Aid

We have seen how Keynes's original proposals for an international bank and an international money system were modified in the face of United States world hegemony and how the plans for SUNFED collapsed. As a State Department bulletin of 1946 put it, 'Congress had decided that the USA should no longer grant large sums under conditions which would leave little or no effective control by the grantor of these funds.' Both the World Bank and the International Monetary Fund came to be virtually controlled by the National Advisory Council, a committee of the United States cabinet. The IMF was not originally intended to meet the needs of the developing countries, since they were expected to have such major requirements for structural adjustment that they would need to go to the World Bank. The IMF was set up to ease the short-term balance of payments difficulties chiefly of the developed countries. The IMF's funds are supplied by the contributions of its members. IMF 'aid' consists in its selling from its fund of hard currencies, that is currencies widely desired generally because the countries' current account is in surplus, in exchange for the soft currencies of those whose account is in deficit. The sale carried a rate of interest of 6.5 per cent. Normally after three to five years, or, by calling on the extended or supplementary financing facility, after 10 years, the borrowing government must repurchase its currencies with hard currency which it is presumed to have earned by then. Each member government has a quota, 25 per cent of which can be drawn without conditions. After that the conditions get increasingly tough. The IMF demands a 'letter of intent', which generally commits the borrowing government to cut its spending and to deflate the economy so as to cut back on imports and expand exports, in order to repay the loan and balance its current account. This is often quite impossible for a developing country's government to achieve without great suffering for the people, and with no necessary advance to a viable economy at the end of such a process.

The World Bank makes long-term loans, but imposes no less stringent conditions of borrowing than does the IMF. Indeed, it can go further and generally requires not only a reduction in state spending, but also less state intervention in the economy and the privatisation of state enterprises. From its earliest days the Bank claimed that it 'had frequently taken steps to encourage a more favourable climate for private business, both domestic and foreign'. These words appeared in the Bank's first report for 1946-53, which claimed also that a stand had been taken against 'excessive emphasis on industry for industry's sake, above all against heavy industry' and against central planning. To confirm this emphasis the Bank launched in 1957 the International Finance Corporation 'to further economic development by encouraging the growth of productive private enterprise in member countries, particularly in the less developed areas' and 'to stimulate the flow of private capital'. The fact is that the Bank borrows its funds from private investors and private institutions in the USA and elsewhere, who do not expect to take risks with their money and are looking for the going rate of return on the money they lend. Governments receiving loans must show that they can be regarded as creditworthy.

These principles led the Bank to discriminate not only against governments of a certain political hue, but also against particular types of aid. In its first few years of operation the Bank refused loans to the USSR and Poland and later refused to lend to Dr Moussadeq's government in Iran and to Col. Nasser's in Egypt, after they had been found 'guilty' of nationalising foreign assets. Immediately after their overthrow, the Bank felt able to provide large loans to their successor governments, whose attitudes were more favourable to international private capital. Much later, at the time of the Allende government in Chile, that government's expropriation of US copper companies in 1971 led not only to the United States cutting off bilateral aid to Chile but to the ending of World Bank finance. The type of aid most favoured by the Bank is funding for specific projects rather than general programmes. Lending for projects involves the Bank in determining many of the details of the project, whether it be land development, irrigation, cash cropping, forestry or power generation. Projects tend to be large-scale — dams, in particular, for irrigation, for export crops and for electric power generation which involve massive land clearance, forest destruction and removal of communities. Very few take into account the actual stage of development of the country. As a result such projects have often worked against the interest of the mass of the people of a given developing country and only improved the position of a small commercial and landowning elite. Details of such practices abound in the many critical books that have been written about the Bank by those who have worked for it or have suffered from its activities. Even more criticism has been directed at the Bank for its recent association with the IMF in imposing conditions on governments, especially in Africa, that involve a reduction of state intervention in their economies and opening up to world market forces the determination of their prices and exchange rates, however painful the result may be for the poorer groups in their populations.

The Bank has generally been sensitive to such criticisms and has at different times attempted to present a rather more human face. This was particularly true under the presidency of Robert McNamara, who was not himself a banker but came to the job from the chairmanship of the Ford Motor Company. A number of innovations were introduced to make funds more easily available to Third World countries adversely affected by loss of export earnings. These have included a supplementary financing scheme which was designed to make up for losses in earnings which seemed likely to upset Third World countries' economic development plans. Such a scheme was also formulated as an insurance fund scheme but came to nothing. More successfully, the International Development Association (IDA) was set up by the Bank to meet the needs of governments which were not deemed to be creditworthy. IDA funds are contributed by subscriptions from the richer members and can be borrowed over a 50-year period without payment of interest but only a small service charge to cover expenses. Unfortunately the total fund is very small in relation to the needs of the poorest countries. In 1975 a so-called Third Window was opened by the Bank, the first being conventional Bank loans, the second the soft IDA loans. This Third Window extended facilities for borrowing to meet purchases of oil after the oil price hike for those Third World countries which were particularly badly affected.

In the rhetoric of the speeches of World Bank presidents, and especially in those of McNamara, there has been much recognition of the inequality of incomes within the Third World as well as between the First and Third Worlds and a commitment to do something effective for the Least Developed Countries. The gap between promise and performance has been most fiercely argued in the case of Africa, many of whose economies were in decline during the 1980s. The Bank has been insisting, as a condition of further aid, on radical measures of reform, balanced budgets, reduced imports, expanded exports and the replacement of public by private enterprise. It claimed, moreover, in a 1988 report that those countries which carried out such a 'structural adjustment' had done better than those which had not reformed their ways. This claim was greeted with outrage from the African governments and a reply to the Bank's report was prepared by the United Nations Economic Commission for Africa (ECA). This was then the subject of a further statement from the Bank. At issue are three main points of fact and method:

(1) Had the Bank been selective in its choice of countries to include as reforming and non-reforming and in the period over which to judge success or failure — the three years 1985-87?

(2) Had the Bank properly allowed for what it called 'shocks', i.e. outside events that affected the economic situation of particular countries, such as changing oil prices, drought and declining terms of trade?

(3) Had the Bank, in judging the success of the reforming measures solely in terms of economic growth, not ignored the effects on the poorest and most disadvantaged sections of society?

Much of the argument must appear to the lay reader to be arcane in the extreme, but the case put forward by the ECA does seem to be the more convincing. It does show that in the World Bank report there were many weaknesses, which the Bank's reply does not satisfactorily answer. Oil-producing countries and non-oil producers are not distinguished; large, wealthier countries such as Nigeria and small countries like Mali, with one-tenth of the population, are given equal weight. Three years is a short time over which to judge reforms. If the seven-year period from 1980 to 1987 is taken, during which reforms were underway, the most active reformers can be shown to have fared much worse than the non-reformers. Outside shocks and particularly declining terms of trade were far more serious than the Bank allowed for; this was confirmed by the Bank's own Annual Report for 1989. Finally, even the Bank had to agree with the third point that the most disadvantaged had suffered disproportionately.

The ECA could point to support from other quarters. An UNCTAD report had shown that of the 12 Least Developed Countries which had reform programmes throughout 1980-87, only three registered higher than average growth over these years and in all there was evidence of harmful effects from the reforms, deteriorating social services and declining living standards especially among the poorest sections of the population. At the same time a United Nations Children's Fund (UNICEF) report for 1989 warned of the social consequences of adjustment policies and quoted the managing director of the IMF, M. Michel Camdessus: 'Too often in recent years it is the poorest segments of the population who have carried the heaviest burden of economic adjustment.'

The reality is that all the funding that the rich industrialised countries have been prepared to make available to the poor people of the Third World has been for a short-term patching up of difficulties, to cover fluctuations in export receipts, the results of disasters, floods, earthquakes and hurricanes, or the unexpected rise in oil prices. These should not be disregarded, but the fundamental need of the Third World and particularly of the Least Developed Countries for a long-term transfer of resources from rich to poor has never been recognised, nor has the need for something other than structural adjustment. The UN Economic Commission for Africa, in its reply to the World Bank, proposed measures of political and economic transformation. Many of these would require major reforms, and especially the ending of corruption in government and the extension of support for grassroots non-governmental voluntary agencies. But, the fact remains that no transformation will be possible without increased aid and in particular the writing off of debts to the bankers and governments of the developed countries. This is not to say that there should be no conditions attached to aid. Susan George in her book *A Fate Worse than Debt* has proposed that requirements of fuel conservation and environmental protection should be attached since such measures are in everybody's interests. Many of these measures of ecological intervention cannot in effect be achieved in Third World countries without outside aid. Some are directly required because destructive practices such as cutting down the rain-forests and excessive cash cropping were taken as a result of the presssure put upon the debtors by their foreign creditors. What else could they do? And the sacrifice has been in vain. Four decades of aid and loans in many shapes and forms have left the gap between the rich and the poor not only wider, but with large parts of the Third World actually regressing under the burden of their debts.

Easing the Burden of Third World Debt

How did Third World countries get into debt to such a serious extent? In the heady mid-1970s, when world-wide interest rates were low in real terms and primary product prices were relatively high, the way forward for economic development in the Third World, and in the Second World of the Communist countries, seemed to be by way of loans from Western governments or commercial loans from Western banks. Where the interference of the World Bank's officials and the criteria of the IMF were equally an affront to national sovereignty, the bankers asked only for cash. Nobody then expected how much cash would be wanted in the end. The banks had money to lend in recycling the vast new earnings of the oil-producing countries following the hike in oil prices. Conveniently, the loans could be used to maintain the essential flow of oil to the non-oil-producing developing countries, as well as to supply plant and equipment and raw materials for industrialisation. Once the loans were negotiated, repayment of the principal could be put off.

While commodity prices were rising and real interest rates remained relatively low, it was easy enough for Third World borrowers to obtain deferment by the banks of repayment of the principal, so long as interest charges were paid. It was possible even to borrow further to keep up the interest payments. This practice of rolling over the debt was unfortunately continued when the prices of Third World products fell — far further than the oil price — and at the same time interest rates rose. The result was that what started as a global sum borrowed by developing countries of $400 billion for purchases of materials, equipment and services had escalated by 1990 up to the then current level of debt of over $1,200 billion. The rise in interest rates between 1976-79 and 1980-82 alone, according to UNCTAD calculations, added $41 billion to the stock of Third World debt. By 1983 the flow of funds into developing countries from export earnings and from new (more probably renewed) borrowing was for the first time exceeded by the outflow of interest and other payments. In other words, the Third World was financing the First World to the extent of some $25 billion a year in the mid-1980s, rising to $40 billion in 1989, compared with about $40 billion net flowing *into* the Third World in the 1970s. This reverse flow was ended in 1990, but only by rescheduling debt which still remains to be repaid. Professor Jan Tinbergen of Holland has estimated that, if the industrialised countries had been fulfilling the target of contributing 0.7 per cent of GNP as official aid, the Third World's debt would have been halved and, if they had paid one per cent, the debt could have have been eliminated before it accumulated to its present size.

It is often said that the developing countries should not have incurred such huge debts, and that much of the borrowing never went into assets which could have generated export earnings or import substitutes. It is certainly true that funds went into prestige projects, massive orders for modern armaments while corrupt government officials siphoned large sums into bank accounts and purchases of property in Switzerland and the USA. Nonetheless, what came to be called 'debt-led growth' did occur in the 1970s. Imports of fuels and raw materials for use in the production process were sustained together with capital equipment purchases for industrial development. Three-quarters of all imports of Latin American countries, which accounted for about one-half of the total debt, consisted of such items. The chief problem lay in the accumulation of debt and compounded interest charges, but the importance of linking external finance to real development programmes cannot be denied. When things went wrong, the bankers turned to the IMF and World Bank for help.

It was such linking that the World Bank and the IMF were expected to ensure. The rejection of their surveillance by Third World countries on the grounds of loss of sovereignty was not just an expression of national pride. We have already noted the threat to all economic development contained in the IMF conditions for aid which include government spending cuts and general deflation of the economy. Recent IMF prescriptions for dealing with the debt problem have been even more disastrous. They have comprised not only public expenditure cuts and restrictions on domestic credit, but also the abandonment of all state subsidies and price controls and the devaluation of the currency exchange rate. The result of these policies, when religiously pursued by developing countries, have been a combination of slump and inflation. Yet, the IMF is regularly required by the industrialised countries to enforce these policies as the condition for Fund aid to any developing country to ease its burden of debt payments. The theory is that the short sharp shock is followed by renewed growth. There is, in fact, no evidence of recovery, let alone of regaining an earlier growth trend, to be found to support such policies.

TABLE 14. IMPLICATIONS OF IMF PROJECTIONS FOR THE EXPOSURE OF THE NINE US MONEY-CENTRE BANKS ($billion)

Country	Exposure in 1984	Exposure as % of capital in 1984	Exposure in 1990*	Exposure as % of capital in 1990
Argentina	5,270	15.4	5,481	10.8
Brazil	15,397	44.9	16,013	31.5
Indonesia	2,871	8.4	2,986	5.9
South Korea	5,874	17.1	6,109	12.0
Mexico	14,553	42.4	15,135	29.8
Philippines	3,868	11.3	4,023	7.9
Venezuela	7,456	21.7	7,754	15.3
Total	55,289	161.0	57,501	113.0

* IMF projections show the total debt of seven major borrowers rising by 4 per cent between 1984 and 1990. The total capital of nine money-centre banks (Bank of America, Citibank, Chemical, Chase Manhattan, Morgan Guaranty Trust, Manufacturers Hanover, Continental Illinois, Bankers Trust and First National Bank of Chicago) was $34.4 billion as of 30 September 1984. The growth of capital, recently high under regulatory pressure, is assumed to be 6.8 per cent, in line with the IMF's projected annual growth of nominal GDP in the industrial countries. Capital in 1990 is thus assumed to be $50.84 billion. The figures for 1984 are from Salomon Bros., Inc., *A Review of Bank Performance*, New York, 1985, Figure 54, p.79.

The author gratefully acknowledges this table which is taken from H. Lever and C. Huhne, *Debt and Danger: The World Financial Crisis*. (Penguin, 1975, p.77).

Various proposals have been made to solve the debt problem. The first, that of Fidel Castro, is default — 'can't pay; won't pay'. This sounds attractive at first sight, especially to those who believe that Third World countries should cut off all relations with the First World and follow policies of self-reliance. We have looked at this view already and concluded that it would not be in the best interests of most Third World countries. They would certainly find great difficulty in ever obtaining loans or credit from the First World again. What is worse, they might find their exports boycotted and their assets, if they had any outside their borders, subject to distraint. The second proposal is that the debt should be converted into long-term stock, either equity or loan stock, attached to particular assets or companies in the Third World country. In other words, the Third World debtor sells its property to its creditors. Such conversions have taken place, but the valuation placed upon the debt has been not far above its market value, which has inevitably been very low. The US economist Professor Milton Friedman believes that all the debt should be auctioned and converted in this or other ways. But, this is not a prescription which the lenders are likely to consider, except as a last resort, and it would almost certainly lead to the borrowers finally deciding to default. A third proposal is that rescheduling of debt should take place over a longer period, as in the Multi-Year Rescheduling Arrangement (MYRA) with Mexico. But this does nothing to end the reverse transfers which are at the root of the debt crisis. This objection could be met by the suggestion of former President Garcia of Peru, that no debt repayments should exceed 10 per cent of a country's export earnings. The ultimate accumulation of unpaid debt would be enormous, but Señor Garcia did not survive to see it.

Why should not the lenders simply renounce their claims at least on the poorest countries, as was once proposed, but never acted on, by the Group of Seven richest countries at one of their summit meetings? It is important to distinguish countries mainly in Africa and Asia where most of the debt is owed to official or multilateral sources and those countries mainly in Latin America where it is mostly owed to private banks. Official loans in the first case could and should be written off. It requires only the political will of enough governments or rich countries supported by the conscience of their peoples. Many aid organisations are involved in concerted campaigns to achieve this end, especially where the Least Developed Countries are involved. The second case is more complicated.

The fact is that the Western banking system is in trouble as a result of the size of the Third World debts which the commercial banks have on their books. These far outweigh the assets which even the largest banks have available to set against them. The nine money centre banks in the USA in 1985 had Third World debt on their books equal to two and a half times their capital assets. Just on their loans to Mexico, Brazil, Argentina and Venezuela two UK banks, Lloyds and Midland, had outstanding debts equal to double their assets. As Keynes once said, 'If I owe my bank a thousand pounds, I have a problem; but if I owe my bank a million pounds, then my bank has a problem.' What the banks have been doing is to make provision for non-payment of debts and, as this reduces their profits, it also reduces their tax liability. In fact, the banks can avoid tax in this way without actually writing off the debt and can continue to collect the interest payments. In this way, the taxpayers in the country where the bank pays tax are making up the difference, while the bank's shareholders lose little and the Third World country gains nothing. The trouble is that it is not reasonable in a competitive commercial world to expect one bank to write off its debts in these circumstances unless all the other banks involved do likewise. Nothing less than overall government action is required to ensure this, but even one government could not act unless all acted together, such are the linkages of state balances in global finance.

It would, no doubt, be possible for the governments of the richer nations to agree to underwrite the Third World's debts to those banks that fall under their jurisdiction. This would achieve the essential purpose of ending the flow of funds from the Third World to the First. But it would leave behind further problems, depending on the way in which it was done. If governments compensated the banks for their losses by tax concessions, then the banks' shareholders would suffer no loss for their share in the errors of judgement committed when the loans were made and extended. If the banks were not compensated in full, then it is highly unlikely that they would make any new funds available to developing countries. Of course, some governments of developing countries would not wish to go through the same experience again. One solution suggested by Lord Lever, the banker and author of a book on debt, is that governments should guarantee new loans on condition that the banks write off the old loans over a period of years. If the governments of the rich countries wish to maintain the IMF, they could make new funds available to it for a guarantee scheme such as the UK Export Credit Guarantee Scheme which many governments offer to their traders to cover possible losses from non-payment of goods supplied.

Whatever new conditions are set for Third World borrowing, and it is inevitable that some will be imposed to reassure the taxpayers who put up the money, it is clear that the present form of IMF conditionality will have to be changed. At present no more money is made available until old debts are repaid. The result is to hold back the development of Third World countries which then have to turn all their resources — goods, land, forests, minerals — into exports. The new requirement would be that money was made available as part of long-term plans for economic viability. This is the basis of the national indicative programmes (NIPs), which the European Community has negotiated with its ACP partners under the Lomé Convention. Similarly, Susan George has suggested that, whether governments act to cancel official debts or underwrite the writing off of bank debt, there should be what she terms 'creative reimbursement'. This would comprise programmes for conservation and trade development drawn up with representative groups in the countries concerned. We shall discuss these in a later chapter.

Many of the programmes suggested would require major structural changes in Third World economies; and it is unfortunate that the term structural adjustment has come to have a particular and rather sinister connotation, suggesting a switch from indigenous practices of subsistence agriculture and local crafts to large-scale, modern agro-industry for export. The aim has been economic growth — so many percentage points a year in dollar values, above the starting level of a few hundred dollars per head towards the 10 thousand dollars and more per head enjoyed in Europe, North America and Japan. This is always measured in conventional calculations of Gross National Product (GNP) or Gross Domestic Product (GDP, which includes all exports of goods and services and excludes all imports), without taking into account social indicators of development, either the damage to the environment and degradation of the soil or the distribution of income and improved life expectancy.

We saw earlier that, when national incomes (GNP or GDP) were measured per head of population, there was little or no growth in many developing countries in the 1960s and 1970s and an actual decline in the 1980s. The main areas of growth were the 'Four Little Dragons' and the oil-producing countries plus Brazil. In the years before the 1980s, life expectancy grew and the poorer the country the faster it grew, despite food shortages. The most striking fact about the nature of the development, which all the forms of aid and borrowing have encouraged in the last three decades, is that it has intensified the inequality of incomes, with the poorest countries most severely affected. Indeed the poorer the country the smaller the share of national income that goes to the poorest groups in society. Thus, in many Third World countries including Brazil, India, Mexico, Malaysia and Peru, the poorest 40 per cent of households received less than 10 per cent of the total income. By contrast, in the developed industrial countries the poorest 40 per cent receive at least 20 per cent of combined income. All the evidence from the last decade shows that the share of national income received by the poorest groups has declined both in the rich and poor countries. The moral must be that in future new forms of aid must be developed and targeted to the poorest groups and must involve them in the decisions about how the funds are to be used to their advantage.

Notes

A history of the Bretton Woods agreements and of international aid provision up to the 1960s can be found in M. Barratt Brown, *After Imperialism*, Heinemann, 1963 and Merlin Press, 1970. H. Singer and J. Ansari take the story up to the late 1970s in *Rich and Poor Countries*, Allen & Unwin, 1978. The two Brandt Reports,

North-South and *Common Crisis* were published by Pan Books in 1980 and 1983 respectively. Susan George's *How the Other Half Dies,* Penguin, 1976 and her *A Fate Worse than Debt,* Penguin Books, 1988 give a radical analysis of world hunger and the debt crisis; Harold Lever and Christopher Huhne offer some moderate solutions to the crisis in *Debt and Danger: The World Financial Crisis,* Penguin Books, 1985. A good introductory pamphlet on the debt problem is Christian Aid's *Banking on the Poor,* 1988.

9. CENTRALLY PLANNED TRADE

Centralised government planning has a bad image today in the wake of the collapse of the Soviet and East European economies. But most economies have been more or less centrally planned in time of war, the British and American as much as the German or Japanese. All trade is planned in wartime with the single aim of winning the war. State orders for the needs of the armed forces take the place of production for the market. The state allocates imports, controls exports and manages the financing of the balance. Many people were surprised that during the Falkland Islands invasion and the Gulf War, ferry boats could be commandeered, factory output diverted, hospitals set aside for receiving casualties and special radio and TV time allocated without any new legislation. Military commanders were brought into cabinet committees and outside experts were recruited for some of the ministries, as in the Second World War, but so long as Parliament voted its support there was nothing the government could not do. Of course, in Britain as in America in wartime, unlike Germany and Japan, the centralised war planning was subject to democratic control. This was much modified by the requirements of secrecy, but nonetheless the government was accountable. The Chamberlain government in Britain was replaced in 1940 by the war-time coalition led by Churchill. We have to draw a distinction, therefore, in judging the Soviet and East European economic collapse, between central planning itself and authoritarian government. President Gorbachev committed himself to seeking not only economic *perestroika* — reconstruction and reform —but also *glasnost* — openness and full accountability.

Planned Trading for Development

Planned trade has in fact a longer pedigree than central planning of the whole economy. Protectionist measures by the state through tariffs and levies and non-tariff barriers, which we looked at in an earlier chapter, are not at all a recent phenomenon. Britain's colonial trade from the seventeenth century was built up by means of Navigation Acts, which directly controlled that trade. What was called mercantilism in France as well as in Britain was a state policy designed to ensure that foreign trade produced a surplus — not of goods but of gold. Merchants had a fear of goods, since an excess lowered prices; but imports of gold raised prices and encouraged business. Only when Britain had established a clear lead in industrial production, not just in merchanting, did she abandon protection, and not fully even then. Other states wishing to catch up had first, as we saw earlier, to protect their trade. The United States, France, Germany and Japan all built up their industries behind protectionist walls until they had reached a stage where they could compete in world markets. Within these walls, moreover, the state established and managed these infant industries until they could safely be sold off to private ownership. It is today, as we have seen, a major complaint against the IMF that it imposes conditions for loans that require client governments to open their national frontiers to free trade and to end all subsidies and protection for their industries.

There are not only many historical examples, but also recent cases, which argue against this requirement of free trade for developing economies. The one country which has most succesfully industrialised in recent years — the Republic of South Korea — has practised the most discriminating policy of protection and support for those industries which it wished to encourage, while opening others to competition in the world market. South Korea, together with Taiwan and some other states of South East Asia, has been following the immensely successful Japanese model of development, which has the planning of trade at its very centre. The Japanese Ministry of International Trade and Industry (MITI) coordinates and directs government action to support the giant conglomerate groups which control the Japanese economy. South Korea has its own MITI supervising, at first in detail and later in strategic terms, the companies under its control. These are in Korean and not in foreign ownership and bridge the whole range of finance, trade and industry. With each new decade Korean industry climbed the ladder from labour-intensive to capital-intensive and finally to high technology products in the wake of the Japanese. It is an interesting commentary on World Bank policies elsewhere that the Bank's officials who prepare its staff working papers show a perfect awareness of the degree of state planning which lies behind this success story of apparently unaided private enterprise.

Many observers have been so appalled at the authoritarian nature of regimes with centrally planned economies, including South Korea, that they have failed to recognise how successful they have been in achieving a rapid rate of industrialisation where more open market economies have failed. They should perhaps recall the strictures of the poet Shelley and others against the repressive legislation of British governments during Britain's industrial revolution. It appears that the role of the state is essential not only to win a war but also to establish the foundations of economic development. The collapse of the Soviet economy and of those of Eastern Europe should not be allowed to obscure the fact that in 50 years, and despite two major wars and an Allied invasion fought over her soil, the Soviet Union advanced from Third World status in 1917 to that of a superpower. She launched the first man into space, developed her own nuclear weapons and launchers and established an industrial base for a modern economy where others, such as India and some Latin American states with similar natural resources, had failed. The rise of China from an even lower level of development to her present position, over a 40-year period, is further evidence of the efficacy of central planning for economic growth, however much we may dislike the methods employed whether in China or South Korea.

We have already raised some doubts about GNP growth as a measure of real development but, since it is frequently used as evidence of capitalist success through following market forces, it seems to be worthwhile at this point to quote comparative figures for the GNP growth of different groups of economies over the two periods 1955-70 and 1970-80.

TABLE 15. ECONOMIC GROWTH RATES, BY REGION 1955-1980

Period	Types of Economy	GNP growth (% p.a.)	GNP growth per head (% p.a.)
1955-70	Centrally planned	9.0	7.0
	'Little Dragons'	8.3	5.7
	All developing countries	5.4	3.1
1970-80	Centrally planned	5.3	4.7
	'Little Dragons'	10.0	7.0
	All developing countries	5.3	3.1

Source: UN *Statistical Yearbooks*, 1960-61, 1981, 1985-86.

Since 1980 the centrally planned economies have nose-dived along with the developing economies of the Third World. Even the growth rate of the 'Four Little Dragons' of Asia has slowed down considerably, but they still maintain their lead. The most important point to note is that in the cases both of full central planning in the Soviet Union and Eastern Europe and of the capitalist planning of the Four Little Dragons we find a most carefully protected economy and full-scale planning of foreign trade.

COMECON

It is necessary to ask why, if central planning by the Soviets and especially the planning of foreign trade, was evidently successful in the first stages of industrial development, it should subsequently have been seen to have failed. In foreign trade the framework provided for coordination of exchanges between the Soviet Union and Eastern Europe by the Council of Mutual Economic Assistance (COMECON) should have been beneficial. Yet, one of the very first steps taken by the new East European governments which emerged out of the mass popular protests of 1989 was to terminate the work of COMECON. What had gone wrong? There can be no doubt that COMECON had provided a framework over many years for planned trade exchanges and joint ventures between the member states. As a result something between a half and two-thirds of each country's trade had been carried on within the bloc. Close links were established between major enterprises in different countries and particularly between Soviet and East European enterprises. Such links appear to be similar in many respects to those which connect the operations of transnational companies in the capitalist market.

A major difference between the First and Second Worlds was, of course, that competition was wholly absent in the Second World. By contrast, the combination of government cooperation with the large companies and inter-company competition has been a key factor in the success of Japanese and South Korean exports. A Japanese economist, comparing the Japanese and British governments' approaches to problems of trade and industry, commented that, 'When our MITI decides on some policy with industry in Japan, they work it out with several of our big conglomerate companies, who then go off and compete against each other for the benefits, while in the UK, for example, your government just talks to ICI'.

A second, and perhaps more important, difference between the planning of trade in the First and Second Worlds was that after the initial period of industrialisation in Japan, South Korea and the other Little Dragons, the use of central commands in planning was relaxed and decision-making decentralised. This was evidently a beneficial move, while the failure to relax central controls in the Soviet Union and Eastern Europe led to decline and collapse. Whether or not this was the main cause of the difference, the fact was that foreign trade in the Second World remained a much smaller proportion of national incomes and failed to grow ahead of them, as it did in the developed capitalist countries, where export-led growth was almost universal. The industrially developed countries of the First World increasingly exchange manufactured goods between themselves, although two or three of the major powers — Japan, West Germany and the USA — lead in technological development. Among the East European countries only in one case — Hungary — has external trade amounted to more than 8.5 per cent of GNP compared with an average of 20 per cent for the capitalist countries — both developed and developing. Soviet exports were less than three per cent of GDP and remained predominantly concentrated on primary products, the share of machinery and equipment in total exports actually declining from 22 per cent in 1970 to 12 per cent in 1987. The Soviet Union failed to become the leading technological centre for East European industry. While her share of total world industrial production rose to one-fifth, her share of world trade actually fell back from a slightly higher figure to just one-twentieth by 1987. Some part of the general failure of Soviet external trade to grow in the Second World in line with the growth of world trade must be attributed to the restrictions on exports of advanced technology from the West to the East, operated by the US-controlled body, the Coordinating Committee on Multilateral Export Control (COCOM) and applied to all the NATO members and Japan.

Nonetheless, much of the failure to develop East-West trade in Europe was certainly due to the inflexible controls operated in the East over hard currency and the ill-considered uses of such hard currency as was available. Thus Abel Aganbegyan, one of President Gorbachev's chief economic advisers, writing about the need for *perestroika* in foreign trade relations, gives the example of imports of foreign excavators when suitable home-produced machines were available at a third of the price:

> All the newly acquired machinery was paid for by the state and supplied to the ministry and to the enterprise as a gift would be. Dependence on hand-outs and attempts to 'live off the state' prevailed. Many purchases of foreign equipment have been made in this way, some of which turned out to be unneeded and incomplete. Therefore, the value of uninstalled and idle equipment has grown, especially in the oil and chemical industry where whole factories have been purchased. Meanwhile, indigenous chemical machine building has been ill-treated, starved of resources and not directed towards producing the equipment needed.

It was not so much the rigid central control, therefore, but the lack of financial accountability that made the Soviet system so inefficient. This can be seen in the whole approach of COMECON to the question of prices. These were allowed to fall steadily out of line with world prices — not because the COMECON producers were more efficient — they were not — but because they were more heavily subsidised. Here it must be said that COMECON experience confirms the warnings of the IMF about a regime of subsidies. Rather surprisingly, the IMF does not issue the same warnings to the United States and European governments in the matter of agricultural subsidies. Protection, we have argued, is necessary to support infant industries, and state grants of aid may be very necessary to support declining or disadvantaged regions, but a regime of state subsidies only protects inefficency and conceals real movements in relative costs.

Subsidies in the Soviet Union and Eastern Europe were paid out by governments partly to control inflation and partly to offset low relative levels of productivity compared with the capitalist world. On the one hand, Soviet fuel and raw materials were being sold within COMECON at well below world prices. At the same time, East European machinery was being sold to the Soviet Union at similarly low prices. On the other hand, some products bought within COMECON such as sugar from Cuba, which was also a member of COMECON, were priced well above world levels. In no case was there any clear relation between production costs and the prices at which goods were traded. A quite irrational system of subsidies held sway. Each of the East European countries had developed the whole gamut of capital goods industries on the Soviet model, even a steel industry in Hungary where there was no iron ore and no coking coal. In the early years of COMECON in the 1960s when commodity prices had been based on world prices, this had led to much criticism from the primary producing countries like Bulgaria, Romania and Cuba because, they said, these prices reflected colonial exploitation, although not exploitation by the Soviet Union, since she was also an exporter of primary products. This criticism was allowed for in the case of Cuban sugar and some other foodstuffs, but despite cheap Soviet oil and other materials, the more advanced COMECON members complained because they believed that for their manufactured products they could obtain better prices outside COMECON.

A further objection to membership of COMECON, from those members who were encouraged to buy their machinery from within the bloc, concerned the poor quality of the machinery compared with what could be bought in the West. Countries wishing to buy machinery from the West had their exports tied in to the East. This became all the more serious as the burden of debt began to weigh them down because they had borrowed from the West in the 1970s to buy plant and equipment for modernising their factories and then found interest rates rising while the prices of their products fell. This was the same problem that faced the Third World. Ceaucescu 'solved' it in Romania in true IMF style by savagely cutting purchasing power at home and switching all production into exports to pay off the debt. The result was a ruined economy, a starving people and the end of Ceaucescu. In none of the other East European countries was anything so drastic attempted, but the declining availability of supplies in local markets as a result of increased exports to meet debt payments, particularly in Poland, was a major contributor to the unrest which led to the overthrow of the Communist regimes.

The main objection to COMECON was again voiced by Abel Aganbegyan; it was that it formed a part of the whole web of bureaucratic controls within which the economies of Eastern Europe and the Soviet Union were confined. After a visit to Prague in the spring of 1968 I made the following observations:

> It was the most insistent argument that was put to me . . . by Czech intellectuals and workers in the factories alike, that Czechoslovak industry was built into the Soviet economic plan. The inputs and outputs of Czech industry were geared to the giant enterprises in the Soviet Union. The Czech Party bureaucracy was there to keep it that way and to grow fat on the proceeds.
>
> (M. Barratt Brown, *Economics of Imperialism*, Penguin, 1974, p.299)

I would only add, 21 years later, that there was no advantage to the Soviet people that this should be so, but there was every advantage for the Party elite in the *nomenklatura*.

Planned Trade in the Developed Capitalist First World

It appears that what is wrong with planned trade is not so much the central planning itself as the way that the planning is done, who controls the decisions and in whose interests. Planning does not need to be authoritarian. The planning of production and trade by the giant transnational companies is of course highly authoritarian at the top, in that company boards of directors are self-perpetuating oligarchies (though still subject to take-over) and not accountable to the public, shareholders' meetings being dominated by a few large family and institutional holdings. But these giant companies have learnt to decentralise to different levels the planning of all the thousands of decisions that go into the productive process and the internal and external transfers which take place between the raw material and the finished product in the shops. Corporate planning today is very far from the earlier hierarchical, bureaucratic model of capitalist development, which we think of as 'Fordism'. It is much more open, flexible and participative, characterised by a 'bottom-up' approach to decision-making based on workplace autonomy, collaborative networks and constant feed-back from practical experience. Despite the giant size of the modern conglomerates, there is still some competition from other companies which makes for efficient responses to demand in the market.

Government coordination ensures that measures are taken to avoid some of the worst examples of wasted resources which we have noted in the centrally planned economies, but that may not necessarily mean efficient use of resources from the point of view of fuel conservation or environmental protection. Even this more open market model is not, of course, so acceptable in the developing countries which supply the cheap labour or the primary products, nor to any others who work for these companies but cannot afford the goods they produce. Much of the criticism which might be made of these companies' international planning is covered by advertising, always selectively directed at the national sentiment of each of their markets to establish the transnationals not only as suppliers of infinitely desirable goods but as patrons of the nation's arts, sport and of many other aspects of national life.

CHART 5. MODEL OF TRANSFER PRICING BY A TRANSNATIONAL COMPANY

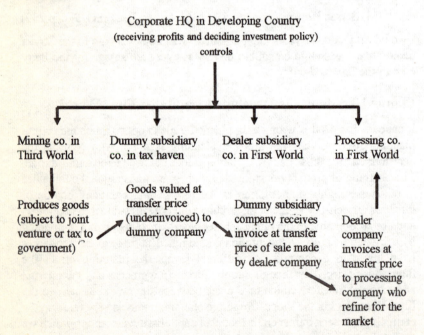

Note: The transfer price at each stage can be fixed according to where the corporate strategy has determined the profit should be made. Since this act will not be the Third World country, if the government has imposed a tax on profits or sales value, the goods are shown as being underinvoiced to the dummy company.

One major criticism of the planning of international trade exchanges by the transnational companies is their use and abuse of transfer pricing. There is some argument about the extent of this practice in the new, more flexible corporate model. 'Arm's length' relations often exist between the several operational centres of giant companies, but transfer pricing appears to have persisted in the case of the export of primary products from developing countries. It is applied especially where a Third World government attempts to impose taxes on the profits of a transnational company's affiliates operating on its territory, or on shares in the profits through a joint venture or draws royalties for mining operations. Production in a Third World country which heavily taxes profits is recorded by the transnational as loss-making, since this is under-invoiced in the transfer to another branch or subsidiary of the company in a country with low rates of taxation. This, then, is where the profit is taken, whether it is at the point of sale or of processing or simply at a forwarding post or one of the tax havens in which the company has a dummy subsidiary or has chosen to have a registered office. Especially favoured for this latter role are countries which combine low tax rates and a shroud of secrecy over all international transactions. Examples are Switzerland, Lichtenstein, the Bahamas and Cayman Islands. However much decentralisation may have taken place to local operating centres, it is the transnational company's headquarters which ultimately controls all the local operations and the movement of goods from place to place in what we called earlier a 'synergy' of capital, labour, materials and locations. Even if company decisions involve full participation of local branches and operating units, little or no account is taken of the wider needs of the peoples involved. The many separate nation-states are only too easily divided and conquered; and this is especially the case where local government officials are open to corruption.

What transnational companies can do, governments can do also, if they will. Many governments plan their trade in great detail and with much forethought, and not only governments in the Second World with their fully planned economies. We have already seen how Japan and South Korea plan their trade through their ministries of international trade and industry. We expressed doubts about the authoritarian structure of these economies. Is there no experience in the more democratic economies of Western Europe from which the Third World could learn in adopting policies of planned trade? There are two countries in Western Europe which have always carried on an important part of their trade in planned exchanges with the COMECON members. These are Finland and Austria with around 20 per cent and 10 per cent of their trade, respectively, with COMECON. It is worth noting that these are the two European countries which have suffered the smallest increases in unemployment in the recent world-wide recession.

West Germany, through its special trade arrangements with East Germany, had five per cent of its trade with COMECON members, in comparison with an average two per cent share of COMECON in the European Comnmunity's trade as a whole. And there are other precedents for successful government trade plannning.

At the end of the Second World War, when the lands of Europe were devastated and production and trade had urgently to be revived, planning of the economy and especially the planning of trade was almost universal. We have noticed already how the Marshall Plan for Europe and Japan financed from United States aid was used by Britain to pay off debts and to strengthen Britain's role in the Sterling Area. But, we noted also how in other parts of Western Europe, where funds were devoted to industrial reconstruction and regional development, these purposes were effected through state planning of production and trade. In France the availability of counterpart funds from Marshall Aid made possible the indicative planning framework which carried the French economy forward from the total stagnation of the 1930s and 1940s to its dynamic growth in the 1950s and 1960s. In Italy two successive long-term economic plans — from 1948 to 1953 and from 1955 to 1964 — were based on the use of Marshall Aid funds for public expenditure in the poorer regions and for modernisation through public enterprise groups. In Western Germany, Marshall Aid was channelled through a public reconstruction loans corporation and, far from the German 'miracle' being a result of the freedom given to spontaneous private enterprise, the crucial role was played by the public authorities in selecting and fostering industrial and regional projects. It is an interesting commentary on the role of the European Commission in its current regulation of the European market that its president, M. Jacques Delors, was one of the most enthusiastic recorders of this key role for central planning at the time.

A somewhat similar need for industrial reconstruction and regional development occurs in Eastern Europe today. While many voices are heard championing the merits of the free market in opening up trade to the East, the lessons of the Marshall Plan as a bridge into future development suggest the need for a strong element of public expenditure and planned trade exchanges. But, to replace the top-heavy planning of the economies of the Soviet Union and Eastern Europe, such planning would require the full involvement of representative governments with the trust of their people. It seems that this is simply not available, and this invidious fact explains why there exists such a strong preference for market forces to decide resource allocation. Even though these forces may be largely controlled by big companies and tend to generate an unequal distribution of income, they do not have total control over people's lives such as is possessed by totalitarian regimes presiding over a command economy.

There are other lessons to be learned in Eastern Europe, and in the Third World too, from the rebuilding of Western Europe's economy after the war. These apply particularly to rebuilding international trade. The disappearance of COMECON does not mean that international trade will simply resume in Eastern Europe without additional means of finance. Some kind of payments system will have to be constructed to clear the new exchanges. The European Payments Union (EPU) played this role in the 1950s by merging bilateral trade balances into a single balance *vis-à-vis* the EPU and providing for varying proportions of credit to gold in the settlement of surpluses or deficits. As a result, there could be no currency incentive to discriminate between member countries in sales or purchases. The EPU paved the way to free trade and currency convertibility, but its winding up left a large gap in available credits for trade. The gap was supposed to be filled by the European Monetary Fund (EMF). This was, however, much smaller than the funds which had been at the disposal of the EPU, and the EMF credits were not automatically available to cover deficits. There are important lessons here for Third World countries trying to emerge from the burden of debt, particularly since the IMF provides no automatic cover for short-term deficits. We shall take this up in the next chapter.

European Community Trade Planning

Over the three decades since the 1950s the European Community has developed far-reaching planning mechanisms, on behalf of the increasing number of its member states, in at least two areas — coal and steel, and agriculture. In both cases the original aim was to make the Community largely self-sufficient in energy and food. But there has been a relative decline in demand for both resources which has required cut-backs in production and even more in employment. The decline in demand has been due to the substitution of other sources of energy and materials in place of coal and iron, and of processed foods in place of cereals and potatoes. The demand is also a result of lower prices outside Europe and especially in the Third World. Thus the European Coal and Steel Community (ECSC) and the Common Agricultural Policy (CAP) have become increasingly concerned with planned trade policies which combine protection from foreign producers with rationalisation of production.

Protection of the steel industry implied not only that imports should be restricted, but that the ECSC should guarantee minimum prices and fix quotas of output from each steel-producing country. In the event, while in the UK under the Thatcher government steel production was slashed and replaced by imports, many of the other producers ignored the quotas and their governments kept plants going by maintaining subsidies. In the case of the coal industry, individual European Community member governments had always provided subsidies. Without subsidies in the UK, even after output had been halved, only the South Yorkshire/East Midland coalfields could have been guaranteed survival; and the UK subsidies were smaller than elsewhere. Without their much larger subsidies, less than half of German collieries would remain and Belgian and French coal production would have been eliminated. The ECSC aim at the end of the 1980s was to end these national subsidies and invest these resources in the affected areas to assist re-employment in more viable industries. The result of such ECSC policies would be to encourage some increase in imports from the Third World — oil and aluminium — and of coal from South Africa. But the main substitutes for the old industries are being found in European-produced nuclear and electric power and in plastics, which are a First World product. It must seem illogical if not hypocritical for First World advisers with the IMF or World Bank to recommend to Third World governments that they make 'structural adjustments' to changing demand through opening markets and reducing subsidies.

We have already considered the European Common Agricultural Policy as a protectionist device, but it is also a remarkable example of planned trade in the First World. In order to bring all West European agriculture into a common framework and ensure self-sufficiency and protection against imports, a target price is agreed which will cover costs of production for each commodity. On the basis of this, after allowing for storage and transport costs, a threshold price for imports is arrived at. The prices of imports, as they move up and down in the world markets, are then studied each day at the Brussels offices of the European Commission. The difference between the threshold price and the world price is then covered by variable levy fixed for each commodity. If the price of a commodity in the local market falls below the target price by a fixed margin, varying from 10 per cent to 20 per cent for different commodities, then the CAP intervention boards will intervene and farmers can sell to them.

As a result of the intervention system, European farmers have an absolutely guaranteed price for their production, and if this exceeds demand at that price then the surplus is stockpiled and released to buyers outside the EEC — in the Soviet Union or in the Third World at prices much below farm costs. Farmers whose costs are above the intervention level will be assisted to sell up or be re-equipped with CAP funding. Jobs in farming have roughly been halved in the European Community since the 1960s; but much increased farm output has been encouraged by the high prices, especially in sugar, wheat and milk production. Whereas the Community was only 90 per cent self-sufficient in sugar and cereals and 110 per cent in butter in 1973-74, by 1985-86 it had export surpluses of 20 per cent to 30 per cent in wheat, sugar and milk. Much of this is stored and then in effect dumped, since Community farmers with commodities available for export can obtain a refund or 'export restitution', as it is called, when world prices are lower than Community prices. Since they usually are, the result of this absolute protection, even for exports, is that Community prices have generally been about 70 per cent above world prices for most agricultural commodities.

The CAP might seem to be a good scheme for Third World producers to copy, if they could just agree to ensure the same degree of unity in planning protection. Unfortunately, in the Third World with so many producing countries involved in primary commodity production and with millions of separate producers, this would be impossible to ensure for most primary products. We have seen already the difficulties attending the several attempts at international commodity agreements. Even if it were possible to transplant it to the Third World, the CAP model might not prove wholly acceptable. About 75 per cent of CAP support for farmers goes to only 25 per cent of the farms. What is more, only 65 per cent of the cost of total agricultural support paid by the consumers and taxpayers in the Community goes to the farmers. The rest goes into storage costs, trading and agri-business. More than this, only one-half of what the farmer receives stays with him; the other half, as we noted earlier, goes to paying for fuel, machinery, fertilisers, pesticides and herbicides, etc. In other words, the beneficiaries are once again not the producers but the giant transnational companies.

State Planning and the Transnationals in the Third World

Most governments, with the exception perhaps of Japan and South Korea, exercise little control over the transnational companies based in their lands; the links between the Japanese government and the big Japanese conglomerates are so intimate that is hard to say who controls whom. Some Third World governments are effectively controlled by transnationals from outside their borders or have little power to control trade exchanges without their consent. Proposals put forward in the 1970s for a Labour government in the UK to establish planning agreements with UK-based transnationals failed to command the Prime Minister's support. France and even Germany have, as we saw earlier, shown a stronger commitment to planning. The United States, the UK and some other governments have attempted to exercise a degree of control over the monopoly power of the larger transnational companies that fall within their jursisdiction, through 'trust busting' legislation and Monopoly and Merger Commission inquiries and the like. The European Community's competition policy has the same aim. So many national and other considerations generally have to be taken into account when reviewing a company's market domination — the strength of the national currency, balance of payments, defence capability, the need for new investment in areas of declining industry, not to mention voting patterns in marginal constituencies and even the contributions that might be expected to flow into political party coffers — that a judgement based only upon degree of market power is most unlikely. No government will investigate sources of finance of a take-over lightly if such investigations are likely to disturb major holdings of the country's currency by an oil sheikh or sultan, or major contributions of a company to election campaign funds.

CHART 6. THE COMMON AGRICULTURAL POLICY (CAP) PRICING SYSTEM

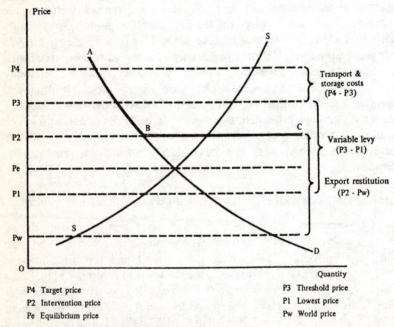

P4 Target price	P3 Threshold price
P2 Intervention price	P1 Lowest price
Pe Equilibrium price	Pw World price

Source: National Westminster Bank Quarterly Review, 1986

If even governments in the First World are hesitant to intervene in the affairs of the giants, the chances for a Third World government successfully challenging the monopolistic positions of a transnational company operating in its territories are hardly bright. The result of doing so is soon made clear by measures of external pressure, including the boycott of trade and even support for military 'contra' forces, such as we have seen introduced against the governments of Nasser in Egypt, of Mossadeq in Iran, Ben Bella in Algeria, Sukarno in Indonesia, Goulart in Brazil, Castro in Cuba, Allende in Chile and most recently Ortega in Nicaragua and against all the Front Line states of Southern Africa. More commonly, such open intervention is not required. The officials and ministers of Third World governments which pose a challenge to the giant companies are quite simply corrupted and incorporated into the network of concealment and transfer pricing which we have described. 'Tiny' Rowland of Lonrho is often accused by his rivals of 'working for the Communists' in Southern Africa. Whatever this means, the result of his work appears to be that the Southern African countries where his companies carry on their trade continue to export through Lonrho subsidiaries like Borma in Switzerland. De Beers, the diamond monopoly in South Africa, and part of the giant Anglo-American group, recently took action presumably as a precaution against what they fear an ANC government might do, and joined the coterie of those companies which have head offices in Switzerland.

Some governments which have succeeded in taking their countries' trade in primary products out of the hands of the giant transnational companies, as Mexico did long ago and Ghana, Kenya, Nigeria and Uganda did in the 1960s, have not been above misusing the power which this gave them. In all these countries marketing boards were set up with the original aim of getting a better deal for the mass of small producers. The government gave to the marketing boards a privileged position in the market, often as sole legal buyers annd sellers of a commodity. The board fixed the price at which it bought, and sold at the best price it could get from the exporting merchant companies or the big transnationals. In this way, the hundreds of thousands of small farmers were to be protected from the exploitation of the local middlemen and the import-export companies. Things turned out differently. When world prices were high, the boards made money and accumulated large funds. These should have been used to finance price stabilisation schemes against a time when world prices fell or for technical research and development of the product. In fact the government used the money for general development expenditure, mainly in the towns and not in the countryside, and some of it was embezzled. The producers benefited little and the smaller producers least of all, since when world prices dipped the boards had no reserve funds and no choice but to lower the prices they paid to the farmers. These low prices would then only cover the costs of the larger and more efficient farmers. This was particularly true in the case of the maize crop in Kenya and the coffee crop in Mexico.

Some people have concluded from such experiences that central planning by governments of their foreign trade is mistaken and should be avoided by Third World countries. But we have already seen that central planning by governments can be beneficial for industrial growth especially in the first stages of a country's economic development, while in later stages a more decentralised form of planning is required. The key question is about democratic and economic accountability. There is no inherent reason why planning at different levels should not also be designed so as to benefit the mass of small-scale producers including those on small farms. For this to happen, however, popular control over marketing boards and over government planners would have to be ensured. This would require effective grassroots involvement by peasants' associations and cooperatives in the marketing system, not only within Third World countries but in links with First World markets. Creating a marketing system of this kind, given the presently existing structures of the world economy, would imply nothing less than a parallel trading system and an alternative trade network within that system growing up side by side with the present organisation of world trade by giant companies.

Notes

For a critical appraisal of Japanese planning in economic development see M. Morishima, *Why has Japan Succeeded?*, Cambridge University Press, 1982, and for the Korean miracle see R. Hopheinz and K. F. Calder, *The East Asia Edge*, Basic Books, 1982. These serve to answer the central argument of Peter L. Berger, *The Capitalist Revolution*, Wildwood House, 1987. Abel Aganbegyan's *The Challenge: Economics of Perestroika*, Hutchinson, 1988, is worth reading for its general critique of the Soviet command economy as well as for the chapter on COMECON and Soviet planned trade. European Community planning is discussed in John Palmer's *Trading Places*, Radius, 1988. A good critique of CAP is *Farming in the Clouds*, Temple Smith, 1984, by the Tory MP, Richard Brody. A very simple introduction to transfer pricing appears in the OECD, *Transfer Pricing and Multinational Enterprises*. J. W. F. Rowe's *Primary Commodities in International Trade* (Cambridge University Press, 1965) has a useful section on marketing boards (p. 34 ff.). An up-to-date study of the European Community's relations with the Third World is contained in M. Barratt Brown, *European Union: Fortress or Democracy?*, Spokesman Books, 1991.

10. A PARALLEL TRADING SYSTEM

How can the small farmers and rural workers in the Third World, who make up more than half the world's total population, get a larger piece of the action in world trade? That is the problem we have been looking at in the second part of this book. We saw in the first part that this is a matter of strengthening their bargaining power in trade exchanges. There are several points at which this is particularly weak. The first is in conditions of direct employment of Third World workers on the plantations of the giant First World companies, whether these are directly owned by the companies or under sub-contracts. There have been heroic efforts to establish trade unions on sugar estates in the Caribbean Islands and in the Philippines, on tea estates in India and Sri Lanka, on rubber plantations in Brazil and elsewhere, and these efforts never cease. Without the support of a radical government, however, they are easily beaten down and their leaders sacked, if not shot. When a government is thrown up which takes the side of the small farmers and rural poor, like Michael Manley's People's National Party in Jamaica in 1980 or Maurice Bishop's People's Party in Grenada or the Sandanistas in Nicaragua, it is subjected to boycotts and military intervention. This is the second bargaining weakness — that in the world market few Third World governments can stand up to the giant transnational companies, especially when they are supported by United States military force; and no Third World governments, apart from those of the oil states, have succeeded in regulating the market. The third point of bargaining weakness for the small farmer arises in relation to his or her own government. When governments do take action to protect farmers in the world market, we have seen that, apart from siphoning off the funds for other purposes, including lining their own pockets, it is the big farmers who get the lion's share of the action.

Barter and Countertrade

Is there no way out? We shall look in the next chapter at the existing alternative trade openings for small producer associations and cooperatives. In this chapter we need first to see if there are not ways of improving the whole situation of Third World producers in the mainstream markets. It should be possible for Third World governments, except perhaps the very smallest, to bargain directly with the transnational companies, taking advantage of the competition which still exists between them. Even the governments of small countries could join together to present a common front to the big companies. Some Third World governments have, indeed, already begun to make direct trading agreements between their state organs or parastatals and First World companies, generally transnationals but also smaller companies and even aid agencies. These direct exchanges may take the form of barter or some other link between sales and purchases which does not involve a money payment, or involves money for only part of the exchange. These arrangements are called countertrade. Such deals began just after the Second World War and were made between governments with planned economies in Eastern Europe and the USSR and the big transnational companies of the First World. They soon accounted for a quarter of Eastern bloc countries' trade and spread to the Third World, where it is now estimated that about 15 per cent of trade exchanges include some element of countertrade.

The reasons that the different parties involved in countertrade have turned to this form of international exchange are various. The Eastern bloc countries wanted to buy plant and equipment from the West and, especially as their debts to the West grew, they were happy to pay with products from their new plant in compensation. In this way they avoided the need in the first place, to earn the hard currency with which to pay. These so-called 'buy-back' deals also overcame both the East Europeans' lack of exports apart from primary products and their lack of experience of selling in Western markets.

Most Third World countries do not have planned economies or full control over their foreign trade in the way the Eastern bloc countries had, but they do share the same problems of debt, hard currency shortage and lack of skills and experience in First World marketing. In the Third World it is not necessarily governments but more often parastatals and even the larger local traders which are interested in countertrade, although government endorsement is generally required. This interest has proved rewarding because, with falling primary product prices, surpluses can sometimes be disposed of only through countertrade. At the same time, the competition among First World companies in a period of recession has forced some to take payment in commodities instead of cash for their exports to the Third World. There is a further reason for Third World interest in countertrade. The structure of prices between industrial and agricultural products is often quite different in developing and developed countries. The developing countries have relatively low agricultural prices and high prices for industrial goods. By adjusting prices in settlements through countertrade, Third World governments can in effect subsidise their farmers and protect their infant industries by what amounts to a tax on imports of manufactured goods.

The aim of transnational companies in countertrade deals is perhaps more obvious; it is to extend their global hegemony and guarantee long-term supplies of primary products or of manufactured goods from countries where they do not wish to invest or are prohibited from doing so. Such prohibitions have been applied in the past not only in the Soviet Union, Eastern Europe and China but in several Third World countries, whose governments have followed protectionist and interventionist policies in planning their foreign trade. Transnational companies' countertrade frequently consists in buy-back deals. The transnational company supplies plant and equipment, e.g. for producing chemicals, and is paid over a period of years with products from the plant when it comes on stream. In this way a transnational company can often obtain its own product from overseas at lower cost than it might from the factories at home because of cheaper labour and no-strike deals in the Third World country. In such bargains the transnational company and the Third World government are negotiating on the basis of a rough equality. Of course, buy-back deals are disadvantageous to the workforce in the First World country, and it will be necessary for international agreements to be reached between trade unions in the First and Third Worlds if transnational company policies of divide and conquer are not to be permitted to force down wages and conditions to the lowest levels world-wide.

Smaller companies in both the First World and the Third World, including cooperatives and local authority enterprises, can also find that countertrade is beneficial. This is generally because of the usual difficulties experienced by newcomers, even from the First World, when entering foreign markets. Countertrade provides an alternative to the practice of going 'pick-a-back' on transnational companies, which has been widely adopted by South East Asian companies riding into world markets on the backs of the Japanese giants. Sometimes, government agencies in the First World have offered special support for exports from companies under their jurisdiction as part of long-term trade agreements reached with Third World countries; and smaller companies have been able to benefit from these offers only by reason of their entering countertrade deals. Aid agencies in the First World have also encouraged barter and countertrade where the aid has consisted in supplying equipment which has enabled Third World producers to improve the quantity and quality of their exports. Then the producers can pay in part with exports using the new equipment and can establish a balance of trade thereafter.

It has to be said, however, that there are many problems and pitfalls in countertrade. Some concern the costs of management and monitoring incurred and the added risks of delays and failure to deliver or dispose of goods or of changes in prices during the period of the deal. Others concern the possible violation of GATT rules which seek to prevent forms of discriminatory practice — exclusivity from most-favoured-nation treatment, for example — which may result where bilateral exchanges in effect rule out competition. There may also be objection from other countries when countertrade in effect conceals an export subsidy or the dumping of goods in unfair competition. There is the danger, particularly for Third World countries, that the goods received cannot be traded normally — for example, because they are below acceptable standards in quality and packaging or incorporate dangerous or obsolete technology.

There are many technical difficulties involved in countertrading, particularly where a long period elapses between the initial outlays on equipment and the final payment in goods. These include the need for cut-off times in contracts, for insurance cover and credit guarantees which will mean obtaining government approval, for special accounting procedures to record payments as they are made (so-called escrow accounts), for calculation of commissions and discounts with inclusion of interest charges for capital locked up in a deal, and provision for arbitration in the event of non-delivery or non-payment. (For an introduction to the subject, see *Countertrade*, published by Third World Information Network.)

Multilateral Trade Deals

Many difficulties arise from the bilateral nature of barter and countertrade — i.e. an exchange of goods or services between parties in two countries. Most East European countries and the USSR and China always had long-term bilateral payments agreements not only with each other but with Third World countries. Some Third World countries have similar agreements with each other. The drawbacks of these agreements are not only that each country is tied down to one supplier or market when other, better alternatives appear, but managing these agreements becomes a bureaucratic task which is both costly and open to corruption. There are, after all, many advantages in a free market, at least where business is open and where the parties are fairly equally balanced in terms of bargaining power. One way of moving beyond bilateral agreements is for a party to such agreements to use payment units received from its sales to one bilateral partner for making purchases from a third party. China, for example, had bilateral agreements with the USSR and seven other COMECON countries, but also with 15 other Third World countries and with France. The USSR had even more such agreements, and India had agreements with the USSR and the East European countries. There was no reason why swapping of payment units could not have taken place between all the parties to any of these sets of bilateral agreements. But this did not happen because, with the single exception of France, none of the parties to these agreements had hard currency and all the governments, especially those with debts, wanted to earn hard currency from their exports.

CHARTS 7 & 8. EXTENDED SWITCH DEALS – ALLER AND RETOUR TRANSACTIONS

These can be of two kinds: ALLER and RETOUR, depending on which country has the surplus balances. They are used especially in trade between Eastern European countries and Third World countries like India. The steps in the two mechanisms are shown below.

Aller Transactions

The Aller transaction involves supply of western goods to India against rupee clearing payment (where India has surplus credit balance). India saves free currency and corrects the trade balance, but may have high financing and discount costs.

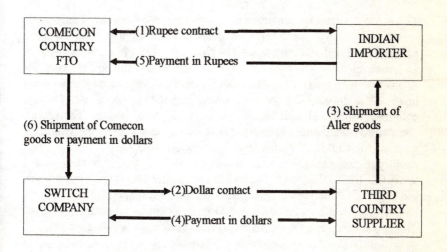

Retour Transactions

The Retour transaction involves purchase of Indian goods by the COMECON country against rupee clearing payment (where the COMECON country has surplus credit balance). India loses free exchange from its sales to the West and COMECON country gets free currency (although at a discount) from clearing its surplus credits.

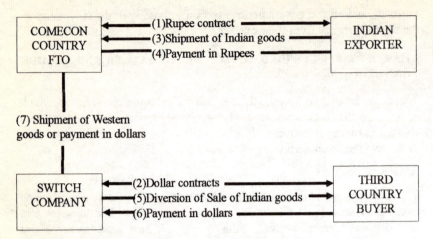

Source: Vijay Chawla, 'Countertrade and Clearing Possibilities in the Indian Market', *Countertrade and Barter Quaterly*, Summer 1984.

There are specialist countertrade companies called 'switch companies' which will arrange three-cornered deals, sometimes involving switches between hard and soft currencies. The chart on p.139 gives the example of an Indian importer who paid rupees to an enterprise in the Soviet Union for goods which he wished to obtain from a third country where the payment had to be in dollars. The Soviet company shipped the goods to the switch company which had a dollar contract with the third country. The second chart shows an Indian exporter who received rupees from the export of goods to a COMECON country. The goods were destined for a third country, which paid the switch company in dollars, that were then passed to the COMECON country. The Indian got a better price in rupees of which the COMECON foreign trade organisation had a surplus. The COMECON country received hard currency, but lost a discount to the switch company. The two transactions are called respectively *aller* and *retour* transactions.

A further step towards multilateral agreements in international trade is the use of international trade certificates (ITC), which can be transferred from one trader to another giving rights to market goods of a certain value, provided that the certificates have been endorsed by a central bank or other recognised authority. Such certificates have been issued by the General Foods Trading Co. of the United States and by the Bank of Boston. In the example given in the chart on page 141, goods are shipped from a Third World exporter to a United States importer. The importer wishes to be assured that what are non-traditional goods and therefore not acceptable in the commodity markets, are nonetheless bona fide. The ITC for the goods is endorsed by the central bank of the Third World country through a transfer agent. The certificate can then be used for exports of a similar value from a United States company to the Third World country, once again endorsed by the Third World central bank through the good offices of the transfer agent. The certificates can be used instead of hard currency, so long as the central bank of the Third World country authorises this, but they are of course restricted to purchases from the USA.

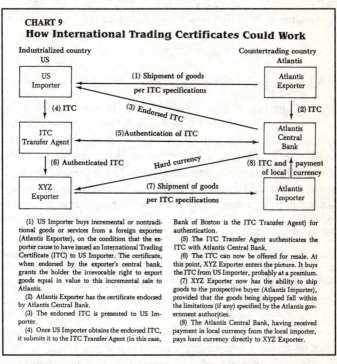

CHART 9
How International Trading Certificates Could Work

(1) US Importer buys incremental or nontraditional goods or services from a foreign exporter (Atlantis Exporter), on the condition that the exporter cause to have issued an International Trading Certificate (ITC) to US Importer. The certificate, when endorsed by the exporter's central bank, grants the holder the irrevocable right to export goods equal in value to this incremental sale to Atlantis.

(2) Atlantis Exporter has the certificate endorsed by Atlantis Central Bank.

(3) The endorsed ITC is presented to US Importer.

(4) Once US Importer obtains the endorsed ITC, it submits it to the ITC Transfer Agent (in this case,

Bank of Boston is the ITC Transfer Agent) for authentication.

(5) The ITC Transfer Agent authenticates the ITC with Atlantis Central Bank.

(6) The ITC can now be offered for resale. At this point, XYZ Exporter enters the picture. It buys the ITC from US Importer, probably at a premium.

(7) XYZ Exporter now has the ability to ship goods to the prospective buyer (Atlantis Importer), provided that the goods being shipped fall within the limitations (if any) specified by the Atlantis government authorities.

(8) The Atlantis Central Bank, having received payment in local currency from the local importer, pays hard currency directly to XYZ Exporter.

Source: Business International Corporation *Threats and Opportunities of Global Countertrade* 1984

Countertrade and barter are primarily sought as the basis for trade exchanges because of the lack on the part of one or other trading partner of cash or credit in a currency acceptable for making the deal. This must be a national currency that is widely used in trade, known as a hard currency, convertible into other currencies and not likely to be devalued. Only the largest trading nations, with no payment problems, will have a hard currency — today chiefly the USA, West Germany and Japan, but also Switzerland not only because of its trade surplus but because it has used this surplus and its neutrality in wartime to build up a role as a safe place to deposit money anonymously. For most countries whose currency is not regarded as hard, it is necessary to borrow or pay in gold if they run into deficits on the balance of their foreign trade. The higher the deficit, the higher the interest charge they will have to pay to borrow. For a long time the South African rand was a hard currency, because of the country's gold production, but this position ended when the value of the gold produced annually fell below the sum of the deficit on South Africa's trade. Countries with continuous deficits have to borrow from the IMF, as we have seen, and as a condition of aid they must agree to draconian cuts in their state budgets and to other measures, including devaluing their currency to make their imports more expensive and their exports more attractive.

The Problem of Creditworthiness

It is a central question in any economy: who gives permission to borrow? It is not correct to say that the banks do. In capitalist economies the banks work on principles of profit-making. They lend money in order to make more money, i.e. by charging a higher rate of interest on the loans they make than that which they pay to their depositors. The owners of the banks, the shareholders, demand this; and if a bank fails to make profits in line with other banks, it will go out of business. So, banks choose to lend only to those who have collateral — an asset which the bank can claim to repay the loan if necessary. Only such customers are regarded as creditworthy. Countries are treated in the same way. Those whose currencies have international value, the hard currencies, or who have access to hard currencies, which are not locked up in debt repayment, are regarded as creditworthy. Others, whose currencies only have local value, find it difficult, if not impossible, to obtain credit; and those who wish to trade with them will not get government guarantees for any credit supplied. This means that down payments will be required in advance of delivery of goods. It is clear from this situation that money has more than one function. It is a measuring rod or unit of acccount, varying in name and subdivisions from state to state. It is a means of exchange which may or may not be acceptable as having international value. Finally, it is an asset, a store of value; it can be used as capital, its long-term value depending on its international acceptability.

Countries which do not have internationally acceptable currencies have had to look for other means of raising credit. Apart from countertrade agreements, several other options have been tried. One system for raising credit without hard currency has been developed by several African countries — Zimbabwe, Malawi, Gabon, the Côte d'Ivore, Liberia, Zambia, South Africa — with the participation of a number of United States banks, supported by the US government. African minerals and agricultural commodities are exported to the United States and warehoused there. The African government concerned retains the title to the commodities. No foreign exchange actually changes hands, but the US government issues a certificate stating that certain quantities of the specified commodity are warehoused at such and such a location. The African government which has the title to the commodity can then use that certificate as collateral to raise credit from US banks for importing US goods. In case of default on payment for US products, the warehoused commodity can be sold, with the proceeds going to the US exporter. The system has several advantages for the African country involved. First, commodities can be used for collateral without violating international marketing agreements to which the government might be a signatory. For example, Nigeria could warehouse oil without violating OPEC quotas, because the oil would not actually have been sold. Second, if the African government is unhappy with the international price for the commodity, it can retain title in the hope that the price will rise, at the same time getting the benefit of using the commodity as collateral for import finance.

Such a system still has the disadvantage of being only narrowly available for a few countries, for a few commodities and is generally tied to particular exports and to particular transnational companies which control such exports. It has the great merit of making use of the capacity of primary-producing countries to produce something which is needed on the world market. The problem for Third World countries is how to convert this capacity into an asset equivalent to the reserves of hard currency or of gold, which more favourably placed states have at their disposal. The IMF arrangements for aid and the compensatory finance scheme for losses due to falling commodity prices, which we examined in an earlier chapter, are merely short-term measures. But the whole problem of the unequal bargaining position of rich and poor countries is that the rich can use their wealth in gold and hard currency to borrow and so to make more money. The poor cannot do this and the gap between the rich and the poor widens.

An attempt to overcome this problem was introduced at the first UNCTAD meeting in 1964 by Professors A. Hart of the USA, N. Kaldor of the UK and J. Tinbergen of the Netherlands. Their idea was that a proportion of the primary commodities which any country produces should be held by that country in warehouses. These might be in the producing country or elsewhere, but they would be given extra-territorial status and the bundle of commodities warehoused would be recognised by the international financial institutions in the same way that gold is, as a currency reserve. On the basis of such a reserve the countries concerned would be able to raise credit. These reserves would both increase international liquidity and encourage a general increase in world trade exchanges. They would go beyond this even and lay the basis for a new world monetary system. The proposal was not accepted as it would cut across the operations of the international·bankers and at once alter the bargaining position of primary producers, which was, of course, what it was intended to do.

Towards a New World Economic Order

There has been much talk in recent years about the need for a new world economic order. The object of all the complicated manoeuvres involving payment units, switch deals, trading certificates and bundles of commodities is nothing less than a series of attempts to replace money as the sole currency of international trade exchanges. The idea of a new economic order refers back to the Bretton Woods agreements at the end of the Second World War which set up the international financial institutions — the IMF and World Bank — and the General Agreement on Tariffs and Trade. It is because they have failed to serve the needs of the poorer countries, and particularly to resolve the Third World's debt crisis, that a new economic order seems now to be required. Some people believe that we should return to the original proposals of J. M. Keynes, which were superseded by a system that recognised the overwhelming political and economic superiority of the United States. Keynes's ideas were based on the assumption of a number of major powers of roughly equal standing — the UK, Germany, France, Japan and the Soviet Union and China as well as the USA — who wished to work together through the United Nations to create a framework for economic recovery and development after the Second World War.

The recent relative decline of the United States, in the face of Japanese and German competition, and the rise and fall of the Soviet Union as a superpower, have once more provided the occasion and the opportunity for international cooperation. Keynes had in mind not only an international banking system with automatic credits for member states incurring short-term deficits and with access to relatively large sums for loans for countries experiencing long-term structural difficulties, but an international currency, which would be universally acceptable and would not be that of any one country, and which would be managed by international civil servants. Challenging the United States' control over the IMF and World Bank presents formidable difficulties, but these cannot be greater than the difficulties presented today by the current United States foreign payments deficit and the funds which Japan and West Germany are having to provide to support it. While these funds make possible the continued level of United States purchases in the world market, they do nothing for the Third World and encourage a level of indebtedness within the United States which may well be unsustainable.

We have seen how gross inequalities are growing between rich and poor not only among different countries but within both rich and poor countries. Wealth polarising at one extreme and poverty at the other may mean more capital available for investment in new productive capacity but the reduced purchasing power certainly means a poorer market for the products of that extra capacity. The capital goes into a property boom and into mergers and take-overs and speculation. At some stage the bubble must burst, unless a major new redistribution of income takes place. There could be such a redistribution if a new Marshall Plan were launched to assist the recovery of Eastern Europe, but it would have to be on a scale far beyond what is now being contemplated except for the single case of East Germany.

When Keynes had proposed the establishment of an international trade organisation, he had intended it to take positive steps to encourage the development of trade exchanges. The organisation which was created, the General Agreement on Tariffs and Trade, has powers only to prevent or reduce obstacles to international trade. In fact, as we have seen, it is only the barriers to the exports of the already developed countries which have been systematically removed. Nothing has been done to encourage the expansion and diversification of exports from the developing countries. However, some initiatives have come from Third World governments, and from First World non-governmental organisations: to use UNCTAD's Common Fund and the European Community's Lomé Convention with the ACP countries for supporting trade development projects. These, which will be looked at in some detail in the next chapter, still fall far short of the kind of international trade organisation which Keynes had in mind.

A new international economic order would require more than just general support for such non-governmental initiatives. The two chief factors which hold back the growth of world trade, and particularly the Third World's share in it, are the low prices now being paid for Third World's primary products and the barriers to entry of many agricultural products and most manufactured products which have been erected, and are still maintained, by First World countries against the Third World. We have looked at both these problems, and saw little hope of a major change taking place so long as world-wide recession continues to lead to competitive beggar-my-neighbour policies being adopted. Could a parallel system of trade be launched which goes beyond the small-scale initiatives of the non-governmental sector and the quite narrow range of countertrading agreements? Such schemes have been proposed in the past, and should be re-examined.

A Trade Clearing Union

The main problem we have identified for Third World countries in developing and diversifying their trade has been their lack of hard currency and access to credit. In particular they lack a generally available system of credit, which would encourage an expansion of multilateral trade exchanges. This is what the international financial institutions, established at Bretton Woods, were supposed to provide but have never ensured on an adequate scale and on terms acceptable to Third World countries. Short of a complete revision of the 1944 agreements, what can be done, and in particular what can be done to pave the way for the renegotiation of those agreements? The obstacle to progress evidently lies with the major political powers and with the giant transnational companies which all believe that they are better off as they are and will presumably continue to believe this until the polarisation of wealth and poverty on a world scale leads to a crisis of 1930s proportions.

What then could be the framework for a system of more easily available credit? We may take a lesson from the giant transnational companies. In the internal transfers of transnational companies money is used only as a unit of account. There is no need for each part of the company which is engaged in exchanging products or services to provide proof of its creditworthiness, even if they deal with each other at arms' length and not via transfers ordered from above. Each part knows that the other will deliver within a framework of planning and regulations set by a central authority, to whom appeal can be made for recourse in the event of failure. A central world trading authority that acted like a giant supra-transnational company would not be at all acceptable to most nation-state governments. It would be altogether too like the monstrous bureaucracy of the now defunct Soviet planning system. How then would it be possible to guarantee creditworthiness without money, but without the complexity and ad hoc nature of bilateral deals and their extension into switches of payments and international certificates? Could not some central guaranteeing organisation be devised which acted not as a command centre but as a trade clearing house? And if the major powers will not join in, could a start now be made between some of the smaller countries and between some of the smaller trading organisations? The idea is not perhaps so utopian.

In the early 1960s there was much discussion among international economists about the need for a supplementary payments mechanism to promote trade among developing countries; and this was indeed the subject of a paper prepared in 1964 by Dr Andreas Goseco, a staff member of the Food and Agricultural Organisation, for consideration by the United

Nations Economic Commisssion for Africa, and subsequently by the United Nations Economic Commission for Asia and the Far East. After the Second World War there was for some time a widespread shortage of hard currency available for facilitating international trade exchanges and particularly the trade of developing countries. All sorts of bilateral trade agreements were being made by governments anxious to ensure that they obtained the goods they wanted to import in exchange for their exports, and not some country's soft currency which could not be converted into universally acceptable money. The Western European countries, as we noted earlier, formed a European Payments Union, through which their own currencies could be exchanged without resort to gold or dollars. The Union provided credit at current rates of interest and in effect made possible the transition to a system of fully convertible currencies. General convertibility into dollars only became possible, however, because of the continuing high level of United States current and capital spending in Western Europe after the initial rapid recovery of European industry with the help of Marshall Aid.

No such good fortune attended the development of Third World countries, except for those where United States military aid was available such as Israel, South Korea and in Central America. Elsewhere some alternative became imperative, and an interest emerged in the idea of regional clearing unions, for Africa, South America and Southern Asia. The scheme proposed for regional supplementary payments unions went one step beyond the model of the European Payments Union in suggesting that money should be replaced by titles to goods and services, money being employed in this case as a unit of acount and not as a means of exchange or store of value. Its place would be taken by commodity credit notes. This was the core of Dr. Goseco's proposal. These credit notes might consist of letters of credit, warehouse receipts or irrevocable contracts to deliver specified goods or services. They would not have been unlike the international trade certificates we looked at earlier, except that the credit notes were to be widely interchangeable, acting in effect as a parallel currency.

The situation in which most Third World countries find themselves today repeats almost exactly that of the early 1960s. Proposals like that of Dr Goseco were forgotten during the years of rising primary product prices combined with expanding demand from the industrial countries which had hard currencies to offer for the products of the Third World. Now demand has fallen back, prices have tumbled and, as debts have accumulated, the shortage of hard currency is once more acute. Trade with and between the Third World countries has slowed down. Stop-gap arrangements involving bilateral barter and countertrade agreements have once more been taking the place of multilateral exchanges financed by hard currency. The need is urgent for a supplementary payments system which could serve to establish a new basis for the flow of trade between the Third World and the First and among Third World countries themselves. Once again, regional arrangements are being looked at to supply a parallel trade system.

What, then, would be needed to start such a system? Can we imagine it starting in Africa, for example, to promote intra-regional trade, but with a link to organisations, governmental or non-governmental, in the First World? Here is how Dr Goseco envisaged a clearing union:

> Under the arrangement a clearing house, established in a suitable city in the sponsoring region, may receive firm offerings and orders for various goods and services (from participating countries) which it may verify and advertise as available much like in commodity exchanges. From such a line of goods and services licensed brokers or jobbers operating in the clearing house may try to fit together specific offerings and needs. Once a feasible deal is constituted the interested broker may then cable his options to his clients or counterparts in the exporting (importing) countries for the quantities of the offerings and orders which he may have been able to fit together. As soon as confirmation is received from all the parties (it has to be from all parties since each deal is inextricably linked with the others, as in a chain), he may then proceed to effect the transfer of titles of the commodity credit notes he has dealt with — the notes themselves representing titles to the offers which had been put together in the deal.

> A potentially simpler procedure would be to accept confirmed and irrevocable letters of credit of specified amounts in payments of goods. This gives a dealer considerable ease and flexibility in closing transactions although it exposes him to the risk of not being able to find the kind and quantity of commodities wanted by the supplier of the commodities he used in acquiring the letters of credit. Needless to say, this problem would not arise if the supplier would unconditionally accept as full payment the particular letter of credit involved. Likewise this problem would be mitigated in the case where there is a wide variety of acceptable commodities to choose from.

The example which Dr Goseco takes comprises a Burmese offer of rice and an order for corned beef, cocoa beans and jute bags; an Indian trader who wants Burmese rice and could sell jute bags and bicycles; an Argentine who has corned beef which he wishes to exchange for jute bags and an Indonesian who wants Indian bicycles in exchange for his cocoa beans. The way in which these dealers in four different countries sort out their problem through the clearing house is indicated in the chart below.

Finally, Dr Goseco addresses the problem of settling balances when

CHART 10. STAGES IN COMPENSATORY TRADE

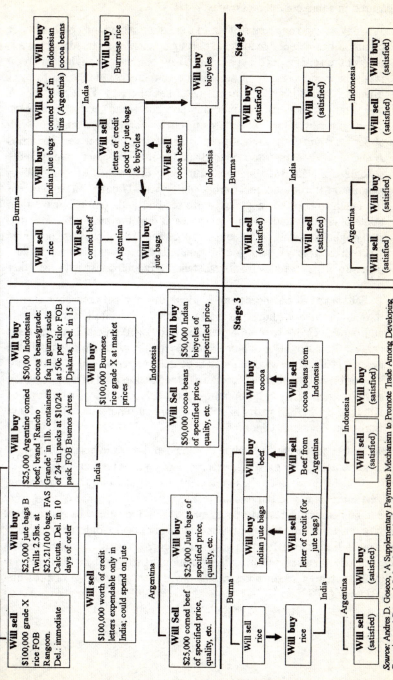

Source: Andres D. Goseco, 'A Supplementary Payments Mechanism to Promote Trade Among Developing Countries — A Proposal, *Indian Journal of Agricultural Economics*, Vol. XIX, No. 2.

various bilateral arrangements are slightly unequal in terms of money, measured in some common currency.

We may now go one step further, to a situation where 'no commodity or commodities acceptable to the exporting country are immediately available in the scheme'. To bypass this likely bottleneck, buying on credit might be made a feature of the scheme; and this could take the form of bilaterally established and maintained lines of credit. Thus countries A and D may each allow the other to import goods and services from each other on credit within set ceilings through intervening exchanges with countries B and C: the mutually arranged credit facility between countries A and D need not be extended to B and C nor to any other country in the scheme. . . . Considering the formidable difficulties encountered in negotiating the now defunct European Payments Union . . . it would seem too much to hope for anything more binding and comprehensive than bilateral credit settlements for purposes of negotiation . . . but an initial step might be to start with a series of bilaterally negotiated arrangements wherein each party would agree to guarantee the forward exchange value, in terms of its currency, of its outstanding indebtedness with the other party.

Settlement of balances may be done directly between countries or through the clearing house on the basis of some bilaterally agreed means and period. Under such an agreement debits and credits may be made against the account of one or the other country with the debit balance being (i) carried forward to the next settlement period and covered with the corresponding letter of credit, (ii) redeemed in gold or hard currency or (iii) settled partly in the currency of the debtor country (in the form of letters of credit) and partly in gold and hard currencies as in the defunct European Payments Union.

It was Dr Goseco's firm conviction that the credit notes in his scheme could come to be used as an exchange reserve, like gold or hard currency — i.e. not instead of them, but as a supplement. He argued that they would not only be more available but less subject to instability, because of their firm base in real commodities. Moreover, unlike gold they could be expected to grow in value in line with the expansion of trade and would not therefore have the deflationary effect that gold has when, as is usual, its supply grows more slowly than the volume of international trade exchanges. Chart 11 below shows how credit notes might move through a series of possible transactions.

Chart 11. Possible Barter Transactions

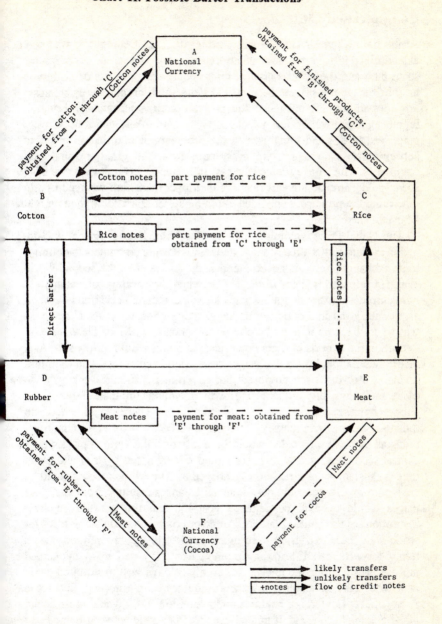

Computerised Clearances

At the time when Dr Goseco was writing, the use of computers was new and confined to governments and large companies. The spread of computers since then and the proliferation of micro-computers and use of electronic mail boxes among private persons and quite small organisations creates a new opportunity. It opens up the possibility of automatically bringing together the bids and offers which Dr Goseco's brokers and jobbers were employed to do, and greatly eases the problems of multilateral payment settlements. Once again, we may learn from the giant transnational companies, which have adapted the new information technology, as we have seen, to decentralise the vast range of their operations, but we need first to determine the principles on which a trading system parallel to theirs might be established.

The Nobel Prize-winning economist, Professor Ragnar Frisch of Oslo, had in the late 1940s already suggested ways of using computers to optimise trade exchanges between governments in the aftermath of the Second World War. He refined his ideas in the 1960s, when the shortage of dollars and hard currencies was still holding back the expansion of world trade. As soon as a country ran into deficit in its balance of payments, its usual response was to cut back its imports by one means or another. Since these were by definition the exports of other countries, the others would follow suit. As a result, international trade exchanges were conducted at less than optimum levels. Professor Frisch proposed that governments should draw up trade plans indicating the anticipated growth in volume of their imports and exports by main categories over a period of years. These would be fed into a central computer. Excesses or deficiencies between different countries' plans as they were revealed would be notified to the various parties by a central secretariat, and a new mix would be attempted by trial and error, until a satisfactory programme was arrived at. The whole process could be subject to regular revision; and financial balances resulting from changing prices would need to be adjusted year by year through the financial institutions of the United Nations. Professor Frisch believed that his ideas for world-wide trade expansion were much superior to the currently negotiated treaty for a (West) European Common Market, based upon unplanned multilateralism inside the market and on a protective wall to surround it. He announced his conviction at a Britain-Commonwealth-European Free Trade Area (EFTA) Conference held in London in 1962. They would in particular make possible the spread of mutual benefits from trade between Europe and the outside world, not a narrowing of benefit within a protected European Community, which is in effect what has transpired.

The objection made to Professor Frisch was not only that his proposals, like Keynes's original ideas for the Bretton Woods meeting, transferred too much power away from the central banks of the major states to international civil servants, but that such detailed planning was impossible. The vast and ever-changing range and complexity of the goods exchanged between modern industrial nations could not possibly be reduced to a package of planned exchanges on a multilateral basis, and to propose to make current price adjustments for many thousands of items was to enter the realm of the unwieldy monster bureaucracy of the Soviet Union. In fact such detailed adjustment of prices would not have been needed. That is why Professor Frisch had proposed volume measurements; the adjustments needed were only in the overall payments position of the several countries as this emerged from time to time from their trade exchanges. Instead of deficits leading to cut-backs all round, the trade plans would sustain trade at a high level; international finance would be used when necessary, as in the various stabilisation schemes we have looked at, to correct major imbalances.

Professor Frisch's critics had a more substantial point in questioning the possibility of governments being able to indicate even volume changes in the movements of thousands of different goods. The same criticism is made, as we have seen, of all central state planning; but the fact is that the very large companies do plan the movements of great numbers of components and products and now, with flexible automation and immediate point-of-sale information retrieval, they can today respond to an immense range of customer specifications. The Soviet central planners had tried to manage literally billions of pieces of information. The tables comprising their plans ran to more than 12,000 pages. But this was quite unnecessary and a hangover from earlier thinking about large-scale organisations shared equally by Soviet bureaucracy and capitalist management, indeed learnt by the Soviets from the capitalists.

What the giant companies had realised in the course of the development of the new information technology was that there are two principles that can be applied in a large organisation to avoid the superfluity of information and decision-making at the centre. The first is that decision-making should be decentralised as appropriate to designated levels of any organisation, and information collection should be limited to what is necessary at each level. The second is that instructions based on information collected should as far as possible take the form of automatic adjustments within a framework of overall aims including a system of priorities to clear bottlenecks, avoid shortages, etc. As we noted earlier, the Soviet central planners' failure to adopt these principles had quite disastrous results. The question for Third World countries is whether they can jump straight into a decentralised planning system without having to go through the stage of a concentration of power at the centre. These countries would have the disadvantage of lack of experience in preparing the appropriate computer software for such decentralised planning. But they would have the advantage of less complex interrelationships and a narrower range of products, at least in the early stages of trade planning. It is this absence of complexity that is generally used as a justification for highly centralised planning in the first stages of industrialisation, but it would be truer to say that it was only the lack of complexity that made the centralisation tolerable. It would certainly have been better to have avoided so much centralised decsion-making from the start if the information technology had then been available.

Now that this technology does exist, how can the Frisch and Goseco proposals be combined in the conditions of the world today and applied specifically to schemes of regional cooperation? It is clear that a scheme does not need to comprise all the goods and services entering trade exchanges but only major groups and sub-groups. Detailed specifications can be dealt with at lower levels. For example the Ford Motor Company has plans for the production and assembly of thousands of component parts of a motor car, but the central planners at Detroit do not need to be concerned with more than the general framework of planning. Even the local plants have no need to plan in advance the range of colours, accessories and fittings of each car that comes off the line. Today you can have any colour you like because flexible automation and computerised control allow the information about customers' requirements to be fed in only at the lowest level — on the assembly line — and then reported upwards as necessary for replacement orders of parts.

With this in mind let us now go back to Dr Goseco's proposals. The author suggested a clearing house with brokers bringing together bids and offers. Today the clearing house could have a large-capacity computer, linked by electronic mail boxes and bulletin boards to all the organisations, governmental or non-governmental, which subscribe to the service. Through the electronic bulletin boards, bids and offers could be circulated with the necessary degree of specification. The computer would be programmed to look for alternative ways of marrying up the several bids and offers presented to it at any one time; it would simultaneously be able to indicate the balance of credit notes in terms of the several soft currencies and of hard currency relativities, which would result from each of the alternatives. Each party subscribing to the system could accept or refuse until agreement is reached. This would require decisions at different levels — at lower levels about the details of price, quality, quantity, specification, packaging, delivery dates, etc.; at higher levels about balances of payments, finance and credit. When all these are setttled deals could be done, sometimes bilaterally, sometimes involving a whole chain of arrangements. Each subscribing member state would be required to make available a line of credit in its national currency up to a certain sum, roughly in relation to the amount of trade which each expected to carry out through the system.

The great merit of a computerised parallel market of the kind here outlined is that it would not have to be centrally controlled or even need to have a large central staff of brokers and dealers. The staff at the clearing house would be required to operate the computer and see that disks were appropriately stored for retrieval, that subscriptions were paid and regulations issued and altered from time to time so that information was made available in standardised forms and in the manner most useful to the subscribers. The staff could also act in an advisory role, suggesting alternative switches and solutions to payments problems as well as answering technical questions on the use of information technology. However attractive such a service may appear, it is unlikely that any large group of states, e.g. in a whole region of the world, would be prepared to enter into such a union unless the system had been tried out on a smaller scale. A prototype for an international clearing union is therefore proposed in the next chapter, based on the alternative trade network of non-governmental organisations, which has been built up over recent years. If a clearing union, and side by side with it a trade development centre, could be established within this network, and could be seen to be running successfully, it would not be difficult to imagine that groups of nation-states might feel able to take up the idea for their own international trade exchanges.

Notes

The publication *Countertrade*, available for £1.50 from TWIN at 345 Goswell Road, London EC1V 7JT, gives a more detailed description of the various forms of countertrade and their drawbacks and has a useful glossary of the key terms. A good general analysis of the several Bretton Woods proposals appears in T. Balogh's chapter on 'International Aspects' in G. D. N. Worswick and P. Ady, *The British Economy 1945-50*, Oxford University Press, 1952. The proposal from Professors Hart, Kaldor and Tinbergen appeared as a paper entitled 'The Case for an International Commodity Reserve Currency' in the first volume of the proceedings of the first UNCTAD meeting in 1964. Dr Goseco's proposals were published in the *Indian Journal for Agricultural Economics*, Vol. xix, No. 2. Professor Frisch's paper, 'A Multilateral Trade Clearing Agency', appeared in *The Economics of Planning*, Vol. 7, No. 2., Norwegian Institute of International Affairs, Oslo, 1967. For the use of computerised information technology in business planning, see M. Best, *The New Competition*, Polity Press, 1990.

11. ALTERNATIVE TRADE: IN AND AGAINST THE MARKET

Where are we now? We have looked at many varieties of supportive, compensatory, centrally planned, supplementary and complementary, and parallel systems of trading in order to find a way to help Third World countries and organisations to strengthen their position in the world market and embark upon a path of independent development. None of them has appeared to offer any real escape from the commercial market as the main channel for international trade exchanges. Is there, then, no alternative within the market? The answer is that there is a not inconsiderable network of alternative trading already in existence. What is more, while the annual growth of world trade has been declining, this alternative network has been growing rapidly. What is meant by alternative trade in this context is a system of trade in which the partners seek deliberately to establish a more equal basis of exchange between the First and Third Worlds. In addition to seeking a fairer relationsip, the aim has been to establish a more direct relationship between groups of producers and consumers in the two worlds and a greater understanding among consumers of the need of the producers for support for their independent development.

From Famine Relief to Economic Support

Alternative trading evolved from the attempts of a number of First World charities to move beyond collecting money for the relief of victims of famine, war and natural disasters. If aid could be given to help such victims in the form of tools and equipment to start working again, and some of the products of their work could be sold in First World shops, a more lasting benefit could be achieved after the immediate relief of famine. Oxfam, the best known of these aid agencies in the UK, moved in this direction from its origins as a small committee of Quakers in Oxford which raised funds for famine relief during the Second World War. In every country in the First World there are at least two or three aid agencies with these wider aims. Most have their origins, like Oxfam, in religious organisations; in addition, there are a number of solidarity organisations created to support popular struggles against outside aggression, as in Nicaragua, the front line states of Southern Africa and now in Guatemala and El Salvador.

Organisations such as Oxfam and TWIN develop alternative trade links by making contact with groups in the Third World, establishing their needs in terms of tools and equipment, and assisting them to find a market for their products. In many cases these are crafts, but the range has been widening to include textiles, canned fruits and jams, honey, nuts and coffee. Most alternative trade organisations (ATOs) then work to distribute these products in the First World — mainly through mail order catalogues and some special shops. In a few countries there are 'Third World corners' in the mainstream supermarkets. This is the case in Finland and the Netherlands and in the Italian retail cooperatives. There is often a link with wholefood retailers and small independent cooperative shops. When TWIN, together with Oxfam Trading and Traidcraft, convened a conference on fair trading in London in the autumn of 1988 nearly a hundred different organisations sent representatives. Their interests ranged from small independent retail cooperatives to large mail order businesses and from electronic mail to mainstream commodity marketing. Their overriding concern was that trade with the Third World should be conducted on the basis of fairness and mutual understanding.

Relative to the Third World's total trade, which amounts to hundreds of billions of dollars, alternative trade is small indeed, accounting only for a few hundred millions. But some alternative trade organisations in the First World have an annual turnover of many millions of dollars, handle a wide range of products and work with hundreds of producer groups in the Third World. The outlets for their products in the First World are to be numbered in thousands. A North American ATO estimated the North American solidarity market to exceed 10 million people. Every major town in Britain has at least one supplier of products from this alternative trade system and the big cities have several. This picture is duplicated in nearly all the countries of Western Europe, North America, Japan and Australasia. In 1989 40 ATOs formed themselves into an International Federation for Alternative Trade (IFAT), headquartered in Amsterdam. Several of these ATOs had been meeting regularly for some years for the exchange of information, coordination of trading arrangements, pooling of resources and support for common campaigns. IFAT provides a central secretariat to formalise and develop these activities, to plan ways of opening up its membership to Third World organisations and strengthen communications with them. At its first biennial conference in Kilkenny, which was opened by the President of Ireland, 40 delegates from 20 Third World countries attended as well as over a hundred delegates from 20 countries in the First World. The Third World delegates presented an agreed common programme for future activity on a regional basis, and this was accepted together with a proposal for establishing a world-wide information service. IFAT will remain an umbrella for the ATO movement and not in any way a directing centre.

A Real Alternative?

Can it be said that these ATOs provide a real alternative to mainstream commercial trade in the world market? The annual turnover is still very small, but in what way is alternative trade really an alternative? How far does it strengthen the bargaining position of small-scale Third World producers and give them a larger piece of the action? We have been looking at these issues in the last five chapters, but testing for success is not easy. At the heart of the answer to these questions lies a fundamental question about the purpose of trade. Today it is very rare, at least in the First World, for producer and consumer to meet in the market. The big companies pull the strings to create a puppet consumer and then lavish their blandishments on what they have created. What has come to be called 'consumerism' pervades the market. Advertising aims to attract attention not only to what is the cheapest, but what is the latest, most convenient and efficient product — and only after the consumer's tastes have been researched, dissected and ever so subtly reconstructed. The essence of an alternative is that the consumer should be told the truth, not only about what is in the product but also the truth about the producer, her or his conditions of life and work, what they get for their work and what it does to the environment — as we saw on the honey label in the introduction. This approach to alternative trading starts from bringing the producer to the consumer. At first, this means asking what resources went into producing the goods, how they will affect the consumer's health and the health and very survival of producers, what effect their production has on environment and the balance of life on the planet. This is the basis of the green movement which is concerned that produce is grown organically and that animals are not ill-treated in the course of manufacturing products or producing food. But the main ideal behind alternative trading is concern for people — the subsistence farmers who are the small-scale primary producers. What is happening to them, when land is converted to producing crops for export, when commodity prices fall, when giant companies take over land and mines and factories in the Third World to produce goods for sale primarily in the First World? What kind of development is this trade making possible?

If trade is looked at from the point of view of the primary producer, the first response may be to wonder whether there should be any trade at all, so disastrous have been the results of cash cropping, tree felling and mineral extraction for the countries in the Third World over the last 200 years and more. And there is a powerful school of thought which argues the case for total self-reliance. Third World countries should, on this argument, withdraw from the world market altogether, or at least from trading with the First World. They should conserve their resources and turn their land back from cash crops for export to food crops for home consumption, putting 'Food First!', as the name of a major North American campaign group suggests. The less extreme version of this view argues for 'trade for mutual self-reliance', that is trade only between economies at the same level of technological development — South-South trade instead of North-South. Most trade today consists of North-North flows. There is much to be said for encouraging more South-South trade, but to end up with two self-contained hemispheres would be unnecessarily limiting. There are real benefits for both from mutual interaction. Markets for much of what the Third World produces exist only in the First World, and much of the equipment which the Third World needs can only be found in the First World. If organisations in the Third World recognise that they have to enter the world market, it is not perhaps for us in the First World to say no, but rather to help them to diversify their trade, increase their control over it and get a better deal, the lack of which has led them to consider taking the path of self-reliance. Making good that lack is the main aim of alternative trade.

The argument against cash crop production arises from the bad experience which many Third World countries have suffered in the past in concentrating on export production. 'It does not make sense to write-off cash crops altogether . . . it was not the production of cash crops *per se* but the social relations that governed their production and exchange that led to the over-exploitation and environmental degradation.' This is the conclusion of a distinguished Sri Lankan agriculturalist, Professor N. Shanmugaratnam, an associate professor at the Agricultural University of Norway. 'Production systems research,' he believes, 'should be carried out in collaboration with the producers to develop ways of combining cash crops and subsistence crops. Moreover, at the current level of population, the alternative production systems have to be sustainable at a higher level of productivity than were the traditional systems . . . . That raises the question of production technology.' And that inevitably raises the question of links with the First World.

However in appropriate much of the advanced technology may be for the needs of Third World countries, to cut them of from access to all First World technology is quite unacceptable. The introduction of electronic communications is an obvious case in point, since this gives to primary producers up-to-the-minute information about markets and the chance to make deals without depending on middlemen. For the primary producers of the Third World to get a larger piece of the action, they need to expand their processing and refining capability, and the fact is that most of the plant and equipment they require for their diversification and development programmes is only available in the First World. The task which the ATOs

BOX 4. FOOD PRODUCERS

Some of our food comes from countries seeking justice for their rural poor through active development policies e.g. Tanzania, Nicaragua, China. The rest come from community groups, such as;

WDM, Assam and Darjeeling teas — supplied by EMA in India. Blended with the maximum possible percentages from acceptable sources, e.g. co-ops in Assam and Tripura.

Nilgiri Tea — This Indian tea comes partly from Incoserve, a peasant farmers' cooperative federation, and Tanfed, government estates providing work for Tamil repatriates from Sri Lanka. The caddy is from Archana.

Encafe Coffee — the value-added by processing remains in Nicaragua.

Campaign Coffee — Tanzania retains the benefit from making this instant coffee at the Bukoba factory, which serves small farmers selling through village co-ops.

central America Dark Roast Coffee — a blend containing at least 55 per cent from acceptable sources, including Nicaragua, and the Cerro Azui cooperative in Costa Rica.

Cocoa — from El Ceibo, a cooperative federation in the Alto Beni area of Bolivia

Raw Cane Sugar — from Craft Aid Mauritius; packagaing sugar provides work for physically handicapped young people.

Muscavado Sugar — from Alter Trade, a marketing organisation based on Negros Island in the Philippines, which assists small farmers by selling their sugar, giving aid and credit.

Papads — from SKVIS, India.

UVA Curry Set — supplied by UVA Spice, a non-profit organisation buying from Cooperatives and small-scale growers in Sri Lanka.

Mango Chutney — from the Academy of Development Science in hill land in Maharashtra, India. An integrated development project working with Takur tribal people.

Brazil Nuts — from gatherers near Puerto Maldonado in SE Peru, who until recently only had exploitative outlets for their nuts.

Hazelnuts — supplied by Fiskobirlik, the Turkish state-sponsored

cooperative which gives guaranteed minimum prices to producers. Also used to make our Hazel Butter.

Cashew Nuts — broken nuts from Mozambique. Whole nuts from the Zambian Cashew Company Ltd. which is promoting the growth and marketing of cashews by 10 farmers in the poor Western Province

Pecan Nuts — from the Rosario de Yauca cooperative in the Inca coastal region of Peru

→

Sultanas — farmers from three villages in Izmir in Turkey get a good price for their organically grown produce.

Apricots — from a family firm in Malatya, Turkey, where apricots are an important cash crop mainly grown in small orchards.

Banana Chips — chip manufacture gives peasant farmers of Negros island an outlet for produce they cannot otherwise export.

Pineapple Rings — processed at the Dabaga factory at Iringa in Tanzania where workers get good pay and good benefits.

Tanzanian Honey — from the 6,000 member Tabora Beekeepers Cooperative, which is exporting after technical, managerial and financial assistance from the Traidcraft Exchange.

Sweet Justice Honey — from the Coalicion de Ejidos de Costa Grande, an association of producers in the southern Mexican state of Guerrero.

Crystals — made at a Zimbabwean factory which provides workers with good wages and other benefits.

Traidcraft Exchange

Traidcraft Exchange is the charity linked to Traidcraft plc. It has two main areas of activity:
1. Support for 'Third World' producers.
2. Education in the UK about 'Third World' issues.

Support for 'Third World' producers

The Exchange has an overseas business development service working with groups in East and Southern Africa, and Southeast Asia. The businesses are chosen for their concern with social as well as financial objectives. The Exchange helps them market their products in Europe and to get the business support they need to meet such orders. Small business development is another part of development in the 'Third World'. We are ensuring that such development benefits the wider community and not just the few.

Education

Traidcraft is about more that selling products. It is also about raising awareness of the issues of fair trading. The Exchange researches and produces a wide range of materials and promotes them through the company. We also supply materials and information directly to the general public.
Just Enterprise is a new pack for schools which links to the enterprise element of the National Curriculum. Through it, young people learn more of the 'Third World' whilst developing an awareness of love and justice in business practices. The pack encourages students to run enterprises with a distinctive 'Third World' flavour. Trials have shown it to be of value across the curriculum for students of 14 years upwards.

Traidcraft Exchange, Kingsway, Gateshead, NE11 0NE.

in the First World have set themselves is to find appropriate equipment for their partners in the Third World so that they can process their natural resources and earn more from them in the market.

We have noted already that much alternative trade so far is in handicrafts. This trade has the special advantage that the people of many Third World countries have retained originality of patterns, colours and designs in their domestically produced household goods, which has been lost to machine production in the First World. 'Ethnic' products have become fashionable. But encouraging craft production for export has other advantages for Third World producers. Handicraft products add value to the local materials: cotton, wool, coir, jute, straw, bamboo. They provide an income for women, who everywhere tend to do the unpaid work, while the men annex the cash. Handicraft production does not interfere with food growing activities. Crafts need little in the way of tools and equipment that is not already easily at hand. Finally, a price can be assigned to the product which takes some account of hours and artistic skill involved in the product, with a bit added for the consumer's commitment to the cause of Third World development. It was thus of special value for people in the Third World to find a market in the First World and to get help with problems of packaging, transport and distribution. Another product which gives similar advantages to small-scale producers in the Third World is honey. There is a growing demand for honey in the First World, as an alternative to sugar which has attracted an unhealthy image. Some ATOs believe it is wrong to import such a valuable food from countries where people live at subsistence levels. But where people are not actually starving the income from exporting a product that can be obtained in the less busy season of the year is pure gain. Imports of honey into Europe and North America have multiplied rapidly. Herbs and spices and several kinds of nuts which are gathered in the forests by peasant families have now been added to the handicrafts on the shelves and in the catalogues of the alternative traders as major items in their business. Again, there is a double advantage: the forests are saved and the forest people with them.

We are beginning to see what makes the trade of the ATOs a real alternative for the producer as well as the consumer. There is a whole range of services which the ATOs provide in getting the products of the Third World into the market. It is not possible to rely on good will, commitment or solidarity for continuing sales of Third World products, where they come into competition with attractive, well-designed goods made in the First World. Successful trading requires professionalism at every stage. Designs have to be adapted to modern tastes and to the arrangements of a modern household. Fashions change and there is an insatiable demand for something new. Packaging is today a large element in what sells a product and often

What Alternative Trade Organisations Do

Bringing consumers and producers together as people understanding each other is what the ATOs are trying to do, but the process requires a considerable effort at understanding on both sides in the development of conditions of mutual trust through cooperation on all the details of commercial trading. The ATO has to become a very special kind of middleman, very different from the sharks, coyotes and piranhas whom we met in earlier chapters. The ATO has first to find the producer groups in the Third World who are looking for a new outlet for their products so as to establish their independent development. Indeed, the most important role of the ATO may be in helping small-scale producers to get organised, to become a stable group and to join up with other local groups, so that there is a firm structure capable of collecting produce from many households, providing storage facilities, setting up processing plant, managing supplies, organising transport and communication with markets at home and overseas. Second, the ATO must be relied on to provide information, which will almost certainly not be available locally — about prices, markets, styling, packaging, quality control, health and safety standards, new uses for old products, transport and shipping and tools, machines and plant for processing, all on an open and fair basis. This information will need to be stored — not just in files and catalogues, but in computers — and to be communicated by modern means of telephone and electronic mail, telex and fax. The chief point is that all information must be available and not restricted by monopolistic operations.

Unlike normal commercial traders, the ADOs do not seek to make a profit for their owners or sponsors. They have to cover their costs and service their working capital, and if they make profits, these are fed back into charitable activities. The aim is to pay as much as possible, not as little as possible, to the producer, yet at the same time to offer goods on the market at competitive prices or at prices that are acceptable to consumers because they know that the extra they pay is going to those who are in need. More than this, ATOs are concerned to help producers to add more value to their produce by enabling them to do more of the processing that is now mainly done in the First World — vacuum-packing nuts and coffee, deep-freezing fruit and vegetables, making margarine from vegetable oils, and chocolates from cocoa, manufacturing garments from cotton, and furniture from timber. We saw earlier how little of what we pay in the shops for produce that comes from the Third World actually goes to the original producer; and the main reason for this, apart from the poor price or poor wages, was that so many stages of the chain of commercialisation are in the hands of expatriate companies from the First World, who invest their profits in their own countries and not in the Third World.

ATOs are, therefore, prepared to undertake business that no commercial firm would risk, often without guarantees for uninsurable losses or for credit supplied. Indeed, one of the main requirements of a Third World organisation wishing to become independent of the local middlemen is for credit. Without cash up front, a cooperative or association of small-scale producers will be unable to get its members to turn down the offers of the middlemen and to make their produce available. Finance in advance will also be required in order to buy the plant and equipment to increase the number of stages of processing carried out locally and to improve packaging and provide transport. Even more funds will be needed to plant new trees, in organic soil conditions for example, or to build new warehouses and factories. Yet the time lapse between the putting-up of money for the purchase and installation of new plant and the launching of a product onto the market (which would enable the original finance to be repaid) may amount to years rather than months. We have already seen that the funds available from the World Bank or the IMF tend not to go to such small-scale projects, but to major schemes such as dams, electrification and irrigation works, and construction of harbours and transport systems, which presume the prior capacity of local producers to make use of them.

The final role of the ATOs that makes them a real alternative is that of carrying out public relations work and promotion on behalf of Third World producers. This must go well beyond the normal commercial advertiser's brief, to include information about the producers, their way of life and conditions of work. This is not just a matter of reassuring consumers about the health and safety, freedom from exploitation and environmental destruction, and possibly the organic origins, of the production process. It embraces many aspects of the producers' lives, so as to bring them closer in the imagination of the consumers, who are used to thinking only of a can of this and a pound of that in the supermarket. For ATOs wish to influence consumer demand, not so much towards the product they are marketing and away from someone else's, as towardsThird World products as a whole and, more important, towards a different attitude to international trade relations. Nor is this just a question of persuading rich consumers in the First World to pay a bit more for the goods they buy from poor producers in the Third World; the hope is to persuade them to think about the need to change the whole structure of world trade exchanges, to bring consumers and producers closer together and cut out much of the money-making that takes place in between the two.

It is evident that the groups that ATOs work with have different aims from those of other producers and traders in the Third World, just as ATOs differ from normal commercial traders in the First World. The descriptions given in this book of how ATOs discovered groups of men and women in the Third World and helped them to set up their own structures suggest that forms of cooperative ownership or of producers' association are typical of the Third World partners of ATOs. Most ATOs specifically look for such democratic structures in the organisations with which they work, and they wish to emphasise the recognition of the role of women, not only in the processes of work but also in decision-making. ATOs will be happiest where their Third World partner is pursuing a programme of all-round development: using its new earnings from trade to build schools, improve the local health service, establish controlled-price village stores, in the way described at the beginning of this book among the *campesinos* of the Sierra Madre in Mexico. Trade development is only a means, not an end in itself —— a means towards a better life for the men and women of the Third World.

One of the main benefits of the trade development projects of ATOs with Third World partners has been that the self-confidence and professionalism which the latter have learned in their entry into the world market have enabled them to become much more effective in their own country markets and in advancing the general development programmes of their countries. This is not just a question of competing successfully against other local producers, but of improving the range and quality and efficiency of their activities, so that the level of the conditions of life of their localities is raised. Initial funding and initial equipment from the First World may be needed to give a start to a trade development project, but the result is likely to be that new sources of local production of tools and equipment are encouraged and new producers are brought in, so that a mutually reinforcing process of economic and social development takes place. It must be repeated that the problems of the Third World do not consist of shortages and inadequate resources, but of rich resources of land and labour that are underused, misused and often abused.

Third World Networking

As we have seen, it is of great importance the the aims and principles of ATOs and their partners in the Third World should be mutually compatible. But how are such mutually acceptable partnerships to be established? The answer lies in the networks that have been created, first for the exchange of information and then for active trading relationships. Earlier, when I described the establishment of IFAT, the International Federation for Alternative Trading, I mentioned the networking principle which is fairly typical of the methods adopted by most ATOs. The relations that they establish with each other and with their Third World partners are not structured heirarchically into holding companies and subcontractors or even into joint ventures of an exclusive kind. They are based on the principles of equality, fair exchange, reciprocal benefits, mutual respect and the avoidance of corrupt practices. The essence of a network is that it is a way of linking individuals and groups that leaves them free to make their own independent decisions within a mutually agreed framework of cooperation. A network is not fixed and rigid but flexible and continuous, capable of growing in many directions, of making connections for many purposes, always open to new members and new initiatives. Typically, a network is a horizontal rather than a vertical system, in that it links mainly those groups of people who have similar functions or aims and who work at the same level. Networks, therefore, differ from the heirarchical structures of most private companies and public organisations, in that they have no directing centre. Nobody gives orders. Partners have to agree. Networks differ also from the market system, in which relationships are essentially discontinuous, ad hoc and always mediated by money. But networks may perform many of the functions of the market, in providing shipping, insurance, broking, wholesaling and many other maketing functions, as well as providing information and research. If networks do not have a controlling centre, this does not mean that they have no centre. They may need to have just one communication centre, but they are likely to have not one but many independent decision-making centres. IRED is a good example. The acronym stands in French for International Network to Promote Development Innovations. IRED distinguishes three kinds of network, and has aimed to move steadily from the first, where all communications go through the centre, via the second, where the centre plays a major role but the partners communicate with each other directly, towards the third, in which there is direct and systematic communication between all the different members, with the centre providing only a support service.

In the third figure, each of the eight angles representing separate partners will have lines going out to contacts peculiar only to that one partner. At the seven points where three or more lines intersect there will be a concentration of messages, which may warrant a separate office, and as the network grows this will certainly be the case. IRED has 600 partners, so that one has to imagine not an octagon but a 600-pointed figure, with a great number of multifaceted intersections. Where many lines intersect, there is an obvious case for a regional office. IRED has five of these already, two in Asia, two in Africa and one in South America. Of course, the partners will not want to receive all the communications between them all. The regional offices can filter messages, or the partners can receive ocmmunications under certain headings and not others.

If networks do not have leaders, they do need networkers. These are people who move easily and freely between groups, making connections, suggesting new linkages, repairing damaged ties. Their detailed interlinking work is what holds the network together. The image of the spider comes to mind, but networking is not a predatory activity and the weaving of the web is not an individual effort. There needs, nevertheless, to be key individuals at nodal points in the network where many connections intersect, like synapses in the central nervous system of a human being. These individuals must have one essential characteristic, that of being entirely trusted by all those with whom they work. Such trust is only built up over time, but it can be destroyed in a moment, by one injudicious act. The role of networkers inevitably varies from place to place and from one circumstance to another. They are not so much themselves organisers or managers, although they must know how to organise and to manage; they are more what we might call enablers or facilitators, what the French would call *animateurs*. Their most important role is that of finding groups that can work together, that are not only compatible but also complementary.

CHART 12. THE IRED NETWORK

The strength of a network like IRED lies in its capacity to organize communication with its partners to enable them, in turn, to communicate and exchange — all with a view to doing things and managing their affairs.

There are many types of network, but there are three main ones (see below):

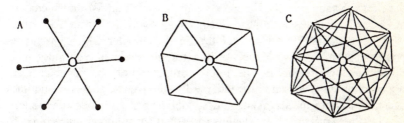

A) All information, support and exchanges go through the centre, a secretariat or a committee. If partners communicate, they do so through the centre.

B) The centre plays a major role but the partners begin to contact each other direct, without referring to the centre.

C) There is direct and systematic communication between the different members of the network. The centre is principally a support service for its partners' activities.

The very essence of a network is that it links groups which are independent but have a common interest and common objectives. There are many networks besides IRED (Innovations et Réseaux pour le Développement) which link together groups in the First World and the Third World. IDOC is a Rome-based communication network, committed to non-dependent development. IFDA (International Federation for Development Alternatives) is linked to Interpress Service, a telecommunications network extending to 60 countries in all continents. UTO (United Towns Organisation) twins towns throughout the world in ceremonial and increasingly in commercial associations. ICVA (International Council of Voluntary Agencies) links 75 such agencies from all continents and religions. FAVDO (Forum of African Voluntary Development Organisations) was recently formed to link African NGOs in the field of development. IWTC (International Women's Tribune Centre) aims to support the initiatives of women in the Third World who are working to promote the more equitable and active participation of women in the development plans and policies of their countries. Its publications are in Spanish, French and English and it has centres in Latin America and Asia and the Pacific as well as in Europe and North America. Women Working World-Wide links women working in the textile and garment industry in both the First and Third Worlds. TICE (Transnational Information Centre Exchange) reports trade union actions in transnational companies throughout the world. In addition to all these non-governmental information networks, there are the NGO/liaison services of the international bodies like the United Nations and the European Community and the World Federation of United Nations Associations, which is more a network than a federation.

It is, of course, the advent of the micro-computer which has made possible such large-scale networking for all kinds of voluntary and non-profit organisations. The micro-computer not only enables any organisation however small to store on disk the names, addresses, outline of main activities, needs, availabilities, publications and other information of all the network members; it allows access, if agreed, to as much of each other's information as each may wish to make public. From a central data base all partners can store what they want under standardised headings which have been agreed in advance. No further coordination is required apart from agreement on updating of information and revision of headings, unless joint action is to follow upon what is in the first instance no more than an extended information system. The use of electronic mail boxes and of electronic bulletin boards further extends the possibility of information exchange at very low cost and without the need for time-consuming travel and conferences. Of course, not all small Third World organisations of producers have electronic mail facilities, but the number who have is growing rapidly.

Alternative Trade Networks

Most of the networks which we have been looking at are concerned with information exchange, but the ATOs have begun to develop an increasingly extensive range of trading networks. But why a trade network? A trade network implies something more than a number of particular projects, linked together by a common catalogue, very much more than a one-off supply of tools and a market boost for the initial output of a group of producers in one of the least developed Third World countries.

A network, as we have defined it, is a continuous and continuing relationship linking its members not only to a common centre but to each other. Trade must comprise regular exchanges, whether by barter or by the use of a common currency. An alternative trade network must, therefore, offer a different set of relationships within the mainstream of trade in the world market. For these relationships to lead to the establishment of regular and continuous trade exchanges a trade development plan is required. Before drawing up such a plan there would need to be a period of initial exchanges between the First World ATO and the Third World organisation, which leads both sides to believe that a fruitful project can emerge from further cooperation.

An outline trade development plan is presented in the Box below. At the centre of such planning there must be people whom we have called 'networkers' or 'animateurs', who will make the links and see through the various stages of trade development.

To go beyond the most limited level of trade development, alternative trade planning between ATOs in the First World and their Third World partners must start from three basic assumptions: that trade should be built up to a scale which is normal in the mainstream commercial market; that trade development should be seen as a working partnership, all the partners sharing information and taking the major decisions jointly; that the ultimate aim is to move towards independence in terms of competence and financial viability. None of this means that there cannot be a division of responsibilities between the First World organisation and its Third World partners, with responsibility assigned for processing and packaging, for transport to a port, loading, shipping, importing and selling in the First World markets. In principle, an ATO from the First World does not seek to retain exclusive rights and will indeed encourage its Third World partners to engage directly in the market, either through trading with other Third World organisations or in the First World markets.

BOX 5. OUTLINE TRADE DEVELOPMENT PLAN

1. Market/Product desk study — to be carried out for each product establishing how to introduce it from a new supplier into the several markets that exist. Information to include:
   — prices
   — seasonal availability/ variability
   — import restrictions, tariffs etc.
   — importers'requirements,health andsafety,etc.
   — international standards and specifications and
     "organic"certification requirements
   — quality premiums
   — pre-shipment processing and packaging
   — transport procedures.
2. Local Study - to be carried out in the Third World country to confirm the desk study, paying attention to availabilities, storage and transport facilities, local markets, local procedures, national regulations, export licences etc.
3. Discussion of findings with the producers' organisation and joint work on preparing the development plan, with all the step necessary to start the exporting process, including:
   — indicative business plan -quantities, costs, prices
   — investment plan proposal
   — equipment selection (if not already decided) for
     a) production
     b) processing and packaging
     c) communications
   — commercial department structuring and staff training.
   — personnel selection and training.
4. Assuming 1-3 are mutually agreed, discussion can proceed to:
   — technical design
   — sourcing of equipment and installation
   — commissioning and training
   — establishing long-term links for the supply of consumable
     materials (for packaging etc.), spare parts and
     equipment maintenance services.
   — marketing possibilities.
5. Trial export, to provide training in
   — export documentation
   — insurance
   — health certificates
   — negotiating with essential intermediaries,
     e.g freight forwarders and shippers
   — monitoring of quality and acceptability to importer.
6. Review of the trial export, leading to:
   — review of business plan, timing, quantities, economies of scale etc.
   — agreement on long-term production plans
   — establishmentof long-termrelationships,

→

e.g. with international buyers, other NGOs
— training in sales negotiations
— setting up of market knowledge information system (including access to market information, prices, trends controls and regulations etc.) with possible use of electronic mail, fax etc.

We saw earlier how IFAT, the International Federation for Alternative Trade, had begun to coordinate the activities of ATOs in the First World and was building links with Third World partners. In the previous chapter we looked at schemes for an international trade clearing union and suggested that a start might be made with the alternative trade organisations. Now that we have looked at the way these work and the scale of their operations, we should be able to decide whether they do really offer the basis for a new system of fair trade inside the market. We are speaking here of non-governmental organisations (NGOs), but, if we are to envisage a major extension of alternative trade exchanges, the views of the nation-state governments in Third World countries will have to be taken into account. This is necessary not only because questions of import duties, export taxes, foreign currencies and trade balances have to be resolved, but because governments are in competition for allocations of aid funds. ATOs need funding for trade development work and there will be many rival claimants in every developing country for a share in these funds. Alternative trade has evolved from projects generated by First World ATOs working with organisations in Third World countries; but increasingly the initiative has come from the Third World. This is taking the alternative trade movement a step forward towards an international network. To take the next step of establishing a wholly new trading system would almost certainly imply international funding from United Nations organisations or possibly from the European Community.

There are in fact already a number of proposals under consideration both in the United Nations forum and in the European Community for consolidating the ATO networks into an alternative trade network. One such proposal is based on the possibility of funds becoming available from the UNCTAD Common Fund 'Second Window', which supports research and development for quality and productivity improvements in primary commodity production. It has been suggested that such funds could be used to finance NGO 'networkers' to engage in trade development projects and to provide a central clearing house for the exchange of information and research combined with a training centre for trade developers. Because the

Common Fund was set up with the express purpose of strengthening the position of Third World primary producers in the commodity markets, the several international commodity organisations must be involved in the allocation of funds, and claims to resources have to be argued out by the various producer countries. Only one example exists of such use of funds: a programme of research and development of jute sponsored by the International Jute Organisation. The purpose of the Common Fund, however, was that a more integrated and cooperative approach to the problems of primary producers could be achieved. Given that the money exists in the Fund, it is most unfortunate that more use has not been made of it and that the suggestion that some of the money be used by NGOs has not been taken up.

Another possibility for the expansion of ATO networks arises from the innovative commitments in the fourth Lomé Convention for trade development between the EEC and the ACP (African, Caribbean and Pacific) countries. These support 'policies of economic reorganisation (structural adjustment)', based on principles of specificity, local responsibility, equity and concern for the social dimension, food security and environmental protection, with 'much greater emphasis on . . . diversifying ACP economies', focusing especially on 'local enhancement of the value of ACP commodities through the development of processing, marketing, distribution and transport activities (PMDT)'. In the execution of these new policies, the Convention speaks of 'an intensification of dialogue in the programming of aid at both national and regional levels' and 'a further opening in the direction of *decentralised cooperation*, designed to facilitate wider participation by the population and give a wide range of non-governmental protagonists the chance to carry out their own initiatives within the framework of ACP-EEC cooperation.' In practical terms, with the extra finance of the Sixth European Development Fund (EDF), 'the Commission undertakes to cooperate with the ACP in the development, at an early date, of a trade development project' where 'the objective is to establish a focal point in Brussels so as to act as a catalyst and driving force in stimulating promotional work' in trade development and marketing.

It is proposed that this trade development centre should parallel the Centre for the Development of Industry (CDI) and should concentrate on agricultural and rural development. Its tasks would include commercial and market analysis, technical and scientific research relevant to trade development, assistance with trade development plans, information exchange between EEC/ACP projects, support for the initiation of trade development plans by 'networkers' from EEC and ACP non-governmental organisations, arranging for training and practical experience for 'networkers' and trade developers. It would seem to be essential that a centre in Europe should soon be followed by centres in each of the ACP regions, if the agreed aim of Lomé IV is to be achieved: 'to intensify dialogue in the programming of aid at both national and regional levels.' At the beginning of 1991 only the opening discussions had taken place in forwarding the Lomé IV commitment to 'a focal point . . . to act as a catalyst and driving force' and in the meantime EEC funds are being committed to Eastern Europe. Instead of seeing this as a diversion from the Third World, it could be seen as a valuable complement, if the suggestions made in the last chapter for a trade clearing union were to be followed up so as to link together the trade of all three worlds — First, Second and Third.

An Alternative Trade Clearing Union

These two proposals for trade development centres, based on ATO initiatives in the EEC/ACP regions and in other parts of the Third World, indicate the possibility of alternative expanding trading into a wider system. When we looked at the idea of a trade clearing union in the last chapter, the creation of such a scheme assumed some planning of trade between several nation-states with common interests, but we suggested that a start might be made with alternative trade organisations. Do these two proposals together offer a foundation for an alternative trade clearing union? The proposals have in common the use of NGOs, in this case mainly ATOs, as agents of trade development. The object is not so much to coordinate their activities from above, to which they would be unlikely to agree, but rather to find a common framework within which their separate networks might be unified. The ATOs have begun to establish their own forms of cooperation through IFAT (the International Federation for Alternative Trade). Their Third World partners are considering the establishment of a regional organisation. IFAT is already planning to establish its own information exchange, in part using electronic mail to record names and addresses of First and Third World organisations, lines of interest, products and markets, trading capacity, current and in prospect — all in accordance with agreed headings. It is possible, as the number of projects grows, that they will need to establish their own presence in the wholesale marketing system for certain major products with a small staff to act in the markets on behalf of all their members. But, impressive as this may sound, the ATOs do not have the resources to establish a framework for large-scale alternative trading of the kind we are envisaging.

Given the availability of extra resources, the next step forward should not be a difficult one. What is needed is a clearing house through which offers of products and bids for products could be cleared and likewise offers of tools and equipment and requirements of the same. Most ATOs in the First World and many of their partners in the Third World have computers and communicate by electronic mail. What is needed is a large-capacity central computer, with a small staff to operate it, accept subscriptions, see that the disks are appropriately stored for retrieval and make proposals for discussion and agreement on headings and sub-headings and other data specifications. ATOs wishing to take advantage of the facility would have to pay a subscription and indicate the range of information they wished to receive and to make available. As well as acting as an information exchange, the clearing house would receive product offers and bids by electronic mail and other forms of rapid communication. These would have to indicate precise specifications of designs, standards, prices, quantities, availabilities, deadlines for delivery, ports of loading, etc. These offers and bids could be processed by the computer for consideration by the parties communicating and they could appear on electronic bulletin boards for the notice of those interested.

The principles applied in creating a clearing union along these lines would be similar to those we considered in the last chapter. Information would be open to all but, in arriving at trade deals, first come would be first served. It would not be necessary, with a relatively small number of ATOs sharing similar principles of cooperation, or at least of non-profit competition, to limit the exchanges to bilateral deals. Multilateral deals could be achieved by using the computer to indicate a chain of linkages which fit together, using the process of trial and error (*tatonnement*), or by calling on the staff at the centre to suggest possible linkages, which members had not thought of or had not had time to investigate. Since all information would be open, there could be no monopoly positions which could be exploited without all becoming aware of what was going on. Members would agree on basic principles of operation including the eschewing of exclusive arrangements; and breach of these would lay members open to expulsion, subject to arbitration before an international court.

Here is an example, which I have used elsewhere. It is assumed that all the organisations involved are part of the ATOs' network of networks, but only those in the same country can make exchanges between themselves without using the clearing union. The organisations are, for simplicity of exposition, given the names of the country where they are established.

It can be seen that no bilateral deals are possible, but all the items which appear as 'offers' appear also in the 'wants' column. If the values of the various offers and wants are roughly similar, which is probably why they will have been picked out by the networkers, then exchanges can be organised by means of credit notes. Since these are in effect money, they

TABLE 16. EXAMPLE OF MULTILATERAL DEALS

Country	Offers	Wants (or will take)
INDIA 'A'	Bicycles	Woodworking tools
INDIA 'B'	Jute bags	Fishing tackle
NICARAGUA	Coffee beans	Bicycles
ARGENTINA	Corned beef	Jute bags
UK	Woodworking tools	Corned beef
NETHERLANDS	Fishing Tackle	Coffee beans

can be used for additional purchases or sales through the clearing union to make up the differences in values of direct exchanges, but they can also, as in the Goseco proposal, be accumulated as a currency reserve held by each subscribing member, which can be used for future purchases.

The last and most important role for a clearing union is that of adjusting and regulating financial balances. In matching up bids and offers, prices would have to be used in line with international markets in convertible currencies, even if such currency is used only as a unit of account. To move beyond barter and bilateral exchanges in countertrade, a system of regular clearances of accounts would need to be established. This could be assisted if each member made available a line of credit up to a certain sum, roughly in relation to the trade which they expected to do. Organisations from the First World would be required to offer more than those from the Third World, some of whom would not be required to offer anything. Accounts would be balanced over a period, either bilaterally, i.e. by simple barter with or without a countertrading cash element, or multilaterally by three-cornered, four-cornered or multilateral swaps. The central office staff would recommend suitable ways of clearing accounts, so that deficits did not mount up.

With these suggestions for an alternative trade clearing union we come to the end of our proposals for initiating changes in the structure of world trade, with the aim of strengthening the position of Third World producers, so that they may expect to obtain a larger piece of the action. For these to become more than wild utopian dreams, it will not be enough to create new structures within which new and more equal exchanges can take place. Side by side with this, a change of attitude will have to take place among the consumers of the First World. The very existence of ATOs in North America, Western Europe, Japan and Australasia testifies to the birth of such a change of attitude. There is still a long way to go. Alternative trade is a baby among giants. The final chapter of this book will examine what we can all do to suckle and protect that baby.

The problem of changing structures and changing consciousness is the old problem of the chicken and the egg: which comes first? The answer in human problems is practice; and generally a crisis forcing a change of practice in which consciousness changes as new structures are built to respond to the crisis. There is no doubt about the environmental crisis, nor about the debt crisis for the Third World and above all looms the crisis of nuclear armaments. This threefold crisis challenges human capacities as never before. Can we look for a major change in consciousness, and in the big economic structures which we have been examining, to be achieved through the practice of alternative trade exchanges such as we have here proposed? Could they be copied on a larger scale? The last chapter will show what has already begun in the practice of organic production and fair trade, as a foundation which could be built on. It will be for readers to decide whether this is indeeed a way forward towards ending the world-wide inequalities which are reproduced and reinforced every day by the way in which the international trading system now operates.

Notes

There is a history of Oxfam's first years written by Mervyn Jones, *Two Years of Corn — Oxfam in Action*, Hodder & Stoughton, 1965. The report of the 1988 conference 'Fair Trade' sponsored by TWIN in association with Oxfam Trading and Traidcraft is available from TWIN at 5-11 Worship Street, London EC2A 2BH. Oxfam's address is 274 Banbury Road, Oxford, OX2 7DZ. Traidcraft's address is Kingsway, Gateshead, Tyne & Wear, NE11 0NE. Both publish regular reports of their activities. TWIN's quarterly newsletter *The Network* carries regular reports on its projects and on the initiatives of UNCTAD and the EEC/ACP. The address for IFAT is PO Box 2703, 1000 CS Amsterdam, Netherlands. The clearing union example is taken from M. Barratt Brown, *European Union: Fortress or Democracy?*, Spokesman Books, 1991, Chapter 7, 'Networks: An Interface for Alternative Trade'.

12. WHAT CAN BE DONE NOW?

At the end of this long journey through the corridors of government, the commissions of the United Nations, the markets of commodity dealers, the complexities of clearing unions and the networks of alternative trade organisations, we come back to the jar of Mexican tropical honey from which we started. If we choose to buy our honey or some craft products from a Mexican women's cooperative, we are doing something that is intended to help people in the Third World to develop their own lives with somewhat greater resources and without so much danger to their environment. Perhaps, as a household, we make one per cent, or even five per cent, of our purchases from ATOs, but what about the 95 per cent — all the rest of our purchases? Sometimes, we may have looked to see if oranges come from South Africa and, if so, we may have chosen not to buy them. We may have begun to look for 'organic' on the washing-up liquid, for unleaded petrol or for 'ozone-friendly' on the aerosol can. But most of the time we do not ask who grew our fruit and vegetables, and prepared them, fresh or frozen, packed or canned, who gathered our coffee or tea or cocoa beans or grapes, who dug our peanuts or potatoes — for what wages and under what conditions. We do not think about the trees that were cut down to make the baby's nappies and all our packaging and wrappings or to give pasture to the cattle which supplied our meat, what food crops were replaced to grow the meal which fed the pigs and chickens for our bacon and eggs, what deserts were created to produce the cotton for our shirts and dresses, what fertilisers and herbicides and pesticides were used to grow the grains for our bread and cakes and biscuits and how the fieldworkers and local communities were poisoned by their application. Except when Friends of the Earth or Greenpeace stir our consciences, we give these things but passing thoughts. Yet, if it were easy to choose a less, rather than a more, harmful product, we would surely do so.

Green Consumerism

The awful threat of disaster for the whole of our planet — of resource depletion, acid rain, the greenhouse effect, deforestation, desertification, loss of wild species, destruction of the ozone layer — is slowly sinking into the consciousness of most people in the First World. The implications for the Third World of these threats to the environment have always been worse. For, while the First World, with only one-fifth of the population, consumes two-thirds of the earth's resources, the effects fall most heavily on the four-fifths of the population which is in the Third World. It is to pay their debts to the First World that Brazilians and Indonesians are cutting down their tropical forests to sell to overseas paper mills and grazing cattle for meat exports or planting trees for export crops like rubber and coffee. It is to build cars for the First World that iron ore and copper, tin and nickel and bauxite are mined, leaving behind a trail of devastation and pollution of rivers and seas. To pay their debts and catch up in the growth race, the Second World of the centrally planned economies was equally caught up in the same system of needless exploitation of the earth's riches, worse even in its results than in the Third World. It is the same wherever economic growth has taken place. Air pollution levels in Third World cities like Bangkok, Bombay, Buenos Aires, Cairo, Calcutta, Manila, Mexico City, Rio de Janeiro, Singapore, are as bad as those in the First World. Seoul's eight million people have one million cars.

Green consciousness is spreading as more and more evidence comes to light of the results of our wanton assault upon the eco-system of our planet. Green parties have appeared in Western Europe and North America, and have begun to win sizeable proportions of the popular vote — 15 per cent in the latest UK elections to the European Parliament. Organisations like Friends of the Earth and Greenpeace and the Worldwide Fund for Nature hammer home the message through their courageous exploits, their campaigns and their literature, to make us aware that every day and in every continent irreparable damage is being done to the land, the waters and the air we breathe and to all living creatures, plants and animals, with whom we share this planet of ours. Most First World governments have begun to express some concern for the environment, and even Mrs Thatcher on appropriate occasions wore green dresses. There is increasing inter-government discussion of environmental issues and the European Community has begun to lay down standards for sulphur emission in the air, sewage disposal in the sea, nitrate pollution in the rivers, and adulterants in the food we eat.

Much of this is the result of the pressure on governments and on the giant companies from consumer groups. Their demands have led to the appearance of organic claims on the packaging of food products and 'green' labels on washing and cleaning liquids. Most of the regulations are still voluntary rather than mandatory, but publications like the British government's *Green Grow the Labels-O!* are having the effect of forcing manufacturers to come into line with the new consumer demands. The regulation of labels is essential because the first result of the growth of green consciousness has been to produce widespread claims that products are 'environmentally friendly' and a proliferation of labels on products bearing pictures of idyllic country scenes to suggest kindness to the environment. The bogus claims will be checked thanks to the appearance of magazines like *The Green Guide to Shopping*, and *The Ethical Consumer*, which are highly critical of those who make such claims without justification. Green consciousness still leaves a large gap in consumer consciousness where the Third World is involved, but green labelling does indicate a promising way forward for those who are concerned to create the basis for fairer trade exchanges and people-friendly production.

The link between environmental issues and Third World development has been recognised now for some years. A first meeting of the CIDIE (the Committee for International Development Institutions on the Environment) was held in 1980. Its aim has been to 'promote concern for the inclusion of environmental sensitivity in the development assistance activities of international financing institutions'. These include the main United Nations, European Community and NGO development banks and funds. The establishment by the United Nations of the World Commission on Environment and Development, under the chair of the Norwegian Prime Minister, Mrs. Brundtland, and the publication of its report, *Our Common Future* in 1987, finally forged the links between development and the environment. 'The planet's main environmental problem,' the report insists, 'is also its main development problem.' As a result of the report's findings, the concept of 'sustainable development' has come to be debated. The detail of the argument cannot concern us here, but two of its conclusions are apposite.

The first conclusion is that the peoples of the First World have to change their ways: 'Sustainable global development requires that those who are more affluent adopt life styles within the planet's ecological means.' This refers not only to their own lives but to their relationship with the Third World. 'Two conditions must be satisfied,' the report stipulates, 'before international economic exchanges can become beneficial for all involved. The sustainability of eco-systems on which the global economy depends must be guaranteed, and the economic partners must be satisfied that the basis of the exchange is equitable; relationships that are unequal and based on dominance of one kind or another are not a sound and durable basis for independence. For many developing countries neither condition is met.'

The second conclusion is the importance of channelling resources for Third World development through grassroots organisations to 'enhance both the environment and the productivity of the resource sectors'. Examples given are 'reafforestation and fuel wood development; watershed protection, soil conservation, rehabilitation of irrigation projects; small-scale agriculture, low cost sanitation, conversion of crops into fuel. . . . Experience shows that the most effective efforts of this type are small projects with maximum grassroots participation. . . . Non-governmental Organisations', the report concludes, 'and private community groups can often provide an efficient and effective alternative to public agencies in the delivery of programmes and projects. Moreover, they can sometimes reach target groups that public agencies cannot.'

A Fair Trade Mark

All this implies the need for a massive expansion of just those cooperative links between NGOs in the First and Third World, which we looked at in the last chapter, and the extension of green consumerism into a much broader movement for fair trade. This is the objective of a group of British ATOs, associated with *New Consumer*, which describes itself as 'an independent, not-for-profit organisation mobilising consumer power for positive economic, social and environmental change'. This group is working on the establishment of a 'Fair Trade Mark' — in their own words: 'to give the world's poor a fairer share of the wealth they help to create.' Alternative trading has found for itself a niche on the margins of the market. The group plans to move the concept from the margins to the mainstream. They feel encouraged by the results of a Gallup poll in Britain in June 1989, and believe that the British public is ready for the introduction of what they call 'a development friendly consumer guarantee in the economic mainstream'. The survey established three clear attitudes in the public:

(1) As a long-term solution to world poverty, 45 per cent favoured fairer trade, compared with 37 per cent who favoured government aid and six per cent charitable donations;

(2) If a higher price meant better wages for the producers, 79 per cent would pay more for a product;

(3) Of these 79 per cent, when buying a packet of tea, 26 per cent would pay 10p more, 44 per cent would pay 20p more and 23 per cent 50p more.

Analysed by sex, age, social class and region, the results remained remarkably consistent.

The general aims of the Fair Trade guarantee are social justice and sustainable development. Within these general aims the criteria for purchasing and the terms and conditions of exchange are being discussed by the group stage by stage, first with Third World producer organisations to discover what products are available under prescribed conditions, what can realistically be achieved and how criteria can be evaluated in relation to identified products. The second stage is to assess consumer attitudes and likely responses in the First World. Finally, it is necessary to determine the potential for involving mainstream retailers in the First World to ensure maximum availability of fairly traded products. Criteria are being set in two parts: a base line that incorporates the most essential factors and a weighted set of desirable factors which could be met over a period of time. The criteria selected which should be followed in choosing products for the 'Fair Trade Mark' appear in the box below:

BOX 6. FAIR TRADE CRITERIA

1. What Kind of Products

a) a product that is traditionally grown in the Third World and of major importance as a source of foreign earnings: e.g. bananas, cocoa, coconuts, coffee, cotton, palm oil,rubber, tea, timber; but not: petroleum, gas, metals and minerals, because the supply chain is not direct to the final consumer, but the product is consumed only after complex processing;

b) a product that enters the mainstream market as a product itself, like tea or coffee, and not as a small component of something else; but cocoa would be acceptable as it forms 60 per cent of chocolate.

2. What Requirements in Product Processing

a) local value added: as much value as possible should be added in the country of origin: e.g. cotton garments preferred to cotton;

b) labour intensiveness: a product that by its nature involves much labour in production and little capital: e.g. craft products, nuts, tea, coffee, cocoa;

c) healthy: not a product that is potentially injurious to the health of consumers like tobacco or coca, or to the health of the producers , e.g through use of sprays;

d)human rights: not a product of slave or prison labour, orproduced in conditions of gross exploitation.

3. What Relation to Other Crops and the Environment

a) not displacing crops on land needed for food consumption;

b) preferably intercropped with other crops to avoid mono-culture;

c) no use of banned pesticides or herbicides, no excessive use of chemical fertiliser, no damage to the environment leadingtotopsoil losses, deforestation, fresh water scarcity or pollution.

4. What Local Producers to Favour

a) organised small producer associations;

b) producer cooperatives;

c) state or private plantations where ILO conventions or recommendations on labour standards for rural workers are properly adhered to.

5. Which Countries to Favour

a) not South Africa, while apartheid lasts;

b) special favour to organisations discriminated against by oppressive governments;

c) special favour to countries — seeking to diversify their products; — damaged by First World trade embargoes and protectionist measures;

d) special favour to areas where large-scale migration or natural disasters have created severe problems.

→

---

6. Other Criteria for the Fair Trade Mark

These all concern the exchange mechanisms which purchasers and suppliers would have to follow in making contracts:

a) Price — mutually agreed with producers for each harvest cycle and not following the ups and downs of commodity exchanges;

b) Commitment to order a certain guaranteed amount from one source, preferably over a number of years;

c) Guaranteed advance of payment agreed before purchases are made;

d) Information freely available on technical and marketing, in order to improve quality and delivery and range of markets;

e) Quality commitment on the quantities agreed and adherence to delivery times specified.

Should these requirements seem to be unrealistically strict and wide-ranging, an example is taken from the Max Havelaar Foundation Coffee Seal. This Dutch charity issues its seal of approval to any brand of coffee that fulfils its criteria. These include sourcing from organisations which represent the interests of small farmers, are democratic in structure and practice, and produce coffee that meets the requirements of the Dutch market. Such coffee comes from Tanzania and Nicaragua and from a number of cooperative farms in Mexico, the Dominican Republic, Zaire and elsewhere. Importers guarantee to buy direct from these sources and agree to a bottom-line price (up to 10 per cent above the world market price), and they underwrite legitimate additional costs and agree to prefinancing (up to 60 per cent) for long-term contracts. Coffee is distributed through regular retail outlets as well as through ATOs. The final price is 15 per cent to 20 per cent above the usual retail price. Small and medium-sized roasters and major supermarket chains take the coffee. Twenty-four brands carry the seal, five sold through regular supermarkets and the rest through ATOs. Penetration of the Dutch coffee market by Max Havelaar has risen to three per cent, and it is hoped to raise this to five per cent. As 72 per cent of the market is held by one giant distributor, the challenge does not seem to be so very big; but it offers a Fair Trade alternative and has encouraged Max Havelaar to look at other products besides coffee, and other ATOs to think about similar schemes.

THE FAIRTRADE FOUNDATION

Guarantees
a **better deal**
for Third World
Producer

Fairtrade

This Charter sets out the principles for responsible sourcing of products from Third World countries. The Charter stands for:

• Buying from responsible producers or suppliers, who provide fair remuneration and conditions of employment, including the right to organise.

• Paying a fair price, which reflects the costs of production and quality of the product plus a margin for investment and development.

• Providing financial credit where necessary to protect the producer against production uncertainties and financial exploitation.

• Encouraging equal rewards for women and men.

• Identifying and encouraging environmentally sustainable production.

• Establishing stable trading relationships on the basis of quality, continuity and mutual support.

Perhaps more surprising has been the response of the giant trading companies to discussions which the Fair Trade Foundation has initiated with them. Awareness of the shopping public's increasing concern about health, animal welfare, environmental damage and genetic engineering was widespread, but ethical trading relations with the Third World were also being recognised as a factor in consumer choice. Not all the traders were interested in discussing fair trade, but the big retailers have been very interested and some at least have regarded the proposal of a Fair Trade Mark as an opportunity rather than a threat. The opportunity, of course, is the chance of gaining a competitive advantage, and this has to be seen as sustainable. Otherwise, ethical considerations become simply another normal cost of doing business, which is how some see their business anyway. There is a change in attitudes to food, which started in the United States and is spreading. What used to be called 'food fads' are now taken seriously. Food products frequently carry the information on the packaging that they contain no artificial additives. Boycott campaigns in the United States have led to major changes in purchasing policies, like the commitment of Burger King not to buy rain forest beef.

Consumer power in the United States has for long been a force for retailers to reckon with. It is beginning to be recognised as such in the United Kingdom. Under the heading 'Now the supermarkets do what we tell them', a report in *The Independent* of 9 March 1991 announced that the Institute of Grocery Distribution had set up a Policy Council to discuss a concerted response to the challenge thrown up by the 'ethical consumer'. The Council is said to be made up of British supermarket chains and key companies in the food and drink industry such as Nestlé, Unilever and Kraft. The chief executive, Dr John Beaumont, told reporters that the industry had to prepare for 'what seems likely to be a completely different business environment' where ordinary people have 'new ideas and concepts outside the basic concerns of every day survival and sustenance.' Dr. Beaumont conceded that 25 per cent of the council's membership may 'merely be going through the motions', but insisted that '75 per cent is genuinely interested in trying to build a keener sense of social responsibility . . . in the name of humanity as well as good business.'

How far the food traders would be prepared to go along the road described above will only become clear with time. Is there a real danger that standards will be diluted and the whole concept of fairer trade discredited? Or should all moves in the right direction be seen as victories? For the time being, the chief limitation on the expansion of fair trade, as on the spread of organic products, is the small scale of the operations of suppliers. To take an example, The Body Shop has built an enviable reputation on being 'animal friendly' and 'nature friendly'. Its management is now showing a great interest in also being 'people friendly'. In looking for certain vegetable oils produced in Africa by associations of small producers, the company has requirements for their chains of shops which far exceed the current capacity of these producers. The large scale of operations of the supermarkets presents even greater problems for small producers.

A Consumers' Union

However far the big commodity dealers and retailers are prepared to move towards the ideals of fair trade and sustainable development, it is clear that there will remain the absolute necessity for watchdog bodies to monitor their performance and for alternative traders to co-exist in order to offer a challenge to what are often the monopolistic positions of the giant companies. What form should this combination of watchdog and competitor take? It is not a very large step for all of us as consumers to go from using the Fair Trade Mark to joining a consumers' union. This should not be confused with a consumer council, such as those that are established by government in many First World countries where industries producing goods and services are run by the state. These councils, like the Coal Consumers' Council and Railway Users Council in Britain, are dominated by the largest industrial consumers. The sheer scale of these large consumers' demands quite dwarfs the claims of the millions of small consumers. A more representative body of ordinary consumers is the association of subscribers to a magazine and information service like the Consumers Association's *Which?* in Britain. There is indeed an International Organisation of Consumer Unions (IOCU). These watchdog organisations offer an essential service and their total absence in the centrally planned economies of Eastern Europe and the Soviet Union was but one aspect of the lack of concern for consumer interests in a command economy. These bodies uphold the four basic consumer rights — the right to safety, the right to be informed, the right to choose and the right to be heard — and have added four more — the right to satisfaction of basic needs, the right to redress, the right to consumer education and the right to a healthy environment. Wide though these rights range, the idea of a Fair Trade Mark goes beyond the tests of personal satisfaction, cost effectiveness and health and safety, to take in the concerns of the producers, their satisfaction, health and safety as well as the environment. A consumers' union, as it is proposed here, takes social responsibility one step further — to act in association with selected groups of producers.

The idea of adding a producer interest to a consumers' union is that subscribers should join an organisation which actually supplies, or organises the supply of, goods and services tested on fair trading principles. It is an interesting reflection of the way that history repeats itself that the origins of the cooperative movement in Britain lay as much in the rejection of adulterated food as in the rejection of capitalist exploitation. The dream after 1834 was of one great national cooperative union to replace the failed national trade union of Robert Owen. The reality was of 'pure, wholesome, unadulterated flour, meal, etc.', which the Rochdale Equitable Pioneers Society offered its members. There was, moreover, in the early linking of cooperative producers and cooperative retail societies a deliberate attempt, in the words of the pioneers, 'to bring the producer and the consumer into more immediate contact'. Sadly, producer cooperatives never grew much beyond the printing and shoe-making industries until their recent revival, and the retail and wholesale cooperative societies which flourished in the UK up to the Second World War, have in the last 40 years failed to keep up with the big, privately owned chain stores. The continuing success of retail cooperatives in Scandinavia and in Italy suggests that the failure in the UK is not endemic to the cooperative principle.

Support for the idea of a national consumers' union with a producer connection was revived by Diane Elson in an article in *New Left Review* at the end of 1988, responding to an ongoing argument between Alec Nove and Ernest Mandel about 'the economics of a feasible socialism'. The argument has become all the more important because of the subsequent total collapse of central planning in Eastern Europe and the Soviet Union. Both Nove and Mandel rejected the command economy of top-downwards orders by state bureaucrats which governed every detail of the input and output of state-owned enterprises. But, there were important differences between the two. Nove, who has since moved back to the Soviet Union as a government adviser, advocated a market system, socialised only by income redistribution in favour of the most disadvantaged members of society and by a broad area of social provision in education, health and housing. Mandel proposed a return to Marx's vision of the free association of work groups, coordinated by a national assembly of workers to make the major sectoral allocation of resources and ensure a measure of reserves for replacement for wear and tear and investment in future development. Diane Elson offered a third way. The state would regulate the market through an economic planning office, a regulator of public enterprise and a prices and wages commission. These would set the norm for self-managed enterprises, which would themselves be subject to the pressure of a consumers' union in the market as a counterweight to trade union power in the management of enterprises. All this was on the assumption of predominantly social ownership of the main means of production, distribution and exchange, whether through government bodies, national or local, or through cooperatives and other associations of small-scale producers.

What is of value to us here is the idea of what should properly be called a consumer-producer union, which would not only provide information based on compulsory registration and reporting by all producing enterprises, but would commission and execute productive activities to meet consumers' needs. This would apply to all consumer goods but also to energy sources, transport, housing, etc. An earlier version of Diane Elson's paper had suggested more than one consumers' union, each having its own network of suppliers. The advantages of having several consumer-producer unions, to which any consumer could belong, are several. First, a plurality of suppliers ensures competition and some very necessary attention of each to costs and efficiency. Second, there are real differences in the levels at which our needs are appropriately met, some by local services, some by district or county suppliers, some on a regional scale, some by national organisations and others still from foreign countries. Third, the essence of networks operating directly between consumers and producers is that a strong element of mutual trust binds them together. This is somewhat similar to the network of suppliers to the giant transnational companies, including the big chain stores. Although the links here are conduits of profit flowing to the centre, the forging of these links requires a respect for contracts. Fourth, and finally, the establishment of some prototypes of consumer-producer linkages in the world market provides a starting point for building a different trading system, which does not require a major challenge to the structure of markets, let alone any revolutionary action to overthrow the existing order.

A Model of a Decentralised Economy

There is a special advantage in thinking of networks of consumer-producer unions at several levels — local, district, county, regional, national, federal and international. It is that elected authorities at levels below that of the nation-state are more responsive to local initiatives. In the market the rich have more pull than the poor; in elections each man and woman has one vote. But, nation-state governments are great centralisers of power. International institutions are little better, because they are nearly always, like the United Nations, associations of states and not of peoples.

Let us for a moment imagine how our needs might be met through a plurality of consumers' unions at different levels, each linked to a network of producers. The following is how I imagine a decentralised model of the economy.

At the lowest level of the housing estate or village or block of flats, it is envisaged that groups would form to elect community councils. These would then have responsibility for certain services — cleaning, laundering, gardening, plumbing and minor building repairs — for which they could make a charge, and also for renting out premises for workshops and retail outlets, shops and restaurants, from which they would receive an income to use as they saw fit, to improve the environment, for recreation grounds, parks, creches, etc. Through horizontal linkages they would network with similar estates and villages and blocks of flats in wards and districts including the surrounding countryside, both to provide appropriate services in housing, health, education, rubbish collection, footpaths, swimming pools, larger parks and playing fields at that level; and so to draw upon those enterprises producing mainly for local needs — fruit and vegetables, bakeries, housing materials, repair shops, etc. Contracts and prices would then be the subject of negotiation on quality and service between representatives of the workers, the groups of households and the elected local authority at district level. These authorities would of course also need to obtain supplies for their activities from outside the district. This could be done by building links with enterprises whose products suited their needs. By adding here the element of networking, these links could be strengthened into firm and continuing relationships allowing for forward planning beyond a single purchase or contract. This happens now, where public purchasing officers have found suppliers that they can rely on to understand their special needs. District authorities could also help to finance specialised networks of groups of people such as ethnic minorities who want to develop provision for their own particular needs and tastes. These could include many of the organisations that are now involved in alternative trade.

In this model the communities and districts form the real building blocks of decentralised power with their own elected councils and much extended responsibilities. For, it is at this level that people can meet each other and get to know each other's interests, share common facilities and feel a common responsibility for the care and protection of the neighbourhood. District and community councils can do much to strengthen social provision for all. But in the provision of personal and household needs we shall have to bring a higher level of power to bear, where large numbers can be deployed to make up for individual financial weakness. Cities and counties comprise populations of several million and it is to them that we must look for the necessary power to influence household provision so that the needs of the poorer households are catered for.

At the level of the city and the county we are not only dealing with a much larger population and with health, education, police, fire brigades and public transport appropriate to that scale, but there will be productive enterprises, factories, mines and quarries, refineries and the like which have a national as well as an international market. It would be reasonable to imagine loosely, vertically integrated competing networks being based on cities and counties. In this case the power of a city or county authority would be enough to ensure that suppliers inside the network catered equally for the full range of income groups. Regional differences in income and in tastes could then be allowed for, as several of the supermarket chains are already beginning to recognise. If cities and counties build up their own networks of suppliers, there is no reason that they should not link with neighbouring cities and counties to widen their network of households, communities and supplying enterprises.

When we reach the level of the nation-state, the question arises of the relationship between, on the one hand, the networks and the enterprises to which they are linked, and on the other, the arrangements to be made for allocating resources between regions, between sectors and between consumption, investment and international trade. Setting the parameters should surely be the limit of central responsibility, whether this is exercised by a state or federal body. For clearing the payments of international trade we have to envisage the need for a much wider international structure than a federation. Within these general parameters of resource allocation, networks should be free to make their own linkages and compete for business. The networks could not be said to be effective competing traders if they could not set their own prices and make their own investments. If there were a great plurality of these networks for households to belong to, and if they were self-financing, not only enjoying the income of grants and subscriptions but also the income of their networking activities in fees, commissions and profit margins, since they would be full trading organisations, they would have as much power as the giant companies today — but they would be subject to the democratic control of their members.

There remains the question of the relationship of the producing enterprises and the networks to the universal international system of resource allocation. Some of the enterprises may be quite large, supplying several, or even many, networks. They will want to have direct relations with the allocating centre. Even if this is not a nation-state it will need to have the capacity to set norms for the operation of enterprises and to see that they are observed. The great remaining problem is the necessity of imagining an international regulator and allocator of resources that does not replicate the bureaucracies of nation-states and of existing federations of states. Given the plurality of networks which is envisaged here, effective international representation of these networks, or of groups of networks, would have to be provided for. The setting of parameters for the operation of both networks and enterprises seems likely to imply something more continuous than occasional rounds of negotiation. One solution to this problem would be a world economic parliament, based on the networks, a second Chamber of Peoples to complement the United Nations General Assembly, which is based on geographical nation-state constituencies.

It is in some model of decentralised democracy, such as outlined above, that one can most easily imagine the emergence of an alternative world trading system; but the argument of this chapter is that a start might be made with a number of consumer-producer unions which deliberately link consumers and producers in the First and Third Worlds. In making such a start we have suggested that the role of non-governmental organisations can be crucial. At some stage in their development, all networks of NGOs are going to need to have the financial support of government powers of taxation and the political influence of government authority over trading practices. Such financial and political support would make possible a broad extension of the kind of policies we looked at under the Fair Trade Mark and would ensure that suppliers met the needs, not only of those who can afford higher prices and visits to hypermarkets out of town, but also of the poorer citizens of the First World, who do not have cars or the money to pay extra for higher priced goods. The one significant variation in the response to the Fair Trade Mark survey was that old-age pensioners were less willing to pay extra for tea bags. Fair trade has to be fair to those who are most disadvantaged, in both the First and Third Worlds, by the insensitive working of the market, whether they be producers or consumers.

Consumer and Producer Unity

The uneven development of the world economy has been gathering momentum for at least 400 years. In the year 1600 the variation in living standards in different parts of the world was not very great, although within each country the gap between the rich and the poor was wide. Since the slave trade and the subsequent accumulation of capital in Europe and North America, the poor have got poorer as the rich have got richer. Only the rise of new centres of accumulation in what were once European settlements, and most recently in Japan and South East Asia and in part in Eastern Europe and the Soviet Union, has prevented the polarisation of wealth and poverty from becoming self-destructive. We have seen in the last decade that the gap is once more widening dangerously. What can be produced with all the new skills of modern technology cannot be sold. Productive capacity has leapt ahead of purchasing power. A great ball and chain of debt holds down more than one-half of the world's people, while the rich employ their wealth in idle luxury, useless speculation and the purchase of each other's assets.

In this book we have looked at many ways to equalise the bargaining power between rich and poor in the world's markets. We have searched for compensatory mechanisms to correct the unequal balance between the First and Third Worlds. We have done this not only on account of social justice but because the economic system has ceased to work on its own terms and has generated a form of exploitation of the earth's resources that is unsustainable. But, it has been like Ptolemy adding epicycles to correct his calculations within an earth-centred system, when all the time the earth was revolving round the sun. For far too long money has been put at the centre of the economic system and human beings have had to circulate around the accumulation of money. If we could but put people at the centre and make money their servant, the problems we have addressed in this book could be solved. But the theme of the last part of the book is that such a reorientation can be achieved, not by dreaming dreams of how it could be, but by practising alternatives for how it is.

Decentralisation of economic decision-making and ensuring that authorities are made accountable to the people for their actions is where we need to start. But such democratic models have generally been based either on workers' control at the work place or on consumer power in the market. The fact is that the two have to be combined. Markets which split us into two halves — into producers and consumers — have to be modified so that we can once more become whole. We have suggested that this can best be achieved by networking between a plurality of forms of enterprise, social and individual, public and private, cooperative as well as competing, at many levels and in many directions. We have also argued that there is a crucial role for voluntary activity on elected councils of workers and of consumers and in non-governmental organisations. This is not to degrade or dismiss the value of professionalism in trade and welfare any more than in government and industry. But human capacities are so much greater than we ever allow for, and the aim must be to encourage them to develop to the full. Failure to do this means that we are all truly impoverished, and that the frustrations of those whose capacities are unfulfilled will only serve to provide the kindling for explosions of violence and the incentive for military adventures. With nuclear arsenals in many countries, which could blow up the whole world, we have to find the means to satisfy expectations which the advances of technology have aroused.

Such a fulfilment of human capacities has to be the ultimate objective of a new economic order, and all our attempts to establish fairer trade relations between the peoples of the First and Third Worlds have to be judged against our success in achieving this wider purpose. As we concluded in the last chapter, we shall only create a new economic order by beginning to build new structures in response to the crisis we all face. The threat of disaster to the very eco-system of the planet and the deteriorating situation of millions of the poorest people on earth sets a challenge which the human race has somehow to find the capacity to meet. The conclusion of this book is that it will be by new forms of cooperation, and not by relying solely on competition, that this will be done. We cannot now foresee what the new structures will be. But we can be sure that they will only be of lasting value, if they are both ecologically sustainable and able to offer a fair share of the resources of the earth to all its inhabitants.

Notes

Jonathon Porritt's *Seeing Green: The Politics of Ecology Explained*, Blackwell, 1987, is the best introduction to the green case. The *Green Guide to Shopping* is available from COMAG, Tavistock Road, West Drayton, England. The *Ethical Consumer* is published by ECRA Publishing Ltd, 100 Gretney Walk, Moss Side, Manchester, M15 5ND. The Brundtland Report, *Our Common Future*, 1987, is published by Oxford University Press. The address of *New Consumer* is 52 Elswick Road, Newcastle upon Tyne, NE4 6JH. A useful book on 'red' and 'green' links is

Ecology and Socialism by Martin Ryle, Radius Hutchinson, 1988. The quotations from my writings on a decentralised model of the economy come from *European Union: Fortress or Democracy* ?, Spokesman Books, 1991.

Note: The Fairtrade Foundation is an initiative of alternative trading organisations, development agencies, cooperatives and research groups, providing an independent guarantee of a better deal for the people who grow, process or manufacture products from developing countries. Council members: CAFOD, Christian Aid, New Consumer, OXFAM, Traidcraft Exchange, World Development Movement.

ANNEXE: ALTERNATIVE TRADING ORGANISATIONS

United Kingdom

ASSEFA
75 Cleveland Road
London N1 3ES

BIASHARA
47 Colston Street
Bristol BS1 5AX

Christian Aid
35 Lower Marsh
London SE1 7RL

CIIR
Unit 3, Canonbury Yard
190A New North Road
London N1 7BJ

Coda International Training
7B Broad Street
Nottingham NG1 3AJ

CRS Political Committee
8 Alma Street
London NW5 3DJ

Daily Bread COOP
The Old Laundry
Bedford Road
Northampton NN4 0AD

Equal Exchange
29 Nicolson Square
Edinburgh, Scotland
EH8 3BX

Essential Trading
Unit 3 Lodge Causeway
Trading Estates, Fishponds
Bristol BS16 3JB

The Ethical Consumer
ECRA Publishing Ltd
16 Nicholas Street
Manchester M1 4EJ

The Food Commission
102 Gloucester Place
London W1H 3DA

Green City Wholefoods
23 Fleming Street
Glasgow, Scotland
G31 1PH

Highland Wholefoods Workers' Coop
Unit 6B, 13 Harbour Road
Longman Estate
Inverness, Scotland
IV1 1SY

ICOM Ltd
Vassali House
20 Central Road
Leeds LS1 6OE

ICOM London
18 Ashwin Street
London E8 3DL

New Consumer Ltd
52 Elswick Road
Newcastle-upon-Tyne NE4 6JH

Oxfam Trading
Murdock Road
Bicester
Oxon OX6 7RF

Shared Earth
Abbey Self Storage
30 Lawrence Street
York YO1 3BN

Shared Interest
52 Elswick Road
Newcastle-upon-Tyne NE4 6JH

Suma Wholefoods
Unit AX1
Dean Clough Industrial Park
Halifax HX3 5AN

Swindon Pulse Wholefood Co-op
27 Curtis Street
Swindon, Wilts SN1 5JU

Traidcraft Exchange
Kingsway
Gateshead
Tyne and Wear NE11 ONE

Tropical Forest Products
Felinfach
Talybont
Aberystwyth, Dyfed SY24 5DJ

Wholesome Trucking
Unit 9 Higgs Industrial Estate
2 Herne Hill Road
London SE24 OAU

World Development Movement
25 Beehive Place
London SW9 7QR
Rest of the North

ACRA
Via Breda 54
20126 Milan
Italy

Afristar Ltd
Kaivokatu 10B
00100 Helsinki
Finland

Alternativ Handel
Kampengt 16
PO Box 2802 Toyen
0608 Oslo 6
Norway

Alternativ Handel
Linnegatan 13-21
Goteborg 413 04
Sweden

Alter Trade Japan
2F Takenoko Building
2-1-1 Nishi Waseda
Ooizumi Nerima-Ku
Shinjuku-ku
Tokyo, Japan 162

Bridgehead Inc.
20 James Street
Ottawa, Ontario K2P 0T6
Canada

Butik Salam
Brandts Passage 34
DK-5000 Odense C
Denmark

CAA Trading
PO Box 184
Kilkenny SA 5009
Australia

Caritas Switzerland
Zentralstrasse 18
CH-6003 Lucerne
Switzerland

Co-op America
2100 M Street NW Suite 310
Washington DC 20063
USA

EFTA
Witmakers Str. 10
6211 JB Maastricht
Netherlands

Equal Exchange
101 Tosca Drive
Stoughton, MA 02072
USA

Eza Drite Welt
Plainbachstr. 8
A-5101 Bergheim
Austria

Fair Trade Foundation
65 Landing Road
Higganum, CT 06441-4140
USA

Gepa Aktion Dritte Welt Handel
Talstrasse 20
D-5830 Schwelm
Germany

International Federation for Alternative Trade (IFAT)
Strijkviertel 38
3454 PM Demeern
Netherlands

Simon Levelt
Prins Hendrikkade 26
1012 TM Amsterdam
Netherlands

National Association of Third World Shops
Westerkade 18
3511 HB Utrecht
Netherlands

North & South Exchange AB
Graddgatan 6-5
41276 Goteborg
Sweden

OS3
Postfach 69
Byfangstrasse 19
CH-2552 Orpund
Switzerland

Sackeus
Tellusborgsvagen 67 B
12637 Hagersten
Sweden

Self-help Crafts
704 Main Street
PO Box 500
Akron, PA 17501-0500
USA

Serry Self-help Handcrafts
500 Main Street
PO Box 365
New Windsor, MD 21776
USA

SOS Wereldhandel
PO Box 115
4100 AC Culemborg
Netherlands

Stichting Goed Werk
PO Box 87
3985 ZV Amerongen
Netherlands

Stichting Max Havelaar
Post bus 1252
3500 BG Utrecht
Netherlands

Tampere ATO
Possijarvenkatu 4
SF-33400 Tampere
Finland

Traideireann
PO Box 20
Athlone
Co. Westmeath
Ireland

U-Landsimporten
Postboks 7
Rolstrubakken 6
DK-7900 Nykobing M
Denmark

Women's World Banking
8 West 40th Street
New York
USA

The Third World

Alter Trade Corporation
Door No. 3 Ground Floor
Baldevia Building
San Sebastian St., Bacolod City
Philippines

ATOYAC — Coalicion de Ejidos
Juan N. Alvarez sur Pt 135
Atoyac de Alvarez
Guerrero
Mexico

Bangladesh Rural Advancement Committee (BRAC)
23/5 Shamoly
Mirpur Road
Mirpur Road ICA
Dhaka 1207
Bangladesh

Bombolulu Workshop
PO Box 83988
Mombasa
Kenya

Candela Trading SA
PO Box 14-0233
Lima 14
Peru

CNOC — Coor. Nac'l de Organizaciones
Cafetaleras
Tabasco 262-301
Colonia Roma
CP 06700
Mexico DF

CORDE — Workteam
PO Box 1895
Gaberone
Botswana

Community Development Society CODES
CODES Christian Medical College
Aramr Road
Vellore 632 002
India

Dorcas
Acpo Box No. 369
Quezon City
Philippines

ECOTA
c/o Oxfam
6-8 Sir Syed Ahmed Road
Mohammadpur
Dhaka 7
Bangladesh

Enlace Guatemala Aj Quen
Apartado Postal 97
04901 Chimaltango
Guatemala

Helang Basali Crafts
St Agnes Mission
PB X 30 Teyateyaneng
Lesotho

Last Hope International
Box 119 Okpala PO, Via Aba
Imo State
Nigeria

Mantis Namibia Ltd
PO Box 22229
Windhoek 9000
Namibia

Minka
PO Box 14-0359
Lima
Peru

National Handicraft Centre
PO Box 66210
Copje
Harare
Zimbabwe

New World Trading
Bustamante 130, Of. 808
Providencia
Santiago
Chile

North Western Bee Products
PO Box 140096
Kabompo
Zambia

Prescraft
PO Box 219
Bamenda, NW Province
Cameroun

Pukara Crafts
Yungay 2866
Santiago
Chile

Radicom
BP 12085
Rue 4 Zone B
Dakar
Senegal

Rakku Handicrafts Training Centre
YMCA Andithevar Rural Health Centre
Muthupatti
Palangagathan Post, Tamil Nadu
India

SIPA
5 HD Raja Street
Eldams Road
Teynammpet, Madras 600 018
India

Skilled Voluntary Workers' Aid
John Kennedy Street
Pamplemousses
Mauritius

SUR-NOR
Talara 483
Jesus Maria
Lima 17
Peru

Toyin
4th KM, Ambala Road
Opp P&T Training Centre
3A Haranpur 247001
India

Trinity Jewellery Crafts
PO Box 16191
Nairobi
Kenya

Tabora Beekeepers Cooperative Society
Kipalapala
PO Box 7017
Tabora
Tanzania

Trade Not Aid — Nyumba Ya Sanaa
PO Box 4904
Dar Es Salaam
Tanzania

Uganda Crafts
PO Box 7047
Kampala
Uganda

GLOSSARY OF ACRONYMS AND TECHNICAL TRADE TERMS

AAA: Agricultural Adjustment Act, USA 1933, to keep farm prices up by ploughing in crops.

ACLI: leading United States commodity trading company.

ACP: African, Caribbean and Pacific, ex-colonies (49 in all), with which the European Community has special trade relations through the Lomé Convention (qv).

ad valorem: in Latin literally 'to the value', a form of tax or tariff (qv) added to the value of goods imported.

Agenda 21: an 800 page blueprint of action agreed at the 1992 Earth Summit setting out wide-ranging but voluntary guidelines for governments to lead development in environmentally sound directions.

Agribusiness: large-scale, highly-mechanised agricultural production using fertilisers, pesticides, herbicides etc.

Aid: in trade relations, assistance by means of grants or credits for purchases, generally by developing countries from industrialised countries, hence aid agencies mainly voluntary organisations providing aid.

Aller: literally in French 'to go'; a trade transaction which the importer finances with credit from some other transaction (cf. *Retour* and see Switch).

ANADEGES: in Spanish short for Autonomy, Development and Self-Management, a Mexican umbrella NGO supporting small-scale producers.

Arms-length Trading: movement of goods and services between different parts of one company as if they were separate companies.

Asset: in economic relations, any property that can be drawn upon to discharge a debt, including capital (qv). **Assets**: the buildings, plant and machinery of a business or government.

ATO: Alternative Trade Organisation, one committed to cooperation with organisations of the poor and oppressed in Third World countries on the basis of justice, aimed at improving living standards mainly by means of promoting trade in products from these countries.

Automation: the use in industry of machines which perform sequences of operations on instructions supplied from other machines, with the minimum of human intervention. (See also Flexible Automation.)

Bandoeng Powers: so-called from the Indonesian city on the island of Java where a conference of heads of Third World states in 1957 established a regular meeting of the Non-Aligned Movement (see Lusaka Declaration and Group of 77 .)

Bankability: ease of access of a company or other organisation to bank credit.

Barrel: measure of capacity, generally of fuel oil, about 35 gallons. 7.5 barrels = 1 metric tonne; an output of 5 million tonnes a year = 100,000 barrels a day.

Barter: direct exchange of goods or services between two parties without the use of money. (See Countertrade)

Bilateral Deal: one that involves only two parties and is made outside the market (qv). cf. Multilateral.

Billion: a thousand million.

Boom: rapid increase in economic activity over a period in one or more industry or nation state.

Brandt Report: after Willy Brandt, ex-chancellor of West Germany, chairman of an independent Commission on International Development which in 1980 published its report *North-South: A Programme for Survival*.

Bretton Woods: after the resort in the USA where the Allied Powers met in 1944 to reach agreement on post-war international financial institutions: IMF, World Bank and GATT 9 (qv).

Broker: an intermediary who deals in a market, bringing together buyers' and sellers' bids and offers.

Brundtland Report: after Mrs Gro Harlem Brundtland, prime minister of Norway, chair of the World Commission on the Environment and Development (WCED), which in 1987 published its report, *Our Common Future*.

Buffer Stock: a stock of commodities held under an international commodity agreement (ICA qv), and increased or reduced with the aim of keeping the price of the commodity stable.

Buy-back Agreement: one made between an exporter and an importer whereby the exporter agrees to supply machinery and equipment and to take payment in goods produced from the machines.

CAFOD: Catholic Action for Overseas Development, Aid Agency (qv), address: 2 Romero Close, Stockwell Rd, London SW9 9TY.

Cairns Group: a number of non-US, non-EC agricultural producers, both in the First and Third World, anxious to reduce US and EC farm subsidies to free up the world's food trade.

Campesino: Spanish word for countryman, whether farmer or agricultural worker.

CAP: Common Agricultural Policy of the European Community, a system of levies and subsidies to protect European agriculture.

Capital: money accumulated for future use or invested in buildings, equipment etc. for conducting a business; ownership distinguished between merchant capital in trade or banking and industrial capital in production.

Cartel: a market arrangement between producers to manipulate prices, generally by controlling output, e.g. OPEC (qv)

Cash Crop: one produced for sale and not for direct consumption, often for export.

CDI: Centre for the Development of Industry, part of the EC programme of aid to ACP countries.

CPEs: Centrally Planned Economies: term used in UN reports etc. for those Communist-ruled countries prior to 1990, i.e. USSR, Eastern Europe, China and Vietnam.

CE: Coal Equivalent, measure of oil, gas or other fuel in terms of its thermal equivalent in coal; e.g. 1 metric tonne of oil = 1.7 metric tonnes CE.

CFAO: large French trading company in Francophone Africa.

CFF: Compensatory Finance Facility, conditional arrangement made by the IMF (qv) in the 1950s to permit member states suffering a fall in price of their export commodities to draw upon the Fund.

CIDIE: Committee for International Development Institutions on the Environment, to promote concern for environmental sensitivity in development aid.

c.i.f.: cost, insurance and freight, the full cost of internationally traded goods at the point of import.

CIIR: Catholic Institute for International Relations, research and publishing centre..

Clearing House/Union: institution for settling accounts between banks or trading partners.

COCOM: Coordinating Committee on Multilateral Export Control, US-initiated organisation for withholding strategic exports of NATO countries and Japan to Communist-controlled governments.

Collateral: a pledge of assets accepted by a lender as guarantee for repayment of a loan.

Colombo Plan: after the capital of Sri Lanka where agreement was reached in 1953 by industrialised countries to provide aid to developing countries in South East Asia.

COMECON or CMEA: Council for Mutual Economic Assistance, organisation in Eastern Europe for coordinating economic plans and trade exchanges, disbanded in 1990.

Commercialisation Chain: stages by which a primary product is refined, processed, transported and packaged etc. until it finally appears in a shop for sale.

Commodity: any good or service produced for sale, and therefore including money and labour, but frequently applied to unprocessed food, fuel and raw materials entering world trade, and hence commodity markets.

Common Fund: fund established through UNCTAD (qv) for financing international commodity agreements (ICA qv), with a 'second window' for improving commodity production.

Comparative Advantage: see Ricardo.

COMPEX: a compensatory fund established by the EC for assisting non-ACP LDCs (qv) which are suffering from a fall in price for the commodities they have to sell: cf. CFF, STABEX (qv).

Conditionality: requirement by aid agencies and financial institutions, e.g. IMF (qv), that certain conditions be agreed by governments before aid is allocated or funds can be drawn (see Structural Adjustment).

Consumer Union: organisation of people according to their common interest as consumers of goods and services to protect that interest (see Ethical Consumer).

Consumer-Producer Union: extension of consumers' union interest into linkages with producers, e.g. in cooperatives.

Constant Prices: a calculation of the value of goods and services by adjusting current prices to the average in a base year or period of years. (See Current.)

Co-operative: organisation of producers or consumers where ownership and control of the business is in the hands of the members.

Corea Plan: the Integrated Programme for Commodities (IPC (qv)) both for production and marketing, proposed by UNCTAD in 1976 and named after the initiator.

Counterpart Funds: monies made available by a government to complement aid received from outside, e.g. under the Marshall Plan.

Countertrade: any exchange of goods or services in which there is a non-monetary element — e.g. barter and buy-back (qv) — in the settlement of sums owing.

Credit: funds provided, generally at a rate of interest, for goods and services supplied in advance of settlement or delivery. (See letter of credit.)

Currency: any form of money which is accepted as a means of exchange over the territory of a nation state, or more widely in the case of hard currencies (qv); convertible currency, one that can be changed for another and is not limited to use inside the country of origin.

Current: as of a certain date, e.g. prices or wages.

Coyotes: Latin American prairie wolf, sobriquet for a middleman in trading.

Cycle: in economics, waves of growth and decline in activity, some short and some very long. (See Boom and Slump.)

DAC: Development Aid Countries, those supplying aid to developing countries under

UN recommendations that 0.7% (reached by very few countries) of the national income of the DACs should be provided in such aid.

Database: collection of information in an organised manner on specific topics, generally available in machine readable form.

Debt: monies owed by one person, organisation or government to another, to be repaid with annual interest or rescheduled with the unpaid interest added to the original capital sum, sometimes, in a Debt-Equity swap settled by sale of property or business enterprise. (See Equity (qv))

Deficit: sum by which outgoings exceed receipts in business, government accounts, international trade etc.

Deflation: action to reduce a price level either by government in a national economy or in a statistical series by adjustment to a base year or to other prices, e.g. commodity prices. (See real terms.)

Demand: in economics, the preparedness to buy a certain quantity of goods or services at a certain price; hence demand elasticity, the measure of the extent to which the quantity sold increases as the price falls or decreases as the price rises.

Depreciation: the amount by which the value of goods or machinery or money has fallen over a period of time; and thus depreciation funds, monies set aside over the life-time of an asset (qv) to replace it at its historic cost.

Division of Labour: distribution of economic activities between persons and countries according to theory of comparative economic advantage (see Ricardo) or historic experience, referred to in this book as 'artificial' and in so far as it is being changed today, as the new international division of labour.

Dummy Company: name applied to a company which does no business but invoices payments for goods or services moving between subsidiaries of a transnational company (qv), so as to conceal the profits being made.

Dumping: exporting goods at prices below local costs of production in order to gain markets, e.g., CAP (qv) subsidised food exports.

EC: European Community, originally six west European nation states, currently (1992) twelve, formed in 1957 under the Treaty of Rome to move towards a United States of Europe.

ECA: Economic Commission for Africa, regional organisation of the United Nations, with offices in Addis Ababa, organises conferences, collects statistics and makes reports on African economies.

ECAFE: Economic Commission for Asia and the Far East, regional organisation of the United Nations, with offices in Bangkok, similar to ECA.

ECE: Economic Commission for Europe, regional organisation of the United Nations, with offices in Geneva, similar to ECA.

ECLA: Economic Commission for Latin America, regional organisation of the United Nations, with offices in Rio de Janeiro, similar to ECA.

Ecology/Sco-system: study of/working of the interaction with their environment of living organisms including humans.

Econometrics: analysis of economic events by statistical measurement.

ECU: European currency unit, the name for the common currency in which the European Community's business is increasingly reckoned.

ECSC: European Coal and Steel Community: organisation of coal and steel industries inside the European Community, established in 1950 under the Treaty of Paris to control production and prices.

EDF: European Development Fund, set up under the Lomé Convention (qv) to provide funds from the EC for ACP countries.

EC: European Economic Commission, original title of the Commission of the European Community (qv) responsible for its economic affairs.

EFTA: European Free Trade Association, organisation of West European states outside the EC, set up in the 1950s for the purpose of encouraging mutual trade exchanges; also European Fair Trade Association — group of European ATOs.

Electronic mail: use of computers connected to the telephone system for transmitting machine readable matter over long distances at low cost.

EMU: (European) Economic and Monetary Union, a series of agreements on economic and monetary matters inside the European Community for moving towards a single exchange rate, a common currency and increasingly centralised economic policies.

Enterprise Zone or Export Promotion Zone: (see **FTZ**, Free Trade Zone).

EPU: European Payments Union, system for clearing payments for West European trade exchanges established in the 1950s when most national currencies were not convertible. (See Currency (convertible)).

Equal exchange: the concept that trade should involve exchanges of equal value in some fairer sense than market price provides.

Equilibrium (price): one at which supply and demand are in balance, achieved artificially under CAP (qv) for example, by varying the levy on imports and refunds on exports.

Equity: see Risk Capital and Debt.

ERM: (European) Exchange Rate Mechanism: agreement among EC members to vary interest rates etc. in order to keep their national currencies in line with each other, within a limited range of variance, in preparation for EMU (qv).

Escalating Tariffs (qv): ones where the rate of taxation on imports rises with every extra degree of processing applied to a primary product in the exporting country.

ESCROW (account): one which records special payments under a countertrade agreement (qv).

Ethical (bank or consumer): one which takes into account moral principles in economic activity, consumption patterns etc. as well as purely commercial concern for price, profit etc.

Ethnic: used to describe goods, especially crafts, which are specific to culture of particular national groups.

Euro-dollar (account): US dollars used for financing trade exchanges outside the United States, and other hard currencies (qv) used similarly, hence Euro-dollar market.

Exchange Rate: the rate at which one country's currency is exchanged for another's, determined by the relative prices of goods and services traded between them.

Exclusivity: in trade agreements, having the aim of keeping out rival suppliers or competing product.

Export Restitution: term applied to a refund or subsidy granted to European farmers under CAP (qv) so as to bring their prices down to world levels for agricultural exports.

Exposure: the outstanding debts of a bank to its customers, generally expressed as a proportion of the bank's capital assets (qv).

Fair Trade Mark: an emblem bestowed by an accrediting organisation on a good or service, to indicate that it has complied with certain advertised criteria of fair treatment of the producers.

FAO: Food and Agricultural Organisation of the United Nations, based in Rome, one of the specialised agencies of the UN, concerned to report on and assist the development of food and agricultural production and trade, especially in the less developed countries.

Farmgate (price): the price at which agricultural produce is sold by the farmer.

FAVDO: Federation of African Voluntary Organisations for Development, a fairly loose association of African NGOs (qv) based on Senegal.

FENLACES: Spanish acronym for Latin American and Caribbean Federation for Trade in the Social Economy Sector, an NGO of small-scale producers in Chile, Cuba, Mexico, Nicaragua and Peru, designed to establish fair trading relations between each other and with organisations in industrialised countries.

First World: name given to the developed industrialised countries, cf. Third World, Second World.

Flexible Automation: is applied to machines in industry which can be adapted easily and quickly to producing different colours, sizes or grades of a product, so as to allow for changing fashions, seasons and other factors in market demand.

f.o.b.: free on board, the value of goods on delivery to the port of export, i.e. without insurance and freight charges, cf. c.i.f.

Food First: title of a North American campaigning organisation concerned to reduce the amount of land in developing countries used for cash crops for export.

Fordism: method of producing and selling goods by large-scale, centralised mass production and distribution, invented by Henry Ford in the USA in the early 1900s. Hence post-Fordism describes the smaller scale, decentralised production and distribution systems made possible by computer control and information technology.

Free Trade: concept of international trade that is unrestricted by tariffs, subsidies or other barriers.

Friends of the Earth: voluntary organisation concerned with the conservation of the global eco-system (qv).

FTA: Free Trade Agreement between the USA and Canada signed in 1989 and being extended to Mexico and possibly other countries in the Americas to provide for free movement of goods and services between these countries.

FTO: Foreign Trade Organisation: the government department having a foreign trade monopoly under a Centrally Planned Economy (qv).

FTZ: Free Trade Zone, enclave in a nation state set apart from the remainder and designed to attract investment by foreign companies by reason of the relative absence of taxes, import and export controls, labour legislation protecting workers, etc.

Funds: sums of money made available for business activities or for government expenditure.

Futures: deals in commodities bought or sold at the prices which are expected to rule when delivery is made at a certain date in the future. Hence a futures market is one where such speculation can take place.

GATT: General Agreement on Tariffs and Trade, agreement signed by the United Nations at Havana in 1944 as part of the Bretton Woods (qv) agreements, to establish ways of reducing obstacles to free trade, to monitor such obstacles and propose measures for ending them.

GDP: Gross Domestic Product, of a nation state, the value of goods and services produced in a year, i.e. including exports but excluding imports.

Gearing: proportion of risk capital to borrowed money in the finance of an enterprise.

Global Environmental Facility (GEF): a World Bank programme to lend money to governments for environmental projects.

GNP: Gross National Product, of a nation state, the value of all goods and services produced in a year, before allowing for depreciation (capital consumption) of assets (qv).

Gold: precious metal widely used by governments and rich persons as an asset (qv) or currency reserve.

Goseco Plan: proposal made by Andreas Goseco in the 1950s for United Nations regional agencies to set up a supplementary mechanism for encouraging trade exchanges by developing countries (see Clearing House/Union).

Greenpeace: voluntary organisation concerned with actions to prevent pollution or destruction of the environment.

Gross: originally large-scale and therefore wholesale in trade, but increasingly applied to products, income, expenditure etc., before allowing for depreciation, taxes or other deductions.

Group of 77: (later to become 96) Third World countries that initiated the establishment of UNCTAD (qv).

Growth (rate): measure of increase in economic activity, generally measured by GDP per capita. A doubling of GDP takes place in 10 years at 7 per cent a year, in 20 years at 3.5 per cent a year, in 35 years at 2 per cent a year.

GSP: General System of Preferences, the system by which industrialised countries grant preferential treatment, through nil or reduced import duties, for certain products imported from developing countries, first negotiated at UNCTAD (qv) in 1968.

Ha: hectare, measure of area, equivalent to 2.5 acres.

Handicrafts: hand-made goods, see also ethnic (qv).

Hard Currency: a currency, convertible and widely acceptable , e.g. US dollars..

Hedging: in commodity markets buying or selling futures (qv) with the aim of compensating for possible trading losses owing to price changes.

Hoarding: amassing stocks of money or goods against future scarcities.

IBRD: International Bank for Reconstruction and Development (see World Bank).

ICA: International Cooperative Alliance, worldwide organisation of cooperatives (qv); International Commodity Agreement (see ICO)

ICCA: International Cocoa Agreement (see ICO).

ICFA: International Coffee Agreement (see ICO).

ICO (International Commodity Organisation or International Coffee Organisation): organisation established to represent producer and consumer countries, in particular, international commodity dealings.

ICVA: International Council of Voluntary Agencies: a coordinating body for voluntary agencies with special representation at the United Nations, World Bank etc.

IDA: International Development Association, set up by the World Bank to meet the financial needs of governments not deemed to be creditworthy for commercial loans, because of the acute underdevelopment of their economies.

IDOC: Italian Documentation Centre for 'non-dependent development'.

IFAT: International Federation for Alternative Trade, founded in Amsterdam in 1989 to coordinate the activities worldwide of ATOs. (qv) in the First and Third Worlds.

IFDA: International Federation for Development Alternatives, linked to Interpress (qv).

IFC: International Finance Corporation, launched by the World Bank in 1957 to further economic development by encouraging private enterprise.

IMF: International Monetary Fund, one of the institutions established by the United Nations at Bretton Woods (qv) in 1944, to provide finance for governments facing short-term deficits on their foreign balance of payments.

Imperialism: protection by advanced industrialised countries of their foreign trade by establishing colonial rule or economic dependency in other countries.

Incentive: extra wage, subsidy, tax concession or other payment to encourage action, e.g. to attract investment by TNCs (qv) in one place rather than another.

Indentured (labour): bound to a master to work, a form of slavery, e.g. Indians and Chinese brought to Latin America by British companies to work on plantations or in mines or ports.

Index: number indicating relative prices or volumes at a particular date compared with those at a base date.

Infant Industry: one established in a developing country and needing protection (qv) from outside competition in its first year.

INRA: International Natural Rubber Agreement. (See ICOs.)

Insider (trading): using knowledge gained as a privilege inside a particular company for personal gain in a market.

Intensive: use of one factor of production (labour, land or capital) more than another. Hence labour-intensive production etc.

Interpress: a non-governmental organisation for encouraging international networking (qv).

Invisibles: the account reflecting income and expenditure from property and services in the foreign balance of any country; cf. the trade account of exports and imports.

IOCU: International Organisation of Consumer Unions (qv).

IPC: Integrated Programme for Commodities covering 18 commodities produced mainly for export by LDCs (qv). See also Corea Plan.

IRED: French acronym for International Network to Promote Development Innovations, a Swiss based international development network of NGOs (qv).

ISA: International Sugar Agreement, see ICOs.

ITA: International Tin Agreement, see ICOs.

ITC: International Trade Certificate, an alternative to hard currency (qv) for facilitating trade exchanges in countertrade (qv).

ITO: International Trade Organisation, proposed by Keynes in 1944 at Bretton Woods (qv) but transmuted into GATT (qv).

IWTC: International Women's Tribune Centre, supports initiatives of women in the Third World.

Laissez-faire: in French, 'let do', phrase used to describe a non-interventionary stance taken by governments in relation to national economies, supposedly especially true of UK governments in the nineteenth century.

LDC: Less Developed Country or more usually now one of the 43 Least Developed Countries so designated by the United Nations because of their low *per capita* incomes and little, if any, industrialisation.

Leads and Lags: transfers of funds by transnational companies to settle their inter-country accounts either ahead of delivery of goods and services or following after, the choice being made according to the advantage or disadvantage to be gained from relative interest rate levels and exchange rate changes (qv), often in fact the cause of exchange rate changes.

Letter of Credit: a promise of credit (qv) which may be used as collateral (qv) for borrowing.

Levy: tax either on persons, capital or goods, often on goods entering a country from outside, as with levies on food imports under the European Community CAP (qv)

Little Dragons: name applied to the four Asian states — South Korea, Hong Kong, Singapore and Taiwan — which may have recently achieved rapid industrial growth.

Lomé Convention: agreement signed between European Community and ACP (qv) governments in 1963, and renewed subsequently to provide aid and guarantee market access in Europe to some products of some of Europe's former colonies.

Lusaka Declaration: statement by heads of state of non-aligned countries made after meeting in Lusaka, Zambia in September 1970 with the aim of committing themselves to mutual cooperation for independent economic development: see Bandoeng Powers (qv) and Group of 77 (qv)

Market: place where commodities, including money and also factors of production: land, labour and capital: are bought and sold, and thence the whole system of allocating resources through supply and demand.

Marketing Board: parastatal organisation, widely found in African countries, for organising trade in certain commodities, mainly for export.

Marshall Plan: programme of United States aid to Western Europe and Japan, supplied after World War Two on the initiative of Secretary of State, George Marshall.

Max Havelaar: trademark of Dutch alternative coffee supplier committed to fair trading, the name being derived from a classic Dutch novel critical of Dutch policy in the East Indies of turning land from food to coffee production.

Merchanting: buying and selling goods and services produced by others so as to make a profit on the deal, applied mainly to foreign trade but also to banking.

MFA: Multi-fibre Agreement, whereby industrialised countries place quotas (qv) on imports of textiles and clothing from LDCs, one of the exceptions permitted under the GATT liberalisation process.

mfg: manufactured goods.

MFN: Most Favoured Nation, the system adopted among nation states in their foreign trade of granting to *all* trading partners the same treatment as to a most favoured nation.

Middlemen: intermediaries between direct producers of goods and services and the market for them.

MITI: Ministry of International Trade and Industry in Japan, the supreme government manager of state industrial and commercial policy.

MNC: multinational company; see TNC.

Monopoly: the position of a single seller of any good or service, but applied also to one with a dominating position in the market.

Monopsony: the correct term for the position of a single buyer in the market or for one with a dominant position. cf. Monopoly.

mt: metric tonnes.

Multilateral (aid): that which is given by nation states through international agencies like the World Bank, FAO etc. cf. Bilateral.

MYRA: Multi-Year Rescheduling Arrangement for debt, applied to arrangements for Mexico's international debt; see Rescheduling.

NATO: North Atlantic Treaty Organisation, military alliance of USA, Canada and most of Western Europe including Turkey against the USSR and Eastern Europe, themselves subsequently allied in the Warsaw Pact until 1990.

National Income: the aggregate annual income of a nation state, gross or net, see GNP.

Net: after deduction of taxes, depreciation or other charges.

Networks: horizontal linkages between organisations, generally NGOs (qv) for the purpose of exchanging information or coordinating action in trade or other matters.

NGO: Non-governmental Organisation, generally a voluntary organisation, e.g. ATOs (qv)

NICs: Newly Industrialising Countries, e.g. 'Little Dragons' (qv).

NIEO: New International Economic Order, the long term objective of the Group of

77 (qv), the first stages proposed at UNCTAD in 1971. See IPC.

NIP: National Indicative Programme, one negotiated between the EC and its ACP(qv) partners.

Nomadic Pastoralist: wandering sheep or cattle grazers.

nomenklatura: Russian word for the elite bureaucrats and ministers in the former Soviet Union.

Non-discrimination: in tariffs, where no preference is given to any trading partner, see MFN.

North: as opposed to South, the leading industrialised nations.

NTB: Non-Tariff Barrier, any obstacle to international trade other than actual taxes on imports. See also Tariffs.

ODA: Overseas Development Assistance, the official name for international aid; Overseas Development Administration, in the UK and elsewhere the title of the government department responsible for foreign aid programmes.

ODI: Overseas Development Institute, a UK parastatal (qv) organisation responsible for research, conferences and publications on development issues.

OECD: Organisation for European Cooperation and Development, the club of the industrialised countries of Western Europe, North America, Japan and Australasia, which holds conferences and collects statistics.

OPEC: Organisation of Petroleum Exporting Countries, set up in 1973 after the Yom Kippur war between Egypt and Israel, in order to control oil production and raise oil prices, includes mainly Middle East oil producers, but also Venezuela, Mexico and Nigeria, responsible for about half the world's oil output in 1990.

Open Outcry: the shouts of bids and offers by dealers in a commodity market, where prices are settled in this manner.

Option: in a market, the right to buy or sell at a certain date, not the actual purchase or sale of goods.

Organic: generic English term for agricultural products grown without the use of chemical fertiliser, insecticides, herbicides, etc. Other countries, like France, Spain, Italy, use the term 'biological'.

Outgrower: a farmer producing commodities on contract for a large company, generally an expatriate company from an industrialised country operating in the Third World.

Oxfam: UK aid agency founded in Oxford in 1944 for famine relief, now includes a trading company. Address: 274 Banbury Road, Oxford OX4 7DZ.

Parastatal: organisation set up by a government, but not actually a government department, e.g. a nationalised industry.

Pearson Report: report of a Commission chaired by Lester Pearson, ex-Prime Minister of Canada, set up under United Nations auspices in 1969 to examine international aid and its effect on economic development.

Peasant: a person (in practice, a household) that works land, which they may or may not own, and who live on the produce of the land, with or without market access.

peon: South American Spanish word for a day labourer who works on the land in virtual servitude to the landowner.

per capita: in Latin 'per head', according to the number of heads, used as a measure of income or consumption by specified populations.

PL.480: United States food aid programme, with the aim of disposing overseas of agricultural surpluses in the US.

Planning: deciding in advance what needs to be done by a person, business or government and working out ways of doing it; in relation to a nation state's economy intervention by government in the working of the market to achieve certain ends, hence Centrally Planned Economies, the name given by UN agencies to (former) communist states.

PPs: Primary Products, those directly produced from the land by agriculture, mining, forestry, fishing etc. and not yet processed or refined.

Preference (s): advantage (s) given by a nation state to other particular states in trade relations, e.g. lower tariffs, duties etc. See GSP.

Premium: extra charge made for extra value or quality in the product or service.

Producer: as used in this book a primary producer (see PPs) and often a small-scale producer.

Product Differentiation: method of attracting buyers to a particular product by advertising its advantages over others and using distinctive labelling.

Productivity: generally labour productivity, measure of output per person, usually in relation to increased productivity resulting from the application of mechanical aids to reduce labour costs.

Profit Margin: an addition to the cost of producing, refining, transporting, distributing and marketing a good or service to provide an income to the owner of a business in any of these economic activities, derived either by means of a monopoly position (qv) or by exploitation of labour.

Protection: in foreign trade devices used by nation state governments to give advantage to their own nationals' products against foreign competitors through subsidies, tariffs, levies (qv)

Quango: Quasi Non-Governmental Organisation, another name for a Parastatal (qv).

Quantum: American term for volume (qv) of goods produced or moving in foreign trade.

Quota: in foreign trade, a fixed share measured in money value or quantity of goods allowed to be produced or imported or exported as a result of agreements reached between governments of nation states.

QM: Quality Mark, distinguishing mark of a quality product, such as Wool Mark, Fair Trade Mark (qv) established by a trading organisation.

RADICOMM: Rassemblement Afrique pour Développement Indigène, large Senegalese consortium of cooperative farmers.

Real Terms: values of goods or services, e.g. imports or exports, expressed at the prices current in a certain base year to enable year by year comparisons to be made, i.e. discounting for price changes.

Reciprocity Principle: in tariff reductions, that one country's reductions should be matched by reciprocal concessions in return, but with LDCs, for example, granted exemption by UNCTAD (qv).

Re-exports: goods brought into customs sheds in one country, not for importing into that country but for export after sale on the commodity markets, especially those in London.

Regression (equation): in statistics fitting a trend (qv) to a series of inexact changes, e.g. in a commodity price.

Regulation: rules imposed by governments, especially for controlling the free working of the market.

Rent: a payment for the use of land or buildings or for access to mineral deposits, oil reserves etc.

Rescheduling (debt): postponing payment of some part or all of the interest and principal on a debt due in any year, by adding to the principal sum to be repaid in the end. See Rolling Over.

Reserves: gold or other monies, especially hard currency (qv) held by a business, bank or government, to finance foreign trade exchanges. See SDR.

Restrictive Action or Agreement: in foreign trade one that limits the ability of a trader to trade in certain commodities or places or with certain partners other than those specified in the agreement.

Retour: literally in French, 'return', a trade transaction which the exporter finances with credit from some other transaction (cf. *Aller* and see Switch).

Reverse Transfer: flow of funds back from borrowers to lenders or from poor to rich countries, as a result of debt repayments.

Ricardo, David: inventor of theory of comparative advantage, to encourage nation states to produce only what they were best at and to sell their surplus in order to import their other requirements.

Risk Capital: that which is put up by the owners of a business, having the last claim to repayment in the event of failure.

Rolling over (of debt): agreement by creditors to defer repayment of the principal, and even sometimes of the interest on loans made to persons, organisations or governments in financial difficulties. See Rescheduling.

Royalty: a sum of money made in payment for use (in the case of books or records), patents or other proprietary claims (including mineral reserves in some cases).

Scale: used in economics in reference to the productive capacity of a business, e.g. small-scale farmer, economies of (large) scale.

S & D: Special and Differential treatment of imports from Developing Countries, allowed after 1964 under GATT rules (qv), thus eliminating the requirement of reciprocity (qv).

SDR: Special Deposit Reserve, a form of money issued by the World Bank and backed by member states to provide a common unit of account and to supplement gold and hard currency (qv) reserves available for financing international trade. See Reserves.

Second World: term given to countries under Communist rule; cf. Third World.

Sharecropper: a farmer whose right to the land he farms depends on his sharing the crop with the landowner.

Shocks: what the World Bank calls events, like falling commodity prices, that occur outside the control of Developing Countries.

Slave trade: trade in human beings as commodities, especially in the eighteenth century transport of Africans to the American continent to work on plantations.

Slump: decline in economic activity in one or more industry or nation state; cf. Boom.

Social (provision or service): one supplied by the state or parastatal (qv), and not by private persons or companies.

Sogo Sosha: current name for the historic Zaibatsu (qv) group of companies in Japan.

Speculation: buying commodities, including money, not for use but for resale in the expectation that prices will rise, or selling in expectation of a fall.

Squeeze: action taken by dealers (qv) or governments to reduce levels of business activity, raise prices, or exclude competitors by manipulating the quantity of commodities entering a market.

STABEX: European Community scheme established in the mid-1980s for providing guaranteed levels of earnings to ACP countries (qv) on certain of their agricultural exports to the EC, comprises about 12 per cent of EC aid to ACP.

Stabilisation Schemes: designed to correct volatile movements in prices of commodities.

Staple: the basic product of a country, either for eating or in foreign trade for exporting to commodity markets. Many countries only have one staple.

Sterling (£): Norman coin with a little star on it, became the currency of the United Kingdom, at one time the main one used in world trade, then in trade among the territories of the British Empire and subsequently among independent Commonwealth countries.

Stock: goods or money accumulated and held for future use.

Subsistence: of an economy, especially of peasant (qv) households, obtaining from the land enough to eat and for other necessities but with no surplus for sale on the market.

SUNFED: Special United Nations Fund for Economic Development, proposed in 1951, but never realised.

Sustainable: in relation to development, what can be sustained without detriment to future generations and the environment.

Sustainable Development Commission: set up by the Earth Summit in 1992 as an organ of the United Nations to monitor UN agencies and countries' observance of Agenda 21 (qv) principles.

Takeover: action by one company to obtain a majority of the shares in another, hence takeover bid.

Tariff: tax imposed by one nation state, generally *ad valorem* (qv) on goods imported from others. (See Escalating Tariffs.)

Tattonnement: reiterative process for reviewing various mixes of products or exchanges in production or trade, so as to arrive at an optimum or required balance, made simple by use of a computer.

TDC: Trade Development Centre, proposed in this book to encourage trade development under EC-ACP or other auspices.

Terms of Trade: relation of the changes in volumes (qv) or in prices of the exports and imports of a nation state or group of states, or of particular commodities entering trade.

Third World: a translation from the French 'Tiers Monde' used to describe countries which are neither industrialised market economies (the First World) nor centrally planned economies (the Second World).

TICE: Transnational Information Centre Exchange, reports on activities of TNCs (qv) and trade unions worldwide.

TNC: Transnational Company, a large company operating in several countries and sometimes (MNC qv) with owners drawn from several countries.

Trader: any person involved in the exchange of goods or services, especially buyers and sellers in markets for commodities, including money, stocks and shares; fundamental trader, one who takes into account all the relevant factors determining prices and not just what other traders are doing; physical trader, one who operates in a market for real and not for speculation; technical trader: see speculation (qv).

Tranche: portion of income or aid drawn upon at any one time.

Transfer Pricing: prices fixed within a large company for the goods or services moved from one part of the company to another, sometimes over state frontiers, and not necessarily the price which would emerge from arms length trading (qv).

Trend: having a certain general direction over a period of time, e.g. falling commodity prices.

Triangular Trade: trade established in the eighteenth century between Europe, Africa and America, as part of the slave trade (qv).

TRIMS: Trade Related Investment Measures, employed by governments to manage the links between their trade and the investments in their countries by foreign nationals, subject to negotiation under the Uruguay Round of GATT (qv).

TRIPS: Trade Related Intellectual Property Rights: the rights of ownership, patents etc. which go with the export of capital goods and services, subject to GATT's Uruguay Round negotiations (qv).

UDCs: Underdeveloped Countries — usually now LDCs (qv).

UN: United Nations, world organisation established after World War Two to maintain peace and assist economic and political development through regional Commissions — in Europe (ECE), Africa (ECA), Asia and the Far East (ECAFE), Latin America (ECLA) and through specialist agencies — World Bank, IMF, FAO, WHO, UNIDO, UNDP (qv).

UNCTAD (United Nations Conference on Trade and Development): established in 1964 as a forum and monitoring centre for advancing the interests in world trade of the less developed countries.

UNDP: United Nations Development Programme, which finances training and other development projects together with governments of LDCs.

UNIDO (United Nations Industrialised Development Organisation): provides advice and assistance to developing countries.

Unit: individual thing or quantity chosen as the minimum in production or trade for calculating output, price etc.

Unity: the number one, in statistics one for one: e.g. in elasticity of demand for a product in relation to growth in an economy when growth of that demand is exactly in line with overall growth.

UNORCA: in Spanish, the National Union of Regional Campesino Organisations, a consortium of small scale farmers in Mexico.

Uruguay Round: of GATT (qv) negotiations begun in 1987, not yet completed in 1992. See TRIMS, TRIPS.

UTO: United Towns Organisation links towns and cities across the world in ceremonial and increasingly in commercial activities.

Valorisation (scheme): for paying farmers in advance of crop delivery, e.g. in case of Brazilian coffee growers, to maintain stable supplies and prices.

Value Added: addition made to the worth of a product by processing, refining, packaging, etc., hence

VAT: Value Added Tax.

VER: Voluntary Export Restraint: agreement by the government of one nation state to limit its exports of certain products in certain markets, e.g. Japanese cars in Europe or the USA.

Volume: the flow of commodities, goods or services in production or in trade over a period of time, measured by discounting price changes over the same period (see Real Terms).

WCED (World Commission on Environment and Development): see Brundtland.

WFUNA (World Federation of United Nations Associations): with offices in New York and Geneva, links national UN support organisations.

WHICH?: magazine of the UK Consumers Association (qv), in which are published reports on the quality and value for money of goods and services in the market.

WHO: World Health Organisation of the United Nations: responsible for conferences, reports, statistics, special studies and consultancies on health matters worldwide, with special reference to developing countries.

Wholesale: sale and purchase of goods in large quantities to be retailed by others, intermediate stage between producer or trader and final seller.

World Bank (International Bank for Reconstruction and Development): one of the international institutions established along with the IMF (qv) at Bretton Woods in 1944. The bank was designed to supply long-term capital for countries suffering structural weakness in the world economy.

WWF (Worldwide Fund for Nature): organisation for protecting wild life, especially endangered species from destruction by pollution, forest clearance, etc.

Yield: the return, generally in money form, on an investment in economic activity, often measured as a percentage of the capital (qv) laid out.

Zaibatsu: historic group of Japanese conglomerate family companies combining finance, commerce and industry. See also *Sogo Sosha*

Zero rating: as in imported goods subject to tariffs, those that are exempt.

Zero sum: mathematical expression, often used in games, meaning that if one player makes a gain, others must lose by the same amount; hence foreign trade is not necessarily a zero sum game because the whole level of international trade may be raised.

Zone: a region specially defined for some purpose, e.g. for industry, trade, etc. See Free Trade Zone.

Index